'Food is the core of culture, and modern industrial culture is rotting from the inside out due to its reliance on fossil-fueled agriculture. The only viable future is one based on small, ecologically regenerative, labor-intensive farming. Chris Smaje's brilliant book presents the rationale, surveys methods and issues, and supplies an abundance of insight derived from the author's twenty years of experience. Every young person should read this book.'

— RICHARD HEINBERG, Senior Fellow, Post Carbon Institute

'*A Small Farm Future* is a solid and truly inspiring book. I have dedicated the last 17 years of my life to creating a micro farm, and what I have learned fully confirms what Chris Smaje says: a small, ecologically inspired farm can produce high-quality, local food while also improving soil fertility, storing carbon, conserving water resources and improving biodiversity. Not to mention creating jobs and improving quality of life. A return to Mother Earth is the foundation on which we can build a new paradigm of sustainable and equitable abundance based on biological resources, renewable energies, eco-construction and solidarity – among individuals and cultures, and across generations. Getting out of a virtual and globalized economy to cultivate the land with love and respect is our only hope to pass on a viable planet to our children. This is also the secret to happiness!'

— CHARLES HERVÉ-GRUYER, author of
Miraculous Abundance; co-founder, Bec Hellouin Farm, France

'We are facing an existential crisis – with species extinction, climate catastrophes, desertification of soil, disappearance of water, pandemics of infectious and chronic diseases, hunger and malnutrition. Industrialized, globalized agriculture based on the myth that it feeds the world is driving the multiple, interconnected crisis. Eighty percent of the food we eat comes from small farms. Chris Smaje's *A Small Farm Future* shows that the choice is clear. Either we have a small farm future, or we face collapse and extinction.'

— VANDANA SHIVA, author of *Oneness vs. the 1%*
and *Who Really Feeds the World?*

T0354032

'Anyone involved in political thought, agriculture, justice, or futurism who is not familiar with Chris Smaje's writing from his blog should do themselves the favor of picking up this book as soon as possible. Smaje's writing is pretty much always worth engaging with – whether for the wry humor, the ways he challenges us to think harder and more boldly, his relentless humanism or his ability to marry nuance with accessibility. He is a visionary in the most interesting and exciting meaning of the word. His writing consistently shows him to be an intellectual tour guide *par excellence*: he may or may not see further than others, but he certainly never fails to help us see what is in front of us *better*.'

— M. JAHI CHAPPELL, executive director,
Southeastern African-American Farmers' Organic
Network (SAAFON); author of *Beginning to End Hunger*

'Chris Smaje brings intellectual rigour to the centuries-old demand for "three acres and a cow".'

— SIMON FAIRLIE, author of *Meat: A Benign Extravagance*;
editor, *The Land* magazine

'Superb! This book shows with great clarity why we are heading for planetary disaster and suggests ways in which new kinds of more stable social and economic practices might evolve around support for sustainable agriculture. A timely and compelling vision of a New Agrarianism. Highly recommended.'

— PAUL RICHARDS, author of *Indigenous Agricultural Revolution* and *Ebola*; emeritus professor of technology and agrarian development, Wageningen University

'Time to tune in – these are powerful arguments for collective action in agriculture. We know that small farms offer solutions to the crises of our time. Stewardship, guardianship and rebuilding biodiversity is real, meaningful work. If each human engaged meaningfully, every day, in their own subsistence, imagine how much more accountable our society would become. This restoration of our food and ecosystems will take many hands, many years, and much patience and goodwill. This means that those of us already farming will need to become well versed in transmitting the *why* and the *how* to those who will join us. The coming radical shifts in ownership, tenure, settlement and structure present an incredible opportunity for sanity, subsistence and self-determination. Onward!'

— SEVERINE VON TSCHARNER FLEMING,
director, Greenhorns; chair, Agrarian Trust

A Small Farm Future

Making the Case for a Society Built Around Local Economies, Self-Provisioning, Agricultural Diversity and a Shared Earth

CHRIS SMAJE

CHELSEA GREEN PUBLISHING
White River Junction, Vermont
London, UK

Cover illustration used with permission from gameover / Alamy Stock Photo

Project Manager: Patricia Stone
Acquisitions Editor: Shaun Chamberlin
Developmental Editor: Brianne Goodspeed
Copy Editor: Deborah Heimann
Proofreader: Judy Napper
Indexer: Nancy Crompton
Designer: Melissa Jacobson
Page Layout: Abrah Griggs

Printed in the United States of America.
First printing September 2020.
10 9 8 7 6 5 4 3   24 25 26 27 28

Library of Congress Cataloging-in-Publication Data
Names: Smaje, Chris, author.
Title: A small farm future : making the case for a society built around
   local economies, self-provisioning, agricultural diversity, and a shared earth / Chris Smaje.
Description: White River Junction, VT : Chelsea Green Publishing, 2020. |
   Includes bibliographical references and index.
Identifiers: LCCN 2020030627 (print) | LCCN 2020030628 (ebook) | ISBN
   9781603589024 (paperback) | ISBN 9781603589031 (ebook)
Subjects: LCSH: Farms, Small — Government policy. | Agricultural ecology. |
   Agriculture — Economic aspects.
Classification: LCC HD1476.A3 S625 2020 (print) | LCC HD1476.A3 (ebook) |DDC 338.1 — dc23
LC record available at https://lccn.loc.gov/2020030627
LC ebook record available at https://lccn.loc.gov/2020030628

Chelsea Green Publishing
London, UK
White River Junction, Vermont, USA
www.chelseagreen.com

CONTENTS

Part III: Small Farm Society

Part IV:
Towards a Small Farm Future

The Civet's Tale

The palm civet is a small omnivorous mammal of Indonesia and other parts of tropical Asia. Emerging from its forest home onto coffee plantations, it's able to sense the finest coffee fruits of perfect ripeness. Eating them, it digests the pulp and excretes the beans, adding a musky scent to them from its anal glands.

In the 1990s, Indonesian *kopi luwak* – civet coffee, made from coffee beans that had passed through a civet's digestive tract – became a new luxury commodity among wealthy coffee-lovers. Market dynamics being what they are, local producers cashed in on the demand by capturing and caging wild civets, force-feeding them coffee beans and selling the produce as cut-price *kopi luwak*. Though cheaper, the resulting coffee lacked the quality of the original conferred by the civet's discerning nose, and came at the expense of ecological and animal welfare.[1]

We live in a world of trade-offs. If you want genuine *kopi luwak* of good quality and low environmental impact you have to pay someone to comb through the forests looking for wild civet scat on your behalf. Humans can simulate the process and produce a similar product at lower cost, but it's not the same.

It may sometimes be possible to find genuine trade-off-free, win-win improvements. But with most things, including *kopi luwak*, and with agriculture in general, there are trade-offs. Improve on price and you lower animal welfare. Increase the yield and you also increase human labour, fossil fuels or downstream pollution. And so on. Whether the cost of an improvement is worth its price is a value judgement that different people will weigh differently. But not everyone's voice is heard, especially when the costs are offloaded onto the future.

In our bid to provide cheap food to our human multitudes, the trade-off is that a lot of people end up eating shit – figuratively and, as we've just seen, sometimes literally. But our culture is drawn to a narrative of constant progress – a narrative that compels us to avert our attention from this possibility raised by the economist Thomas Sowell: there are no 'solutions', only trade-offs.[2]

There are different ways of dealing with troublesome trade-offs or, in the words of futurologist Peter Frase,[3] of 'loving our monsters'. If human actions are driving pollinators to extinction, Frase suggests we 'deepen our engagement with nature' by developing robotic pseudo-bees to do the job instead. I won't dwell here on how fanciful that is, but I will suggest a wholly different 'monster' we could choose to love if we so wished: an agriculture that doesn't use poisons that kill bees, and instead favours more complex biological interventions, including more human labour. We could learn to love the immediate work of acting on the natural world as much as the mediated work of developing machines to do it. And we could also love the limits to action imposed by nature as much as we love to transcend them.

An obstacle to that kind of love is the narrative of progress I mentioned. Adopting low-tech, labour-intensive approaches to solving a problem or meeting a need, rather than high-tech, labour-substituting approaches is considered regressive, a nostalgic turning back of the clock, as if a historical ratchet prevents us from doing anything in the future that looks like things we did in the past. Actually, there *is* a ratchet that works like this – the capitalist political economy. The mistake we often make is to suppose that this ratchet is some implacable force of nature rather than just a particular way of organising society, itself with a history that may someday end.

These two monsters of overcoming versus restraint are becoming as significant a divide in contemporary politics as old schisms between right and left. Thomas Sowell distinguished between what he called 'constrained' and 'unconstrained' visions of human well-being, the former emphasising the optimisation of trade-offs within relatively immobile constraints, the latter emphasising perfectibility through the overcoming of constraints. The former is usually associated, like Sowell himself, with conservative thought. It encompasses a popular notion of capitalism as market exchange, the sum of innumerable transactions with no higher purpose or guiding hand emerging from the bounded rationality of people acting in their own immediate here and now. The unconstrained vision has usually been associated with the political left and its ideas of remoulding people to work collectively, achieving new goals and great things.

But these certainties are now dissolving. The neoliberal turn in global capitalism invests the hive mind of 'the market' itself with a kind of limit-busting, self-perfecting intelligence that brooks no opposition to any constraints human reason tries to put around it. And various strands of unconstrained leftism sign themselves up to this programme, becoming almost indistinguishable from the capitalism they supposedly reject. Witness books with titles like *Fully Automated Luxury Communism* or *The People's Republic of Walmart: How the World's Biggest Corporations Are Laying the Foundation for Socialism.*[4]

In this emerging political landscape, conservatives inclined towards the constrained vision are discovering that there's nothing especially constrained or conservative about corporate capitalism, while those on the left like me, unpersuaded by either corporate capitalism or attempts to tame it with glib left-wing versions of global industrialised plenty, are discovering a need to reappraise the idea of constraint and aspects of conservative politics informed by it. If we're to bequeath a habitable and abundant planet to our descendants, a key part of that reappraisal involves rethinking the relevance of small farm or 'peasant' societies that are often dismissed for their 'backwardness' or buried under an unusable legacy of romanticism and nostalgia.

For these reasons, we need to consider some questions that modern political traditions have scarcely equipped us to answer with subtlety, or even to ask. What if the route out of widespread farming towards urban-industrial prosperity that today's rich countries followed is no longer feasible for millions of poor people in 'developing' countries? What if that urban-industrial life in fact becomes increasingly unfeasible even in the rich countries in the face of various political, economic and ecological crises? How might the future of humanity then unfold?

When I started asking myself these questions about 20 years ago, the best answer I could come up with was that the most appealing future for humanity would be a small farm future. It's still the best answer I can come up with. For a good stretch of those last 20 years, I've tried as best I can to be a small-scale farmer. The results have varied from the worthwhile to the hapless, always constrained by a world geared to treating the efforts of farmers in general and small-scale farmers in particular with indifference at best. But this book isn't about those efforts, or that indifference. Instead, it considers what may be impelling humanity towards a small farm future, what (in broadest outline) that future might look like, and the forces that may deliver it – or something worse.

Still, let me start that journey with my feet on my farm. When people visit it I notice three main responses. One is an unbidden enthusiasm for the rural paradise we've created, the beauty of the place, and our great good fortune in avoiding the rat race and producing honest food from the land. Sometimes the words are spoken and sometimes I only see it in their eyes, but the sentiment that usually accompanies it is: 'This is great. I wish I could do something like this, but I can't because – '

The second response takes in our rustic accommodation, the compost toilets, the rows of hard-won vegetable beds, the toolshed speaking of the work to be done, the reek of manure and compost with a kind of recoiling pity. It seems to say: 'You went to graduate school and got a well-paid job. Then this. How did it go so wrong?' Or the more actively disdainful: 'Each to their own. But nobody wants to farm any more. All that back-breaking work!'

The third response is that of the harsher critic, whose gaze homes in on specifics – the tractor in the yard, the photovoltaic panels on the roof, the tilled beds in some of the gardens. 'Look how tied in you are to the global fossil fuel economy and its cash nexus.' This critique comes from both sides of the green divide. 'You haven't *properly* escaped and found a truly natural way of life,' from one side. 'You talk about sustainability, but you're no better than the rest of us. Besides, small farms like this can't feed the world,' from the other.

I begin with this story because I'm going to be arguing not only that, yes, small farms like this *can* feed the world, but also that in the long run it may *only* be small farms like this that can. Therefore I'm going to have to address the other criticisms – the compromises with the status quo, the low prestige and toil associated with an agrarian life, the global flight from the land. So I have a lot of work to do in these pages. One thing that encourages me is that, of the three responses I mentioned above, the first seems much the commonest – it simply isn't true that nobody wants to farm.

But people aren't willing to farm under just any circumstances. Too often, farming is still a life of unrewarded toil, not because that's intrinsically how it has to be but because farming is, as it were, the engine room of every society – including our present ones – where the harsh realities and dirty secrets of how it achieves its apparently effortless motion are locked away below decks. I argue here that they need to be unlocked and shared more widely. But for now my visitors who say 'I can't because . . .' are correct. A congenial small farm life is a viable option for few – not for the massed ranks of the employed, unemployed or underemployed in the cityscapes of the world, and not for its multitudes of rural poor, who can scarcely make a living from the land. But in both cases the *dream* of the small farm lives on, and that's an important place to start.

Of course, it's only a place to start, and a sketchy one at that. Notions of the agrarian good life are commonplace around the world, but often they figure as little more than bucolic symbols, empty of pragmatic content. They seem to lack the power of the urban case for supremacy, which has deep historic roots. City, citizenship, civilisation, civility: so much that we value about our world shares an urban etymology. But if we want to build good lives on lasting foundations for the future, the time has come to abandon the unilluminating oppositions of city versus country and factory versus farm, as well as associated oppositions like progress versus backwardness.

Regrettably, that's not how public debate seems to be going. There's a veritable industry of opinion-formers laying their bets only on the first half of those dualities and exhorting us to be 'optimistic' about a future presented as urban, capital forming, high-tech and non-agrarian. This neo-optimist or progress-literature often invokes recurrent myths of human technological problem-solving as an inspiration for transcending present problems. Take, for example, London's Great Horse Manure Crisis in the 1890s, where it's said that people feared the proliferation of horses would bury the streets under their faeces, only to find horses were soon displaced by non-defecating motor vehicles. Or take the idea that fossil fuels saved the whales when kerosene-burning lamps displaced demand for whale oil.[5]

I call these myths partly in the everyday sense that they're untrue. There never was a Great Horse Manure Crisis in the 1890s. And it was the industrialised whaling of the 20th century powered *by* fossil fuels that really put whales in danger.[6] But they're also myths in the deeper sense that they're mystifying and over-simplifying stories that reveal cultural self-conceptions. The self-conception of our modern culture that's revealed in these myths is that the problems we face are discrete, technical ones with one-shot solutions.

These stories are mystifying because they tell tales of fossil fuel–based solutions to predicaments in the past at a point in our current history when fossil fuels present us with problems for which there are no obvious solutions. Right now, we need more than banal assertions that someone's bound to think of something. And they're over-simplifying because human capacities for technical innovation aren't in doubt. What's in doubt is the human capacity to find purely technical solutions for a plethora of current economic, political, cultural, ecological, biological and geophysical problems with complex, interrelated feedback loops exhibiting imperfect information in real time.

In this book I try to provide a different narrative that's less impressed with techno-fixes or dominant notions of civilisational progress. I don't deny that our contemporary civilisation has its successes. But it has its failures, too. I see it in the eyes of those visitors to my farm – who in material terms must surely count among the richest people in the world, ever – which betray a life diminished, trammelled by too many of the wrong kind of obligations. More importantly, I see it in the fact that the world we live in today is just about the most unequal one ever, where somewhere between 800 million and 2.5 billion people are physically undernourished, about as many (or more) than the estimated 800 million population of the entire planet in 1750 at the dawn of the modern age.[7]

These undernourished people haven't missed out on progress, but in large measure are its victims. If global industrial civilisation ever had the capacity to lift the poor and undernourished people of the world to something like the standard of living we experience in the richer countries, the chances of it doing so now have been extinguished in the face of the numerous internal and external threats that have emerged globally during the questionable march of modernisation. So I'd counter the neo-optimist view that the world's problems can be solved with high-tech fixes delivered by the reigning capitalist economy, not with pessimism but with an alternative optimism – an optimism that this reigning economy won't endure much longer, and will be succeeded by something that offers a better future.

The better future I write about here is a small farm future. I'm not completely optimistic that it's the future we or our descendants will see, but for the numerous reasons set out in the book I think it's our best shot for creating future societies that are tolerably sustainable in ecological terms and fulfilling in nutritional and psychosocial ones. Now is a key moment in global politics where we might start delivering that future, but also where more troubling outcomes threaten. Here I try to herald the former by sketching what a small farm future might look like, and how we might get there.

The small farm isn't a panacea, but what a politics geared around it can offer – what, perhaps, at least some of the visitors who come to our farm can glimpse in outline – is the possibility of personal autonomy, spiritual fulfilment, community connectedness, purposeful work and ecological conviviality. Relatively few farmers past or present have enjoyed these fine things. Throughout the world, there are long and complex histories by which people have been both yoked unwillingly to the land and divested unwillingly from it in ways that are misrepresented when we talk of agricultural 'improvement' or progressive 'freedom' from agricultural toil. The improvements haven't been an improvement for everyone, the freedom hasn't been equally shared, the progress has landed us in a whole raft of other problems that we must now try to overcome. And none of it was preordained.

For a Small Farm Future

That's why it's urgent at this point in history to think afresh about a small farm future. Taking each of the three words in reverse order, we need to think about the *future*, because it's clear that present ways of doing politics, economics and agriculture in much of the world are reaching the end of the line. Wise authors avoid speculating on future events because time usually makes their words look foolish, but such dignity isn't a luxury our generation can afford. We need to start imagining another world into being right now.

Modern thinkers have coined numerous terms for the way we now live to distinguish it from the past: the affluent society, the effluent society, industrial society, post-industrial society, Industria, consumer society, postmodern society, the information society, the virtual society. These all capture something significant about our times, but they too easily allow us to forget that in fact our modern societies are *agrarian* societies, just like almost all other human societies over the past few thousand years. Humanity today relies heavily on just three crops – wheat, rice and maize – all of which had been domesticated by about 7000 BCE and which are still mostly grown using techniques whose basic outlines would be instantly recognisable to any ancient farmer. Despite the recent hype over industrially cultured nutrients, the future we face is probably a *farm* future.[8]

Computers nowadays have millions of times more processing power than the ones available just 50 years ago, whereas average global wheat yields are less than nine times higher than those achieved in the Roman Empire.[9] In dimensions that matter most to our continued existence, we're less distant from our ancient counterparts than we sometimes think. And the agricultural improvements that we've achieved since those times have often come through processes that draw down on non-renewable sources of energy, soil and water while imperilling climate and ecological stability.

Whether individually we farm or not, almost all of us ultimately are farming people. In fact, there are more farmers in the world today by formal definition – somewhere between 1.5 and 2 billion – than at almost any point in history.[10] There are good farmers and bad farmers. The best ones learn to produce what's needed with a minimum of effort, without compromising the possibilities of their successors doing the same or losing sight of their obligations as members of communities. It's about time we started trying to tell the story of our world from their perspective – not a story of how we transcended agriculture, because we never did, but of how we might transfigure it, and ourselves in the process, to deal with the problems we now face.

This is a story I try to tell in this book. It's not particularly my story. Although I started by talking about my farm, I'm not going to say much else about it in the book. For one thing, I don't think I have much to teach other people about how to farm, nor do the precise techniques that are used from place to place seem the most important focus of attention. But I *am* a farmer, and so are you if you grow any of your own food or fibre or would like to increase your community's capacity for self-provisioning.

It's the importance of this local self-provisioning that turns a farm future into a *small* farm future. I'm not suggesting there's no place in the future for any larger farms, or that large-scale farmers are always the bad guys. In itself, small isn't necessarily beautiful and I won't be proposing any cutoff points by acreage to define the small farm in this book. But I'll be emphasising some broad differentiating features that will be justified in greater detail as the discussion unfolds: small farms play a key role in creating local autonomies from global flows of capital; they involve a degree of self-provisioning at the individual, household or local level; they employ labour-intensive techniques applied more often by family or household labourers than salaried workers; they adjust their activities to sustain the ecological base in their locality that underpins their productivity; and they tend to operate in a de-commodifying (but not necessarily un-commodified) way compared to large farms.

'Local' or 'locality' looms large in many of those features, perhaps merely displacing the need to define the 'small' into a need to define the 'local'. Again, on this point I refuse hard and fast delineations. The local isn't a matter of prior definition but emerges out of how autonomies and self-provisioning are achieved in practice. One thing I can say for sure, though, is that the small farm future I'm describing isn't the same as a green consumerism future, where shoppers with lives much like the ones most people lead in rich countries today buy their food in stores like the ones they shop in today, except that the food is more local, more sustainable, more organic or whatever – and where, like today, people spend time fruitlessly arguing about whether local really is more sustainable. Instead it'll be a future where you or your descendants are trying to figure out how to furnish your needs from your locality, probably by furnishing many of them for yourself, because you have few other choices.

For some, that may sound too dystopian, apocalyptic or declinist. There certainly may be some dystopian or apocalyptic futures awaiting us unless we play our present hand of cards with skill. But a small farm future only represents a decline from the large farm present if you consider the latter to be a lofty civilisational summit to which humanity has laboriously climbed. That's a view I resist. If we play our cards well, the small farm future I describe here could make for a much more congenial life for most of the world's people than the one they experience today. But we do need to play them well. This is a time in history to be open to a fundamental rethink of how we organise ourselves globally. Too much of our present futurology aims to double down on existing technical and social logics, and dismiss radical alternatives out of hand. At the same time, there's a good deal of received wisdom in the alternative agriculture and alternative economics movements that could use more critical scrutiny.

I don't claim to have fully achieved that rethink here, or to have produced a thoroughly worked out alternative. The idea of a small farm future is so marginal and ill-developed within contemporary thought that at present merely laying out its broad outlines is a daunting enough task. So I offer this book as a kind of critical introduction, a way of starting to organise thinking about what a widespread turn to agrarian localism might look like. This seems worth doing because even though the idea of a small farm future is currently marginal to mainstream thought, it's probably the best future now available for most of humanity, and we don't seem to be discussing the implications of that nearly seriously enough.

PART I

A Small Farm Future?

A fundamental departure from the long-established pattern of maximizing growth and promoting material consumption cannot be delayed by another century. . . . Before 2100 modern civilization will have to make major steps toward ensuring the long-term habitability of its biosphere.

VACLAV SMIL[1]

CHAPTER ONE

Ten Crises

It shouldn't be controversial to suggest that we're living in an age of crisis, if only because everybody always lives in an age of crisis – crisis, that is, in the sense of a decisive moment, a turning point when things could go in one direction or another, rather than in the sense that everything's falling apart. Still, some epochs are more crisis-ridden than others, and though the view that we're headed for hell in a handcart has been popular through history – far more common, for sure, than the actual occurrence of its worst-case scenarios – portents of a troubled future haven't invariably been wrong. Humanity is always in crisis but, peering as we now must into the future's murky glass, there are suggestive hints that the crises we currently face are at best deep and systemic and at worst that the handcart is approaching the fire this time.

So I begin by outlining ten aspects of our biophysical and social worlds whose dynamics suggest we might be edging towards, at the very least, some radically different circumstances for humanity to wrestle with in the future. Each of them properly deserves more than a book to itself. Here I offer the briefest of brushstrokes, focusing particularly on the issues that are most relevant to my arguments for a small farm future later in the book rather than attempting even-handedness.

Those arguments for a small farm future are based on the view that the various crises humanity faces aren't best considered in isolation and remedied through piecemeal solutionism. Instead, I try to identify common, underlying and systemic factors impelling them. It's in seeking remedies to these crises at that systemic level that the case for a small farm future strongly presents itself.

Crisis #1: Population

Whenever a troubling global problem is raised in public discussion, the view that the real problem is human over-population invariably gets an airing. I've lost count of the times in online forums I've seen population described as 'the elephant in the room that nobody talks about'. So I want to acknowledge the elephant, and talk about population at the outset.

At one level this populationism seems plausible. The emergence of global resource and pollution problems coincides with the vast growth of the human population, which has increased ninefold in little more than 250 years. The impact of each new person on these problems is more than zero, so their solutions would surely be eased if the global population were lower. But research suggests that population control alone isn't enough to prevent future decline in human well-being.[2] If population is a problem, it's not entirely clear what kind of problem it is. And what, if anything, can or should be done about it.

Relationships between impact and population exist, but direct proportionality is questionable. So, too, is the underlying web of causality. On the first point, for example, population grew by 45% in low-income countries over the period 2000–2014, while their carbon dioxide (CO_2) emissions grew by only 15%. Across all the other countries of the world over the same period, these figures were almost exactly reversed – a 17% increase in population but a 47% increase in CO_2 emissions.[3] At the individual level, a person's emissions can vary by a factor of 2,000 depending on the circumstances into which they're born and their life choices.[4]

It's therefore misleading to impute climate impact to global population increase per se. In relation to CO_2 emissions – certainly one important measure of environmental impact – the places that are adding the most people to the world aren't the places that are adding the most CO_2, and to raise the spectre of population as the problem effectively offloads the blame where it doesn't belong and diverts attention from specific damaging practices to a more superficial calculus of human numbers. So in relation to CO_2 emissions, population growth may be *a* problem, but it isn't *the* problem. Since far greater decarbonisation can be achieved by acting directly on emissions than by population policy, it seems fair to say that if human population is the elephant in the room, there are some even bigger critters roaming elsewhere in the house.[5]

On the other hand, the places that are adding the most plastic pollution to the oceans *are* located in lower-income countries. Ten heavily populated river catchments in Africa and Asia are responsible for 90% of marine plastic pollution, whereas pollution from populous catchments in wealthy countries is minimal. The significant factor isn't bald population levels, but effective waste collection.[6] With both examples there's no simple and uniform relationship between population and impact.

Another complicating factor is that, unnoticed by many, the world is now experiencing an unprecedented demographic transition. In just 50 years, global fertility has more than halved, from an average 5.07 live births per woman in 1964 to 2.45 in 2015. In three of the five most populous countries of the world, fertility rates are considerably below replacement rate; in fact, this is true in about half the countries of the entire world. Fertility is generally higher in poorer countries, especially in sub-Saharan Africa where most of the highest-fertility countries are located. But fertility is also declining in these countries – faster, in fact, than in the wealthier ones.[7]

Some argue this still isn't good enough, because although fertility *rates* are decreasing, the total global population is still rising and will probably continue to do so into the next century. This is true, inasmuch as fertility rates first have to decline before population does, just as a car first has to stop accelerating before it can start to slow. Also, increasing life expectancy drives global population increase as well as fertility. Still, for those who'd like to see a smaller global population, the fact that fertility rates have fallen prodigiously since the 1960s is surely worth celebrating.

Exactly why they've done so is less clear, but the expert consensus focuses around issues like improving infant and general health, changing social norms, increased education and increased female agency both inside and outside the home.[8] A good deal of the impetus behind this last point arises from women in poorer countries gaining more paid off-farm employment, which has troubling implications for the theme of this book. Can a small farm future encompass persisting female autonomy? (I consider this question in Chapter 12, 'Households, Families and Beyond', page 165.)

A more general problem is that economic development seems to be the main force behind both fertility decline and ecological breakdown, such as increased greenhouse gas emissions, other kinds of pollution, biodiversity loss and so on. Increases in these latter trends are proportionately greater than population increase, suggesting they can't simply be explained by it. Ultimately, it's the material and energy throughputs underlying these trends that must be explained and, more importantly, reduced, and these aren't straightforwardly indexed to population levels.[9] Widely cited equations such as I = PAT (human environmental impact = population × affluence × technology) are misleading here inasmuch as they imply that population is directly, proportionately and causally linked to impact.

The truth is that humanity's environmental impact isn't simply the aggregate of individual humans' impacts, but a result of systems – agricultural, economic, political, cultural – that humans have invented and that affect both the environment *and* our human numbers in ways that can't be reduced *to* human numbers alone. Here, we come to the complexities of the underlying causal web mentioned above, where it's worth introducing a distinction between proximal and underlying causes. A patient's death might be recorded as lung cancer, but this is only the proximal cause. Perhaps the underlying cause was that they smoked heavily. But even that only takes us so far. Not all heavy smokers get lung cancer, and not everyone is a heavy smoker – why *this* disease, why *this* person? We can pursue underlying explanations at many levels.

So perhaps if global population is a problem it's a proximal problem, and it's as well to seek the underlying ones. Behind the recent rise of human population and the fall of human fertility is the longer-term history of globalisation, modernisation and an expanding world economy. Global population trends have been conditioned by this history and undoubtedly have some independent impacts on the human and natural world. But in an expansionary world economy, system impacts may increase even as population decreases, while in other economic contexts population increase may have small effects.

Here, it's worth summoning the ghost of a familiar bogeyman on matters of population – Thomas Robert Malthus (1766–1834). Malthus notoriously argued that humans, especially poor ones, tended to increase their numbers through reproduction at a greater rate than they could increase food to satisfy the elevated population, prompting the checks of hunger, disease and war to fell the surfeit.[10] His analysis was a key influence on Charles Darwin and Alfred Russel Wallace in their theories of evolution by natural selection. Darwin and Wallace both enjoy a secure place in the canon of history's greatest scientists, while Malthus wallows in a slough of intellectual derision for his wrongheadedness. Why?

One much-touted reason is that while the Malthusian analysis may work for wild organisms of the kind studied by Darwin and Wallace, humans are a special case. Rather than overshooting a fixed productivity limit we can, unlike other creatures, use technical innovation to increase the limit. Economist Ester Boserup developed an influential statement of this argument in her book *The Conditions of Agricultural Growth*,[11] showing that when populations have expanded throughout history, people have responded by intensifying agricultural production and producing more food from a given area.

But Boserup didn't argue that this intensification was trade-off free. In premodern agricultures, one of the main forms of intensification was labour intensification. People worked longer hours to bring forth greater productivity. Sometimes this resulted, ironically but rationally, in even more population growth to meet labour demands.[12] In modern agricultures a lot of work is done by machines, but again not without trade-offs, including greenhouse gas emissions, soil erosion, water scarcity, agrochemical pollution, wildlife loss and land extensification. These problems form other productivity limits, which may or may not prove surmountable. Certainly, there's nothing in Boserup's analysis to suggest that productivity limits can always be overcome, and if they can't then her account is more of a qualification than a negation of Malthus. Perhaps one reason why Malthusianism gets such short shrift is because it touches a nerve. We may not be quite so different from other organisms as we think.

It's common nowadays to dismiss virtually any analysis that invokes external limits upon human action as Malthusian, thus making it guilty by association with Malthus's sour reputation. This makes for good propaganda but it's not intellectually rigorous.[13] One reason it's not intellectually rigorous is because it mixes up Malthus and Boserup, supposing that because it's possible to overcome the problem of a given productivity limit then productivity limits are not a problem. Let me instead make this suggestion: to overcome the negative outcomes imposed by modern society and its mechanised agricultures, we should follow a Boserup path of agricultural intensification – a labour-absorbing small farm future with a low environmental impact. I don't expect anyone to accept this suggestion at face value as obviously the best response to current problems. That's a case I hope to build as the book proceeds. But it's important to stress that my case is not Malthusian. I propose labour-intensive, small-scale agriculture as a positive, technological response to current constraints.

A better reason to criticise Malthus than human exceptionalism is that his analysis depoliticised hunger and poverty, which he blamed mostly on the excessive reproduction of the poor rather than on the politics of how some people get to be poor in the first place. Maybe approaches that continue to depoliticise poverty are better dismissed for their Malthusianism than ones that invoke external limits to human action.

There seem to be two variants of this depoliticised Malthusianism nowadays. The first holds that population growth or high fertility is a cause and not a consequence of poverty in high-fertility countries, and that migration from poor to rich countries should be prevented so that the latter aren't dragged down – an argument that mercifully commands little expert support, though it's heard often enough in political debate.[14] The second is a historical argument. Before the onset of the modern age, human populations were caught in a 'Malthusian trap' where income increase prompted population increase that diluted away any net increase in individual well-being. But with the onset of the modern industrial world, the argument runs, self-sustaining growth slayed the Malthusian demon and created the possibility of improved well-being for all.[15]

This second argument raises questions that have been addressed in intricate scholarly debates. Did a premodern Malthusian trap really exist? Is modern industrial growth truly self-sustaining, or is it a different kind of trap? How did it bootstrap itself out of the supposed Malthusian trap? Is greater income the same as greater well-being? What about its wider effect on planetary biophysics? We'll touch on some of these issues later in the book. The point I want to emphasise now is that the 'escape from Malthus' narrative coincides with a conventional view of economic development as a benign global force that's available to all the world's people if they follow the industrial path out of farming and into urbanism. Development isn't seen as something that concentrates resources to the benefit of some places or people at the expense of others, and that may not be generalisable to the global poor. In that sense, it's a depoliticised – perhaps Malthusian – narrative.

Take these excerpts from Stewart Brand's book, *Whole Earth Discipline*:

> *Life in your village is dull, back-breaking, impoverished, restricted, exposed, dangerous, and static. Brigands get you, an accident gets you, disease gets you, and there's no help nearby. You work like hell; then the weather*

changes, and you don't have crops to eat or sell. . . . In the city, life is exciting, work is less grueling; you're far better paid; you're free to move around and change jobs; you have some privacy; you're less vulnerable; and you have upward mobility. Will you put up with slum conditions for all that? In a heartbeat. . . . Let no one romanticize what the slum conditions are. . . . But the squatter cities are vibrant. *. . . What you see up close is not a despondent populace crushed by poverty but a lot of people busy getting out of poverty as fast as they can. . . . Everyone is working hard and everyone is moving up. . . . Peasant life is over unless catastrophic climate change drives us back to it.*[16]

Leaving aside the question of whether calling slums 'vibrant' constitutes romanticism, the sentiments in this passage are widely asserted, are perhaps sometimes accurate, but are also misleading. It's true that people in towns are better off on average than people in the countryside. But that's not the same as saying that poor people from the countryside will get rich by moving to town. Evidence suggests chronic, multi-generational slum poverty, which often bites hardest on rural newcomers. In practice, the lives of the global poor rarely follow the Dick Whittington narrative conjured by Brand, but involve a complex patchwork of livelihood strategies that juggle both urban and rural sources of family income over time and often retain a footing on rural farmland for income security.[17]

The rhetoric of choice and open opportunity in Brand's writing belies how economic chances are systemically structured so that poor people, rural or urban, have few opportunities for solid improvement wherever they go. If you believe in what Brand calls the 'urban promise' where 'everyone is moving up', then indeed peasant life is over and there's no case for a small farm future. But if the urban promise isn't kept – and there's plenty of evidence to suggest that it isn't now and won't be in the future – it's worth considering alternatives.

All this takes us a long way from questions of global population, but it underlines the point that where people are and where they're going – the global *flows* of people set in train by modernisation – may be more important than bare numbers. Brand's enthusiasm for people voting with their feet and quitting the impoverished *countryside* in favour of urban promise is widely endorsed in arguments for development. Despite the identical logic, the idea of people likewise voting with their feet and quitting the

impoverished *countries* in favour of 'rich-country promise' isn't so enthu-
siastically aired, especially in the rich countries where anti-immigrant
politics and border policing are amplifying.

International migration remains numerically small globally. In 2019,
3.5% of the world's people lived in a country other than their country of
birth. But across seven of the world's ten largest economies the average
proportion of the population born abroad was about 13%. These countries
had a 10% share of the global population and a 46% share of global economic production.[18] This suggests that people go if they can to where the
economic opportunities are greatest – towards prosperity, away from relative want. In the process, their fertility tends towards the typically lower
level of their rich country hosts, but their patterns of consumption also
tend towards typically higher host-country norms.

In a sense, these global patterns represent the core tension I explore in this
book. The world divides very roughly into high-fertility, low-consumption
(poor) places and low-fertility, high-consumption (rich) places. People
want to live in rich and not poor places, but there are only two ways this
can happen. One involves physical movement from poor to rich places or
countries, but this isn't possible for everyone and it's often unpopular with
people already there. The second involves endorsing the right of people not
to have to migrate afar in search of prosperity, instead spreading the low-
fertility, high-consumption way of life of the rich countries across the whole
world. The problem with this is that although fertility rates are declining,
this spreading of wealth isn't happening and can't happen within the existing
global economy. And if it did, it would create intolerable pressure on global
resources because the high-consumption part of the second lifeway more than
makes up for the low-fertility part, pushing beyond planetary boundaries.

A different future is needed, and what I suggest is a small farm future, ideally
a low-fertility, enough-consumption future, widely shared around the world.
It would be based neither on vast global flows of people nor on implausible
levels of worldwide economic growth, but instead on settling in to our existing local places for the long haul at historically high, but soon to be declining,
numbers in more sustainable, steady-state cultures and agricultures.

It's often assumed that relatively low-tech smallholder or peasant agriculture inevitably involves high fertility, in order to generate the hands
to work the fields (one possible route of Boserup's intensification). But

studies of smallholder agriculture in situations of relative land scarcity suggest that this isn't necessarily the case.[19] What's probably more important is a policy environment harnessing the same forces that have historically pushed fertility rates downwards – a sense of relative prosperity, a sense of security, and female agency. So these are crucial to the possibilities for a congenial small farm future.

I don't underestimate how daunting that challenge is in the face of the dominance of the present migration–urbanisation–economic growth model, though in the long run I suspect it will prove less daunting than dealing with that model's increasingly dysfunctional consequences. As is often pointed out, the world's population is now more urban than rural – though it's still a close-run thing, and around half the world's urbanites live in cities of under 500,000, suggesting at least some possibility of fruitful local urban–rural linkages.[20]

But this urbanising trend isn't some force of nature. It has occurred as a result of active policies that often haven't greatly benefited many of the people they've affected, and it could be reversed over time by other active policies oriented to different ends. One reason to think that this is likely to happen is that most of the world's population (and probably most of its capital) now lives near the ocean, often in giant port cities. The chances are high that a good deal of this land area will soon no longer be land. Or if it is, it will be considerably less amenable for human habitation.

The chances are likewise high that the economic dynamism that has drawn so many people into capital-concentrating coastal urbanism over the last century will waver over the next one. Before we can 'settle into our local places', a lot of the world's population will have to find a different local place to live. Climate change is already the main driver of global migration.[21] Perhaps the real population-related 'elephant in the room' for our times will be climate-fuelled migration, particularly from urban to rural areas. In the words of one recent report, the future is rural.[22]

Crisis #2: Climate

Climate change is the most widely discussed global crisis of our times. Unfortunately, wide discussion has trumped wide action. It's possible that the past three decades spent debating whether it's happening, whether it's caused by human actions and whether its consequences are anything to worry about may come to seem criminally complacent in the future. The bottom-line answer to all those questions is 'yes', but how serious the consequences are remains uncertain. At worst, a civilisation-ending catastrophe in which a small farm future of a sort for a remnant of humanity in a hot and hostile world is the only hope available. At best, numerous difficult adjustments in different places to various combinations of drought, flood, tempest, coastal storm surge, heat wave, wildfire, diminishing crop yields and crop nutritional content, sea level rise, and the spread of human diseases and crop pests.

I won't attempt to summarise the latest scientific thinking on the likely shape of future climate change,[23] but I will summarise its main proximal cause: the extraction and combustion of the fossil fuels (coal, oil and natural gas) that power the modern human economy. Their combustion releases as waste products greenhouse gases (GHGs), especially CO_2, which trap re-radiating sunlight in the atmosphere, prompting global average temperature increases, which currently stand at about 1°Celsius (1°C) above preindustrial levels. Within the next 10–30 years the increase is set to reach 1.5°C, the level at which the world's governments agreed to try to stabilise temperature increase on a voluntary basis at the United Nations Framework Convention on Climate Change meeting in Paris in 2015. The impacts on human well-being beyond 1.5°C are likely to be severe. Projecting the current emissions profile forwards on a business-as-usual path without mitigation suggests catastrophic global heating estimated at 3.7°C and possibly as high as 4.8°C above late-20th-century levels by 2100.[24]

A further problem is the long-term persistence in the atmosphere of much of the already emitted CO_2. To reduce temperatures to a safe level it will probably be necessary not only to stop further GHG emissions but to actively remove CO_2 from the atmosphere.

Soils and plants can emit or absorb GHGs at different stages of their life cycles and in response to different human management regimens, so farming can in theory be either a net source or sink for GHGs. Currently it's a net source, possibly responsible for 10%–16% of total human GHG emissions.[25] This will have to be reversed in the future. A good way of doing that is to move towards a small farm future. Not everyone will agree, but if we're to get emissions under control it's hard to dispute that we need a *different* farm future, in which agriculture becomes a sink rather than a major source for GHG emissions.

At the same time, it's easy to overdo the focus on agriculture and land use as GHG sources and sinks when the real culprit, overwhelmingly, is fossil fuel combustion, both directly in its own emission profile and indirectly in terms of the kind of farming and land use it makes possible. My main climate-related arguments for a small farm future aren't directly about the net emissions achievable through small-scale and low-impact means relative to other possibilities. Bigger questions turn on what kind of societies, economies, infrastructures and politics will be possible in a world that by design or default is decarbonising or warming. It's in this situation that the case for a small farm future presents itself most strongly.

It's conventional to distinguish between *mitigating* and *adapting to* climate change. The former involves reducing or removing carbon emissions from the atmosphere while the latter involves finding ways to cope with the effects of climate change. Both of these are necessary, but the case for small-scale farming revolves mostly around its potential value in social adaptation to climate change.

Fossil fuels, the main proximal cause of climate change, were first used industrially in China more than 2,000 years ago.[26] Although human activities have left an ecological imprint at least since those times, it's only in the last two centuries that the fossil fuel economy has taken off, culminating in the climate forcing of contemporary human activities. Without the geological accident of fossil fuel reserves, it's unlikely that humanity would be facing its current climate crisis, but fossil fuels alone aren't a sufficient explanation. As with population, the *underlying* cause is surely to be found in the specific histories of modernity, capitalism and globalisation, and the expansionary economies resulting from them.

Arguments in the form of 'only the capacity of capitalism to innovate technological solutions can now save us' therefore neglect the fact that the social and economic logic underlying modern societies continues to generate GHGs despite these societies' high levels of innovativeness. In a recent article, Ted Nordhaus put his finger on the dilemma: 'the only remotely plausible path to the sorts of changes that many environmentalists now demand, such as zero net emissions by 2030, or stabilizing global temperatures at 1.5 degrees Centigrade above preindustrial levels, would require top-down, centralized, technocratic measures that most environmentalists are unwilling to seriously embrace'.[27]

That's probably true. It also seems overly optimistic to judge the chances of such top-down measures to deliver those outcomes as even 'remotely plausible'. And even if they do, the proximal solution involved still doesn't address the factors underlying GHG emissions likely to threaten planetary boundaries in other ways. So if there's now time only for the global capitalist political economy to save us, then the time when we were salvageable has probably passed.

Nordhaus lambasts such thinking: 'There has never been any actionable agenda that green radicalism will actually embrace. . . . It is postmodern nihilism dressed up with the trappings of moral seriousness.' I see things otherwise. It's worth green radicals supporting the mitigation measures that governments do take, because mitigating climate change is usually better than failing to mitigate it. But we now also need to build autonomies from the global capitalist political economy orchestrated by those governments that continues to generate climate change – autonomies that will enable us to adapt to climate change as best we can and work towards a better future than those governments can deliver. The actionable agenda for a better future I propose is a small farm future, which is not a nihilistic one.

Similar issues arise with the view that climate change is so urgent that we need to keep all solutions on the table. This usually turns out to be a justification for high-tech interventions like nuclear power rather than real open-mindedness about the full range of climate mitigating and adapting interventions. In theory it might be possible to construe all-solutions approaches – a mixture of low-carbon, labour-intensive, horse-powered agriculture along with low-carbon nuclear power, for example. In practice this seems unlikely, not least because technologies aren't just technical. They involve different and often incompatible social logics around issues like the deployment of capital and labour, the concentration of state power, and more philosophical questions like humanity's place in the universe, of a kind that puts horse-powered agriculture and nuclear power on diverging conceptual tracks.

But given our exceptional capabilities in the modern world it's worth pondering why climate change seems to pose such an unsolvable problem. In an influential though widely criticised paper, the controversial ecologist Garrett Hardin discussed what he called the 'tragedy of the commons,' in which a resource open to all, like a common pasture, might be depleted if its users each pursued their own self-interest without regard to the wider common interest.[28] His critics correctly pointed out that this isn't how a commons actually works, although private property or state control have generally been favoured over common resource management in modern times anyway. Ironically, the result has arguably been a global tragedy of the commons, in which various agencies and individuals pursuing numerous ends through the medium of fossil fuels have offloaded the consequences onto the wider world and prevented collective action against their effects on Earth's climate.

It would be wrong to suggest that localised economies that bear the consequences of their own actions more directly can simply step in now and provide a complete solution to climate breakdown. But such economies involving low-emission, labour-intensive farming can help to mitigate it and, in some places, adapt to its consequences – one reason why a small farm future may be well fitted to future scenarios of climate change.

Certainly, the notion that increased organisational reach, knowledge, specialisation and complexity equate with greater climate security and resilience no longer seems as persuasive as it once did. Archaeologist Joseph Tainter, whose 1988 book *The Collapse of Complex Societies* is still among the best general discussions of how civilisations can fail, questioned simple theories of external, environmentally caused collapse:

> *Complex societies are characterized by centralized decision-making, high information flow, great coordination of parts, formal channels of command, and pooling of resources.... With their administrative structure, and capacity to allocate both labor and resources, dealing with adverse environmental conditions may be one of the things that complex societies do best.... It is curious that they would collapse when faced with precisely those conditions they are equipped to circumvent.*[29]

In the decades since he wrote those lines, it's become easier to see why societies might collapse when faced with such conditions, as we've witnessed our own put its impressive resources to work in understanding the threat of climate change and then do . . . almost nothing. Indeed, by 2014 global CO_2 emissions were 68% higher than in 1988[30] – not only the year that Tainter published his book, but also the year when global governments established the Intergovernmental Panel on Climate Change (IPCC) to analyse the risks of climate change and possible responses to it.

To be fair, Tainter does identify part of the problem: 'Once established a civilization's capacities for change become limited. Collapse results from sociopolitical ossification, bureaucratic inefficiency, or inability to deal with internal or external problems.'[31] This is a reasonable summation of where we seem to be right now. Despite the increasing urgency of the IPCC's warnings, global politicking over the period has produced nothing more than tepid voluntary accords, such as the 2015 Paris Agreement, that fail to address the gravity of the issue.

This inability to deal with climate change seems to have three main causes. First, countries that control large fossil fuel reserves (which are mostly rich and powerful) stand to lose economically from emissions restrictions. Second, within the present structuring of the global economy, the only route to development and prosperity has involved greater and greater amounts of fossil energy. And third, economic, political, energetic and climate-impact inequities between countries are grounded in long-term histories of colonialism and domination whose modern-day consequences would have to be confronted and settled if poorer countries were expected to limit their energy use and emissions.

In other words, most countries have short-term self-interests that militate against creating joint agreements with other countries on emissions limitations that would ultimately benefit everyone. We could view this as a tragedy of the global climate commons, or as a tragedy of *failing* to create a climate commons. What's more important than the terminology is recognising that sometimes people fail to come up with collective agreements that are in their long-term interests. More important still is figuring out what to do when that happens.

Creating and maintaining commons is hard to do (see Chapter 13, 'Complicating the Commons', page 173), so it's not necessarily surprising that we've failed to create one globally around climate change. But the cost of that failure will likely be huge. The projections vary, but typical scenarios suggest the need to reduce emissions globally by 45% within the next decade and to net zero by 2050 to keep warming within 1.5°C of pre-industrial levels.[32] Various ideas have been presented at national and international levels for how to achieve such cuts. I don't propose to evaluate them here, but it seems fair to say that the possibilities for implementing them without fundamentally disturbing the economic status quo are low.[33] Meanwhile, emissions continue

to rise. Currently the world is nowhere near being on a climate change mitigation pathway. In that light, three main future scenarios present themselves:

1. Rapid techno-fix: Existing net GHG-producing forms of production
   are replaced with GHG-negative equivalents, starting immediately,
   allowing economic and political business as usual to continue.
2. Political cap: Global governance breaks out of its present impasse,
   imposing drastic carbon limits that fundamentally restructure the present global economy.
3. Climate breakdown: This is the default in the absence of (1) or (2),
   unleashing chaotic consequences.

Much discussion understandably focuses around (1), emphasising
technological developments that, in the words of environmental writer
Emma Marris, 'have already allowed humanity to squeeze more out of
less' without relying on a 'sudden and unprecedented improvement in our
moral character' or 'grand sacrifices'.[34] The problem is that while these
developments certainly have enabled us to squeeze more out of less (relative
decoupling), they haven't led us to *actually use* less (absolute decoupling),
let alone to reduce emissions at an adequate rate. The real challenge is not
to produce *existing* levels of economic outputs like food or construction
materials more efficiently with respect to GHG-emitting inputs, but to
produce *adequate* levels of output with no GHG-emitting inputs at all. In
this the world is currently making less than zero progress.

In the likely absence of rapid techno-fix, it's possible that governments
will rise to the occasion and collectively impose the drastic emission cuts
implied in the second scenario. The IPCC states that holding global
warming to 1.5°C requires rapid and far-reaching transitions across most
economic sectors at unprecedented scale.[35] It's hard to imagine how these
could be achieved in the relevant time frame without more localised
economies (including agricultural economies) that largely jettison fossil
fuel inputs in favour of reduced and more labour-intensive production. So
the second scenario probably points to something like a small farm future.

At present, though, there's not much sign of governments rising to the
occasion, so the third scenario appears likely. It's hard to predict what this
world of climate breakdown would look like in political and economic

terms. Probably, it'll be quite varied from place to place, but it seems unwise to assume that the present world economy and world system of states would survive in anything much like its present form. As ex-CIA director James Woolsey has written, in a world with a 2 metre (~6 foot) sea level rise – which is eminently likely within a century under current emissions trends – 'it will take extraordinary effort for the United States, or indeed any country, to look beyond its own salvation'.[36] In other words, political uncertainties are looming that undermine confidence in the possibilities for centralised, technocratic climate change mitigation of the kind favoured by Ted Nordhaus.

So, short of some eleventh-hour techno-fix, the present climate crisis suggests a need to think seriously about local, labour-intensive, small-scale farming economies as an adaptive response. One aspect of this thinking is suggested by Emma Marris when she equates consumption and morality. If it requires an 'unprecedented improvement in our moral character' to consume less, this suggests that consuming large quantities of material things must be morally suspect, but also an unavoidable human failing. That seems a plausible description of how people often think about consumption nowadays, but it's an odd one historically. Most societies, including the forerunners of the rich countries comprising today's Global North, have been simultaneously less focused on extravagant material consumption as a prime route to fulfilment and less anxious about its moral implications when they do focus on it. The all-too-physical realities of climate change may ultimately have a culture-historical or, dare I say it, a spiritual grounding in the way we've come to think about consumption, morality and sacrifice. I return to these themes later in the book.

Crisis #3: Energy

All living things require external energy input to function, whether by obtaining it directly from the sun as plants do or indirectly by eating other organisms, as animals like us do. An adult human requires about 2,200 calories of energy per day (3.4 gigajoules – GJ – per year) from food to keep ticking over. But nowadays humanity uses a lot more direct energy than that: around 80 GJ of primary energy consumption per person annually as a global average, excluding food intake. On a country-by-country basis, the amount varies from less than 3 GJ per person in South Sudan to more than 750 in Iceland and Qatar.[37]

These high levels of energy consumption are a recent phenomenon. In 1800, average global energy consumption was 20 GJ per capita.[38]

To get to grips with the critical energy issues it's necessary to review some energy basics. Almost all the energy that's tapped by humans ultimately derives from the sun. Solar energy manifests on Earth in the form of relatively transient *flows* – the wind that's blowing or the sunshine that's beaming outside my window right now or, less fleetingly, the water that's flowing down the river nearby. The annual energy input from this solar flux is vast, dwarfing what even contemporary humanity uses by a factor of many thousands to one. But it's diffuse and hard to capture. On my farm, for example, we have some photovoltaic panels and a small wind turbine that turn solar flux into useful electrical energy we can store in batteries, but this is a costly, high-tech apparatus that only captures a tiny fraction of the incident energy falling on the farm.

Another way of capturing the flow is letting the plants on the farm do the work. My farm's trees, grasses and crops turn solar energy into plant biomass, giving wood and potentially other biofuels to burn for heat, edible crops, and fodder for livestock that produce food and fibre. On the farm, our inputs of time, energy and other resources to get these outputs are low (at least relative to the turbine and solar panels), but we still only capture a small proportion of the incident energy. Like the electricity we store in our batteries, the plant and animal biomass we create on the farm fixes solar energy flow into something a little more enduring: wood, plants and their oils, animal hides and carcasses. These are *stocks* instead of flows, but relatively short-lived ones.[39]

Fossil fuels are enduring energetic stocks. They derive mostly from dead plants that decayed in ancient geological eras, and therefore also originate from now long-gone solar flows. But they've kept that energy intact and available for aeons as a long-term stock, until humans began excavating and using it. They've also concentrated it physically. Crude fossil fuels contain up to three times more energy per kilogram than short-run stocks like wood or grain. And of course they are distributed non-uniformly across the Earth's surface, impelling a good deal of modern geopolitics.[40]

The idea of using energy raises other issues. It's a scientific axiom that energy can't be created or destroyed. It can only change its form. Without going into technicalities, the way this works in everyday human situations is that flows of incoming solar energy are fixed in intermediate stocks that then do useful work for us – a full battery, a sack of coal, a cord of firewood, a bag of wheat. When the work is done, the intermediate stocks are degraded and no longer available, their energy transformed mostly into low-grade heat that we can't recapture. Sometimes, the degraded product has another use – ash from burnt wood can be used in soapmaking, human excrement from wheat can be composted to stimulate new plant growth – but the degraded product can't do as much generalised work as the pristine one. Unless we obtain fresh energy inputs and start the process again, the system reaches an equilibrium with its surroundings in which no more useful work can be done. With technological improvements, we may be able to decrease *energy intensity* (the input of intermediate product needed to produce a given quantity of output) – 'squeezing more out of less'. But we still need new energy inputs.

Three points to notice about these energy basics. First, in situations where the available energy mostly comes in the form of flows, you'd expect people to spread out in the landscape to make best use of local flows, though with some concentration around points of greater energy potential such as rivers. This is essentially the situation of premodern societies and agricultures. When concentrated energy stocks are available, this restriction is removed and it becomes possible (though not necessary) for people to cluster in conurbations, as in the modern, fossil-fuelled urban world.

Second, inputs of energy are required to create the intermediate stocks. Wood must be cut and collected, oil must be extracted, solar panels must be assembled. There's no point creating stocks that require the same or more energy input than they furnish, and energy sources with a higher energy return on investment (EROI) are usually favoured. Generally, fossil fuels have high EROIs while low-carbon, renewable sources have lower ones (as do unconventional or 'tight' fossil fuel sources like oil sands, on which the oil industry increasingly relies). In low EROI situations, economic growth and labour productivity are less, because more investment must be diverted to furnishing intermediate stocks.[41]

Third, there are 'energetic ecosystem' dynamics that parallel ecological succession: an early, resource-rich energetic ecosystem enjoys few resource limitations and a high energy throughput. Later, resource limitations start to bite, energy throughput relative to production decreases, and low, efficient energy use and resource use is emphasised.[42]

As Figure 1.1 shows, the high levels of primary energy consumption among modern humans rely overwhelmingly on accessing stocks of fossil fuels. Hence the problem of climate change. The fact that fossil fuels are source-limited or non-renewable is potentially another problem, since ultimately reserves must deplete and fossil fuel energy prices escalate – the much-touted problem of 'peak oil'. But the real problem currently is at the sink, not the source. If humanity continues to burn fossil fuels as at present, we'll make the world uninhabitable for ourselves through climate breakdown long before the fuels are gone. So the main worry right now isn't the scarcity of fossil fuels but their abundance. The necessity is for us to impose 'peak oil' (and gas, and coal) on ourselves.

Figure 1.1 isn't too encouraging in that respect. It shows climbing levels of fossil fuel consumption globally, from about 3,500 million tonnes of oil equivalent in 1965 to nearly 12,000 million tonnes in 2018. The thin slivers at the top of the graph show consumption of lower-carbon, non-fossil fuel sources of energy, including nuclear power and renewables like hydro and solar electricity, wind power and biomass. The proportionate contribution of these lower-carbon forms to the total energy mix has increased from 4% in 1965 to 13% in 2018. But these lower carbon forms of energy haven't substituted for fossil fuels. They've merely added to a total energy con-

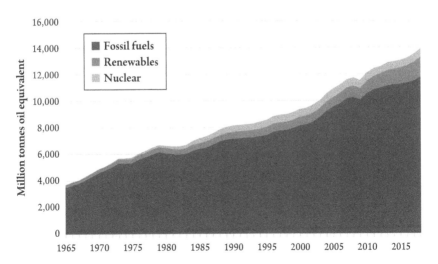

Figure 1.1. World Energy Consumption, 1965–2018. *Source: BP Statistical Review of World Energy 2019*

sumption dominated by high-carbon fossil fuels, whose consumption has risen inexorably. Even if we correct for population increase by considering per capita rather than absolute fossil fuel consumption, there's still been an increase in fossil fuel consumption globally from about 1.05 tonnes of oil equivalent per person in 1965 to 1.55 in 2018 – another piece of evidence to suggest that the problems we face aren't just population-related.[43]

The downward kink seen in Figure 1.1 around 2008 reflects the financial crisis of that year and its chilling effect on the global economy manifested in energy use. But, as you can see from later years, this turned out to be a short-run downturn in the longer upward trend. As this book is going to press, the global pandemic caused by the new SARS-CoV-2 virus seems certain to cause another and probably larger downward spike. Collapsing demand for fossil fuels arising from the pandemic has caused an economic crisis in the oil and gas industry that's prompted some analysts to question whether it can survive. But what's clear from Figure 1.1 is that the modern global economy is utterly dependent on fossil fuels, whatever short-run price fluctuations the sector experiences in crisis conditions. No fossil fuels, no capitalism in its modern form and no globalisation. So if the pandemic indeed puts paid to the oil industry and helps save the climate, if the downturn becomes permanent, we'll need to devise a different kind of economic future for humanity. In fact, we need to devise a different kind of economic future for humanity anyway – however the long-term effects of the pandemic play out.

While proponents proclaim the virtues of low-carbon energy technologies, Figure 1.1 shows that these technologies aren't even close to replacing fossil fuels or mitigating their impact right now. The next energy revolution – if there's to be one – is yet to begin. This is especially problematic because meeting the 1.5°C global warming target of the 2015 Paris Agreement is already unlikely in view of committed emissions from existing fossil energy infrastructure,[44] unless it's prematurely decommissioned at high cost and without low-carbon replacements available at volume. Currently available low-carbon replacements such as nuclear and renewables also have significant limitations as complete substitutes for our fossil-fuelled present. And even if they were rolled out now at faster rates than current implementation, their impact on GHG emissions wouldn't itself be enough to prevent dangerous warming.[45] To be clear, I'm not arguing against transitioning urgently from fossil fuels to low-carbon energy sources. Hopefully it'll be possible to carry some of these sources through with us into a climate-stabilised future. But it seems wise to assume that people in the wealthy countries at least will have to get by in the future with lower per-capita energy consumption.[46]

The rising global consumption of energy, fossil fuel energy in particular, shown in Figure 1.1 is mysterious in that it isn't driven independently by population, affluence or energy intensity but seems to follow its own internal dynamic – 'energy begets energy' in the words of two writers in the field – prompting humans to persist in furnishing as much of it as they can.[47] The sobering implication of this is that the small but growing slivers of low-carbon energy sitting atop the thick wedge of fossil fuels in the figure aren't the beginnings of a transition out of fossil fuels – they're *additions*, not replacements, to humanity's voracious energy consumption.

But the idea of energy begetting energy is odd. As we saw above, energy furnishes intermediate goods that do useful work for us. People surely don't just toil to create intermediate energy stocks for fun. Instead, the present structure of the global economy involves a spiral of ever-growing capital investment, which is physically manifested in (fossil) energy use. Further, as this capital is put to work in ever more complex and interrelated ways, the amount of energy used to produce the final outputs increases (there's greater investment in the final and intermediate energy economy), even if the intensity of energy use to produce a given level of output diminishes.

This has two further sobering – though perhaps in some sense liberating – implications. First, it seems impossible to 'degrow' the global economy in its present form energetically without fundamentally changing it. Otherwise, degrowth would equate simply with recession, joblessness and economic stagnation. Second, even if energy use could be made carbon neutral and effectively limitless, it's likely that the compounding material trace of capital growth would then butt up against some other physical limit – soils, water, phosphates, pollution abatement and so on.[48]

But these sobering implications are potentially liberating because they suggest the present structuring of the global economy can't continue, freeing us to work towards other kinds of economy. This is the lodestar of an emerging movement in economics working under the banner of 'degrowth' that aims to rethink the whole basis of economic action.[49] It speaks to the mature human energetic ecosystem, in which energetic throughput is reduced relative to the fossil-fuelled bonanza of the 20th-century economy, while human well-being is retained or enhanced.

My position in this book is in keeping with the degrowth project, but I argue for a strong focus on agriculture as the key point of energetic transformation. I also have some sympathy for mainstream economists who struggle to differentiate the unfamiliar new world of degrowth economics from the familiar scourge of negative gross domestic product (GDP) growth, or recession. Moving to a mature post-carbon human energetic ecosystem would probably involve junking billions of dollars of fossil fuel investment and infrastructure, which would take a lot of movement out of the global economy of both a fiscal and physical kind. It would generate multitudes of people looking for new kinds of localised, low-carbon work.

One of the most obvious and necessary forms of such work in a low-energy throughput economy is farming, which can absorb a lot of labour. A human energetic ecosystem of this kind would probably look a lot like the diffuse, rural world of premodern agriculture, oriented to skimming energetic flows rather than mining energetic stocks. And that, perhaps, is a problem. Nobody wants to turn the clock back to the hardscrabble life of toil retained in folk memory from the small farm past.

I have two responses to that over and above the old parental stock-in-trade that in a tough world what people want isn't necessarily what they get. One is to probe at the gaps, slippages and weak points in the folk memory of small farm toil to come up with a more congenial cultural package for a small farm future. The other is to address in more practical terms how such toil might be avoided, especially by retooling the energetic economy of the traditional small farm.

One piece of happy news is that even in heavily mechanised modern agricultures on-farm energy input is only a small fraction of society's total energy use. To take the example of wheat production in the United Kingdom, in 2017 nearly 15 million tonnes (16 million US tons) were produced, about enough to provide for the annual food energy needs of the country's 66 million people. The on-farm energy use associated with this harvest was approximately 35 million GJ, less than 1% of the country's total energy consumption. Or, to put it another way, it requires the equivalent of about 16 litres (4 gallons) of gasoline on-farm to produce one adult's entire annual food energy requirements (which are the equivalent of about 100 litres of gasoline) from wheat. Incidentally, nearly seven of those litre-equivalents are devoted to producing synthetic fertiliser; organic wheat uses less energy.[50]

This is just an illustrative example. It would be naïve to assume that in a future decarbonising world of small-scale farming, refineries would still be trickling out a 16-litre-per-head allocation of gasoline so that farmers didn't have to bend their backs. And it wouldn't be a good idea to grow only wheat. But the wider point is that a little fossil or concentrated energy can go a long way on the farm. In Part II, I advocate for a farming that uses less fossil energy and more human muscle than is now standard in wealthy countries. But to really 'squeeze more out of less', we should probably start thinking about a small farm future with a lot of people spread out over rural landscapes to skim their energetic flows, and apply our minds to how we might ease their burden by providing a modicum of more concentrated energy. There are jobs on the farm where they'd certainly want machine power, but the extreme mechanisation of modern agriculture is driven more by profit margins in a competitive, fossil-fuelled economy than by any rounded view of what counts as rewarding human work.

Another piece of (mostly) happy energetic news about a small farm future is that even though it may represent a path of agricultural *labour* intensification, it's also a path of energetic deintensification and greater resource efficiency. There are economies of downsizing which arise from devoting less energy and economic activity to producing intermediate goods and more to end products, another symptom of the mature energetic ecosystem.[51] This may not be such happy news for those of us perched atop the global income distribution. Not only do we have large quantities of fossil fuel energy available to do our bidding, we also have a large number of poor people, mostly in faraway countries, toiling in the primary and intermediate economies who are also doing our bidding via the mechanism of market demand. In a small farm future, it's unlikely you'd be able to drive to the supermarket and buy wine from somewhere like South Africa that's furnished by the multitudinous and often poorly paid labours of estate workers, packers, drivers, miners, roughnecks, merchant seamen and so forth. But you might be able to make some wine yourself from the fruits in your garden, and so might all those workers who certainly can't while they're working for you. Overall, if we get it right the energetic deintensification of a small farm future may enhance aggregate human welfare – possibly even in the richer countries if we learn to appreciate the virtues of making wine instead of buying it.

Still, a low-energy small farm life isn't all about ferments from the hedgerows. Energy analyst Vaclav Smil has argued that it takes annual energy consumption of around 84 GJ per capita for a society to gain a modicum of affluence.[52] As noted above, the variation from country to country is huge, ranging from less than 3 to more than 750 GJ per capita. Only a minority of countries fall above Smil's 84 GJ cutoff, not many of them notable for an extensive small farm sector.[53] But there are grounds for questioning the idea that high energy use is inherently necessary for a decent life. Cuba, for example, achieves life expectancies in excess of the United States, with 20% of its workforce in agriculture, despite per capita energy consumptions in recent years hovering around the 40 GJ level and per capita GDP only 14% of US levels – all of it achieved historically in the face of embargoes and enmity from the world's major superpower. At the other end of the scale, once energy consumption exceeds 110 GJ per capita there's no improvement in standard quality of life indicators.[54]

We can infer that within the present global economy, per capita annual energy consumptions over 84 GJ are necessary for buy-in to industrial success, but countries that emphasise self-reliant agricultural production and egalitarian social provision can achieve good social outcomes at much lower levels of energy consumption. It's therefore possible that the mature energetic human ecology of a small farm future could achieve a reasonable level of well-being for most people at much lower levels of energy consumption than our current fast-throughput energy ecology delivers. That's a happy conclusion if it's true, because transitioning to a low-throughput energy ecology seems increasingly unavoidable if we're to avert climate breakdown. Some less happy conclusions are that energy transitions usually take a long time, and we haven't yet started one.

Crisis #4: Soil

Farming, and therefore human life, depends upon the soils in which crops grow. Despite the attention garnered by various costly forms of modern soil-free cultivation like hydroponics, vertical farming and cultured protein, that fundamental truth is unlikely to change in the foreseeable future.

The soil crisis exists because human agriculture is causing the physical erosion of soils or the degradation of their capacity to sustain healthy plant life at faster rates than they can reform.

Gardeners can build soil quickly by assembling decayed organic matter, but it's an energy- and labour-intensive process, and there's only so much organic matter to go around. Working on a larger scale, farmers – and civilisations that depend on them – are effectively limited by the soils already in place. Their job is to try to retain them.

They haven't always been successful. Agriculture largely depends on annual crops that have to be established anew each year from seed, usually after tilling the soil. Annual plants are relatively rare in wild ecosystems, where soils are typically covered and bound together by perennial plants that offer protection from the erosive effects of wind, rain and surface water runoff. In annual-dominated human agriculture, the soil is at high risk of physical erosion, especially in tropical and arid climates. Whereas soil-forming and soil-eroding processes in natural ecosystems more or less balance each other, erosion can exceed formation by one to two orders of magnitude under annual tillage regimens, suggesting that current methods of farming aren't sustainable in the long term.[55] Poorly managed agricultural soils eventually get blown into the atmosphere or washed into watercourses, where they're of no use.

Cautionary tales abound concerning soil loss, both past and present. The demise of ancient civilisations is routinely attributed to poor soil management, and the same goes for more recent events, such as the US Dustbowl of the 1930s. In the present day, it's even been claimed that Britain, with its forgiving climate and long history of tillage farming, only has a hundred harvests left in its soils as a result of modern farming methods, though in this case the issue is soil nutrients and carbon, rather than physical loss of soil as such.

Most of these tales turn out to be more complex and perhaps less dramatic than first they appear. The Dustbowl, for example, arguably resulted more from unusual climate extremes to which farmers eventually adjusted than from irredeemably bad farming practices, which is maybe just as well in view of the climate extremes to come.[56] Still, there's no doubt that soil loss and soil degradation are major problems, with an estimated 25%–33% of world soil already moderately to highly degraded due to human-caused erosion, nutrient depletion, acidification, urbanisation and chemical pollution, and 12 million hectares (30 million acres) of soil 'lost' annually to degradation.[57]

Another aspect of the high-yielding annual crops favoured in agriculture is that they demand nutrients more heavily than most wild flora. In the case of nitrogen, an abundant element in the atmosphere and a key plant nutrient in soluble compound form, it's possible for farmers to get it to their crops renewably in various ways, albeit at the cost of significant energy input, or labour input, or additional land-take, and sometimes at the cost of downstream fertiliser pollution. But most of the other plant nutrients aren't so easily cycled. There's a danger of mining them from soils and dumping them wherever human effluent goes, often ultimately into the sea, where they're essentially lost to agriculture while polluting marine ecosystems. The long-term availability of agricultural phosphorus is a particular concern, since global agriculture currently relies on mining it non-renewably. With global reserves concentrated in just five countries, the prospect of 'peak phosphorus' has been described as a 'geostrategic ticking time bomb'.[58] Again, the case for a low-energy agrarian localism presents itself: closing the loop by returning phosphorus from crop and human wastes locally to soils, instead of mining it globally.

The global distribution of nutrient inputs is also relevant. Farmers in wealthy countries often apply them heavily for diminishing marginal gains, resulting in runoff that causes problems for drinking water supplies and the eutrophication of aquatic ecosystems resulting in anoxic dead zones. Farmers in poor countries often can't afford them, resulting in low yields that can compound poverty or, among the very poorest farmers, over-exploitation of soils leading to erosive loss. So 'fertiliser equity' is an issue. And farming geared to local demand is probably more likely to achieve efficient fertiliser use.

In summary, soil is a non-renewable resource that farm practices can physically destroy, mine of its nutrients, pollute or denude of its vitality – all of which are occurring. This, in essence, is the soil crisis. Whether small farms are less culpable than large ones is debatable. A hundred smallholders armed with spades may be no less destructive than a single farmer working the same area with a tractor. But small farms are probably better equipped to conserve the soil than large ones, for both social and agronomic reasons connected with their capacities for closing the loop of local flows. More important still is a question that can't be answered by comparing soil degradation on large and small farms under present economic conditions: What would farming look like in an equitable, low-energy, non-expansionary civilisation that emphasised the preservation of the soil?

Another point we'll consider in Part II is the capacity for good soil management to turn not only the soil crisis but also the climate crisis on their heads. It's possible to adopt farming practices, the argument runs, that can *build* soil rather than deplete it, absorbing atmospheric carbon in the process while furnishing us with our food. That win-win-win would be very good news indeed – if it's true.

Crisis #5: Stuff

Soil is only one of the material things upon which current human civilisation depends. Nowadays we rely on a bewildering multitude of materials in unprecedented quantities. I see four potential dimensions of crisis with this plethora of 'stuff'.

First, the processing of certain materials is energy intensive. Iron, for example, is abundant and likely to remain so, but turning it into useful metal consumes a lot of energy. Currently, there are no plausible substitutes for fossil fuels to smelt iron (or to produce other key resources like fertiliser) at existing prices and volumes.[59] In this respect, there are material implications to the climate and energy crises.

Second, discarding certain materials causes pollution and toxicity. Plastic waste pollution in the ocean is an example of the former, while numerous substances from modern industry to which humans and other species haven't long been exposed are actually or potentially toxic. This includes agricultural inputs such as fertilisers and pesticides, as well as materials from other industries such as heavy metals in mine tailings. We have little idea of the long-term consequences.

Third, there are issues with the non-renewability of certain materials. In 1980, biologist Paul Ehrlich and economist Julian Simon famously placed a bet on whether the price of five industrial metals would be relatively higher or lower after ten years. Ehrlich argued for the former on the basis of resource exhaustion, and Simon for the latter, mostly on the basis that human ingenuity, helped along by economic incentives, would find substitutes for scarce resources. Simon won the bet, providing ammunition for the view that human innovation always overcomes resource constraints.

Other analysts have argued that Simon just got lucky. Ehrlich would have won the bet in most decades since 1900. The issue remains controversial, especially in view of the poor correlation between price and abundance, but recent evidence of increasing metal prices and price volatilities, decreasing ore quality, and a tripling of the resources and materials required to generate a given quantity of some ores compared to a century ago suggests that Ehrlich's view might be sound.[60] Besides, the problem modern civilisation faces isn't just finding substitutes for a few resource inputs but for many, at a time when demand is growing and pollution sinks are shrinking. And consider rebound effects or the Jevons paradox: increased efficiency in resource use, which potentially delays its exhaustion, is counterbalanced by greater usage due to lowered price. (Evidence in this area is complex, but often suggests strong rebounds.[61])

So, to put it mildly, Simon's case against resource scarcity seems unproven. Others put the matter less mildly, including chemical engineer Harald Sverdrup and his colleagues:

> *Several metals, elements and energy resources are about to run into scarcity within the next decades, and most elements within some centuries. . . . [T]his scarcity will lead to 'peak wealth,' 'peak population,' 'peak costs,' 'peak junk,' 'peak problems' and possibly 'peak civilization,' unless some urgent measures are systematically taken throughout the world. . . . The future resource supply is thus unsustainable as long as resource use continues as today. . . . [G]overnments must take this issue seriously and immediately start preparing for legislations that can close material cycles, optimize energy use and minimize all types of irreversible material losses as soon as possible.*[62]

Yet governments are stuck with a single model of development that makes it hard for them to do so. United Nations (UN) data suggest that use of material inputs increases in proportion to income with no apparent limit, to the extent that the resource use of the wealthy countries can't realistically be generalised worldwide.[63] Since a major justification for the present economic order is precisely its possibilities for generalising such wealth and well-being, this portends a looming crisis in political economy (see 'Crisis #9: Political Economy', page 53).

That, in essence, is the fourth dimension of resource crisis. Unquestionably, human well-being requires stuff but not at currently proliferating levels of resource extraction. The inability to discern the difference between what the richest people in the world want and what's necessary for human well-being is a proximal resource crisis, which is the material embodiment of an underlying cultural crisis (Crisis #10). I submit a small farm future as a possible corrective.

Crisis #6: Water

Water is part of a perpetual hydrological cycle, and therefore unlike fossil fuels or soils it can't be 'used up'. However, the availability of water in a given place varies due to short-term fluctuations and long-term climatic and topographic change, and when it comes to meeting human needs it's possible to abstract it faster than it's replenished. These factors combine to make water availability a critically limiting resource in many places, with global supply projected to meet only 60% of demand within 20 years.[64] A further problem, returning to the Ehrlich–Simon debate, is that while people are ingenious at replacing many depleting material feedstocks with new ones, we haven't been so successful at finding substitutes for water.

The concentration of water needs prompted by urbanisation is another complication. Furnishing people's water needs and dealing with their wastes are demanding businesses in cities. There are parallels here between the provision of water and energy. With cheap energy, we can turn water flows into stocks by building reservoirs and elaborate pipe infrastructures that enable us to aggregate into conurbations rather than spreading over landscapes to make the most efficient use of water flows and human wastes. But there are limits to these processes imposed by hydrological factors, energy costs and labour dynamics, all of which are likely to press on future water supply. One estimate suggests that two-thirds of the global population may be living in water-stressed conditions by 2025.[65]

A lot of water use occurs in agriculture, where irrigation accounts for 70% of global freshwater withdrawals (rain-fed agriculture constitutes an additional usage). Without irrigation it's been estimated that global grain production would decrease by about 20%, but inevitably irrigation by some methods for some crops in some places is more efficient than in others.[66] The food system doesn't bear the long-term – or even short-term – costs of local water depletion, leading it to over-produce water-intensive crops, particularly cash export crops. This is particularly so in the case of non-renewable water from aquifers such as the Ogallala aquifer, which transects several Midwestern states in the United States and holds 'fossil' meltwater from the Ice Age. The depletion of such aquifers has major consequences for future crop selection and yield.

Global water abstraction is affected by numerous factors: changing technologies that make it easier to draw down on non-renewable resources (as when petrol-powered pumps replaced wind-powered ones over the Ogallala) or easier to conserve water (as when drip irrigation replaces sprinkler irrigation); changing economic incentives (water usage agreements, agricultural subsidies, food and energy prices); changing crop choices and varieties; and perhaps above all, the changing climate. Issues of water quality, water abstraction and water rights all condition agriculture-related water crises.

It's worth asking if current patterns of water use are sustainable in relation to climate change, energy availability, non-renewable (aquifer) availability and so on – and, if not, what the implications are for human well-being and crop production. Efforts are under way to develop more drought-resistant crop varieties, though yield penalties may be unavoidable. There's also an argument for choosing better-adapted crops in certain situations, such as unirrigated sorghum over irrigated wheat. Sometimes such choices may involve embracing neglected local or indigenous knowledges, a point developed in detail by Gary Paul Nabhan in his reconstruction of local foodways in the arid US Southwest.[67] But it seems unlikely that such parts of the world will be able to sustain current population levels, and certainly not in the manner to which they're currently accustomed. There's a social sustainability dimension here: in the absence of subtle, imaginative and benevolent governance, such mismatches between population needs and water availability often fuel violent human conflict.[68]

Globally, people are beginning to turn attention from high-tech, high-energy forms of water management to whole-landscape management that integrates watersheds, woodlands and farmland. In the words of International Fund for Agricultural Development president Gilbert Houngbo: 'For too long, the world has turned first to human-built, or "grey," infrastructure to improve water management. In so doing, it has often brushed aside traditional and Indigenous knowledge that embraces greener approaches'[69] – knowledge that, once again, is typically based on diverse skimming of flows in order to create local livelihoods of the kind that small farms furnish rather than the concentration of the stocks required to generate large-scale profit.

Water is likely to emerge in the future as a critically limiting resource for human well-being in general and food production in particular. It's possible that, as with energy and soil, a more water-conserving mature human ecology will emerge in which people spread out in the landscape to tap flows rather than concentrate at the cost of pricey energy and labour inputs. This is in keeping with a small farm future, especially because small farms often generate more product per unit of water input, despite poorer access to water overall.[70] Again though, the main impetus towards a small farm future in relation to water probably isn't the relative water-use efficiencies of small and large farms under present conditions so much as the combined macro effects of future water scarcity on issues like urbanisation, migration and grain prices, which are likely to prompt a more distributed and localised human ecology.

Crisis #7: Land

Crises of energy, stuff, soil and water are one thing, but is there even enough land? The answer depends, of course. Land for whom, and land for what? Some analysts predict a 21st-century 'looming land scarcity', suggesting the need for additional global farmland of anything between a challenging 210 million hectares (519 million acres) to an impossible 10 billion hectares (25 billion acres) over the coming decades. The drivers of this upward pressure divide fairly evenly between population growth, urbanisation, cultivation of biofuel crops as fossil fuel substitutes, pasture for increased meat production and demands for industrial/plantation forestry.[71]

But these projections are based on business-as-usual assumptions about growing demand that may not come to pass (the same is true of the much-repeated but misleading factoid that humanity needs to grow 70% more food by 2050[72]). Another way to think about land is to compute a per capita global footprint on the basis of existing farmland, which works out at 0.65 hectares (1.6 acres) currently, falling to 0.5 ha (1.2 acres) by 2050 at the UN's mid-level population estimate, maybe less with the effects of climate change and sea level rise. Trying to hold those 0.5–0.65 hectares in mind as a rough rule of thumb for how much land you have at your disposal to furnish all your food needs is a worthy exercise. Country by country, the allocation varies from 37 ha in Mongolia to 0.006 ha in Bahrain. Looking at *cropland* specifically, the most generously provided country is Kazakhstan, with 2.5 hectares – 6.2 acres – per capita. The United States is quite well placed, with 2.5 hectares per capita of total farmland currently; water rather than land is likely to be the critically limiting resource in much of the United States.

The places with the most potential for environmentally tolerable agricultural expansion are sparsely populated parts of Eastern Europe, Central Asia, sub-Saharan Africa and Latin America, some of which are currently experiencing population outflows. Various possible future agricultural pathways present themselves – new expansionary frontiers in these lightly farmed areas, perhaps in the form of smallholder in-migration or the neo-plantation model of corporate and governmental land grabs; increased pressure at the margins of more sensitive biomes like tropical rainforests; intensification of agricultural production on the 'global 0.5' hectare by various possible means; or a lowering of land demand by reductions in meat consumption and food waste.[73]

We'll consider some of these issues in more depth later. For now, I'd like to extend the gaze beyond humanity and ask whether there's also a crisis of land scarcity for the rest of Creation.[74] The answer is a resounding yes. Such a precipitous decline of wild organisms and species is occurring that our present era has been dubbed the sixth mass extinction, taking its place alongside ancient traumas that have left their imprint in the fossil record. This time, we can blame humanity's climate-changing activities, our destruction of wild habitats, chemical pollution, intensive agricultural practices that erase wild species from farmland and our introduction of exotic organisms and pathogens to new habitats at accelerated rates.[75]

The decline of some species – such as the insects that pollinate human crops or oceanic microorganisms whose life cycles mitigate climate change – threatens human well-being directly. In other cases the human consequences are less clear, though the evidence suggests that cascading ecosystem stresses rebound negatively on human welfare.[76] The effects on the well-being of the species concerned are clearer – a kind of Malthusian crisis deflected from humanity onto the rest of the Creation. Assessing the rights and wrongs of these effects takes us into realms of moral enquiry beyond the scope of this book, but humanity's inability to respond to them with clear philosophical confidence may be another morbid symptom of a cultural crisis (Crisis #10) underlying many of the other crises discussed here.

But we aren't completely getting our way in our current battle with the Creation. Bacteria, weeds and crop pests are increasingly resistant to the medical and agricultural antibiotics that we've been throwing at them in recent decades, threatening a rockier road ahead for human and crop health. It seems wise to take this as an advisory note from forces larger than ourselves that full-frontal, broad-spectrum, labour-saving human assault on the wider Creation won't pay in the long run. The shorthand mantra of the alternative farming movement is to 'work with' rather than against nature, which is sensible so far as it goes. But, as ever, there are trade-offs, and nature can be a capricious work colleague. We'll return to these issues in Part II.

Sparing, Sharing and Rewilding Land

The most important link between the extinction crisis and the concerns of this book hinges on how exactly to trim the human impacts on nature. This is addressed in the land sparing sharing debate. The idea is that it's good to have as much undisturbed wildlife habitat as possible and it's also good to make farming as wildlife-friendly as possible. But if wildlife-friendly farming produces lower crop yields and therefore occupies more land while remaining less wildlife-friendly than true wilderness, then it may be better to adopt higher-yielding, less wildlife-friendly farming that concentrates agriculture in smaller areas, leaving more space for wilderness.

Other things being equal, this is logically possible in theory and in some cases and some geographic levels appears to be true in practice. But other things aren't equal, and the sparing-sharing debate mixes up too many issues that need to be separated out.

First, it's commonly assumed that higher-yielding, less wildlife-friendly farming means large-scale, high-tech, energy-intensive, mechanised farming of the kind practised in wealthy countries today. This assumption isn't necessarily true. Organic and small-scale farming in poor countries often out-yields larger-scale and more high-tech agriculture, using low-tech inputs like additional labour. In other words, higher-yielding land-sparing strategies might actually point to small-scale agriculture.

Second, the land-sparing framework typically assumes that total production is fixed, so if per acre yields increase then land-take is bound to fall. This is rarely what happens in practice. There can be a Jevons paradox in land use, as with any kind of consumption. For example, improved yields in staple crops for which demand is relatively fixed can make land available for cash crops like biofuels, coffee, and meat for which demand is elastic, prompting increased land-take. Generally, greater market linkage can increase land-take, even when per acre yields are higher. The acid test is whether land intensification *actually does* result in more wildlife habitat rather than *theoretically might*, to which the answer seems to be – not usually.[77]

Another complication is that animals and other organisms often need to move across farmland between wilderness areas. This is possible if the farmland is diverse and extensively managed, but not necessarily feasible under a land-sparing, intensive agriculture. It's also worth questioning how amenable different styles of farming are to wildlife, something that might point to the advantages of smaller-scale and more labour-intensive farming. The possibility that poor people released from farming by large-scale capital and energy-intensive land-sparing agricultures will move into wild habitat margins if they can't find other employment is also relevant. So the sparing-sharing framework is incomplete without considering wider political and economic issues.[78]

Although the sparing-sharing framework originated in serious ecological studies, it's often deployed by partisans of large-scale conventional agriculture to criticise organic farming in rich countries for its lower yields. This is a questionable focus in view of the vastly greater land hunger of non-organic pure livestock systems. Meanwhile, the ecological literature is quietly ditching the sparing-sharing framework in favour of more sophisticated models, while low-input agroecological intensification is probably a more promising route for delivering an ecological and economic win-win for poor small-scale farmers than large-scale 'land-sparing' agriculture.[79]

Another inflection of the sparing-sharing debate is the case for replacing extensive farmland with reintroduced wild species, such as the proposed Buffalo Commons in the US Great Plains. In the United Kingdom, the focus has mostly been on upland sheep farming. The idea is that sheep farming creates low-grade grassland, producing little food for consumers and little money for farmers while preventing woodland growth that might not only enhance wildlife but also mitigate lowland flooding.[80]

If the United Kingdom eliminated upland sheep farming, it would clearly be problematic to substitute with imported sheep products unless it could be shown that the sheep industry in the exporting countries had a lower environmental impact. Some analysts argue that such globalised trade-offs do sometimes actually minimise net impact across the world.[81] But this requires expert monitoring and is prone to 'leakage' or rebound effects, so there's a case for keeping trade-offs and ecological feedbacks local – which is one of the strongest arguments for small farm localism. Even then the trade-offs are complex. Without inclusive governance involving farming communities themselves, it's easy to impose top-down conservation models that can alienate those communities and produce various counterproductive outcomes, a common problem globally when the voices of traditional agriculturists are politically silenced.

Generally, then, there's a need within the sparing-sharing debate to attend carefully to which human and wild ecologies are being promoted and to what larger ends, especially when small-scale farmers are less prominently represented in the debate than familiar agri-industry and conservationist viewpoints. As Welsh sheep farmer Dafydd Morris Jones put it: 'Rewilding portrays itself as being a way of reconnecting people with nature. . . . The question I'd ask of it is which people and which nature? . . . Aren't you actually disconnecting people from nature in order to reconnect other people with a different nature?'[82]

This question of *which* nature people choose, locally and globally, is an important aspect of the contemporary crisis over land.

Judging Nature

In her book *Rambunctious Garden*, Emma Marris discusses the dilemmas faced by conservationists as they wrestle with curating the natural world on what she terms a post-wild planet. With climate change, we're beginning to discover that the world may not be quite as post-wild as we thought, but Marris does identify a genuine problem, the same one hinted by Morris: nature offers no benchmarks or authoritative scripts from which we humans can determine what kind of ecosystems 'ought' to be in place beyond our own interventions, and how to use them to guide our conservation efforts.

There's a trap here inasmuch as the lack of any single 'right' nature doesn't mean that anything humans do is as good as anything else. But Marris's ironic take on 'nature' is useful in alerting us to the absurdities inherent in trying to define 'proper' wilderness or 'official' countryside. On the face of it, this seems in keeping with a land-sharing view that wildernesses without human inhabitants aren't some gold standard of conservation, and that farmers might share space with wild organisms and seek a dialogue of mutual accommodation. Surprisingly, Marris draws a different conclusion: 'Preserve open land. Don't ignore green, growing land just because it isn't your ideal native landscape. Protect it from development, even if it is just a "trash" ecosystem. Build your cities in tight and up high, and let the scenery take over the suburbs. In a nutshell: give up romantic notions of a stable Eden.'[83]

But the real heft of the Bible's Eden story isn't a romantic notion of stability. It's a recognition that, unlike other organisms, humans can't just 'be' – we have no choice but to consciously transform the natural world and, in the process of transforming it, judge what kind of nature is 'right'.[84] And on this point, there's no good reason to suppose that the correct judgement is for people to live 'in tight and up high' in cities and make room for 'scenery' any more than spreading out and learning to inhabit the world of plants, animals and other organisms around them as another one of its denizens.

One benefit of the idea that we live in a post-wild world is that it allows a fresh look at traditional land management practices among aboriginal foragers and farmers around the world, seeing these people, too, as authors of post-wilderness. Too often, incoming colonisers imported a modernising perspective through which they disparaged or failed to notice long-term and thoroughgoing practices often carefully calibrated to local circumstances through which indigenous peoples altered their surroundings to satisfy their needs, assimilating colonised people themselves to the status of the wild. Take this passage from John Locke's *Second Treatise of Government* (1689): 'For I ask whether in the wild woods and uncultivated waste of America left to nature, without any improvement, tillage or husbandry, a thousand acres will yield the needy and wretched inhabitants as many conveniences of life as ten acres of equally fertile land do in Devonshire where they are well cultivated?'[85]

The *Second Treatise* was perhaps the original land-sparing manifesto, albeit with a focus on sparing land for colonisation, not wilderness. It thoroughly disregarded Native American practices of fire management, watershed management, game management and soil husbandry. Not all aboriginal practices have always had benign effects on their local environments, and not all arguments for agricultural 'improvement' are always ill-founded. But the language of modernisation, rationalisation and agricultural improvement has a long history, from John Locke in the 17th century to the *Ecomodernist Manifesto* in the 21st, which heavily emphasises the relative efficiency of modern land use practices over historical and traditional methods, while underplaying their aggregate destructiveness.[86]

It's hard to argue that the effects have been wholly or even mainly positive for either the people or the wild organisms targeted for modernisation. Stretching far back into the Palaeolithic, humans have had a profound impact on their surroundings – we're 'patch disturbers' in ecological parlance – but it's only with the fully 'improved,' modern, rationalised global economy and its 'productive' agricultures that we've started engineering the systematic extinction of our fellow species, and perhaps ultimately ourselves, on a global scale.

The line I take in this book is not against improving agriculture. It's against agricultural improvement. It's for farming oriented to a renewable local ecological base, and for a doctrine of post-wilderness which, in contrast to Emma Marris, I'd summarise as follows: embrace the message of the Bible's Eden story. Like other creatures, you must work to secure your livelihood. But unlike them, you must also unavoidably stand in judgement of your fellow creatures, deciding their fate. Try to judge well. Protect green, growing land from 'development' and preserve it for agricultures, forestry and industries that answer to your needs, not to every conceivable want. Learn from your fellow creatures – spread out and make yourself a denizen of your landscape, skimming its bounty renewably. Work it well and try to leave some space for other people and other creatures.

Crop Biodiversity

This isn't what's actually happened, however. As we've seen, there are now more people living in urban areas than in the countryside. Since 1991 the proportion of the global labour force employed in agriculture has declined from 44% to 27%,[87] though this conceals a more complex reality we'll examine later.

An associated change in the aftermath of the Green Revolution, which introduced input-intensive, high-yielding cereals to global agriculture, is that humanity is now more reliant than ever on a handful of major commodity crops increasingly traded on global markets.[88] Three in particular – rice, maize and wheat (all cereals, and members of the grass family) – are responsible for providing humanity with around 40% of its energy and protein (more if indirect sources are included).[89] Paddy rice excepted, much of this global crop is grown in semi-arid continental grassland areas which are increasingly threatened by water scarcity and climate change.

The major cereal crops fit well with the logic of an 'improved' agriculture and economy. Few other crops can match their per acre productivity of protein and energy. They're also amenable to a mechanised agriculture, store well, can be efficiently transported, are more visible to government taxation and record-keeping, and can be easily processed into a wide variety of other readily tradeable foodstuffs.[90] Without dwelling on the downsides, maybe 'don't put all your eggs in one basket' is enough to suggest why global reliance on just three crops is probably unwise. The alternative is to grow a wider variety of energy-rich and more localised 'peasant' staples like potatoes, cassava, plantains, yams, sweet potatoes or taro, as well as other vegetables and fruits, which can be more productive per unit area than cereals.[91] But this kind of production is usually more labour intensive, less mechanisable, less bureaucratically visible and less amenable to trade, transport and industrial processing – not a problem for the 'more than one basket' small farm future I advocate, but possibly a problem for the large-scale global commodity cropping that stands in opposition to it.

In addition to the diversity of crop species themselves, genetic diversity *within* given crops is also an issue. In a locally oriented farm economy where farmers save their own seeds and breed their own new plant varieties, such diversity happens more or less by default. That's not necessarily the case in a globally oriented farm economy where farmers buy commercial seed and sell crop varieties that must be chosen on the basis of a few demanding characteristics: yield, pest resistance, shelf life, transportability. It's possible to overstate the benefits of local seeds, some of which don't gain wider popularity for good reasons, and to understate the advantages of a professional seed industry able to breed desirable characteristics into new varieties efficiently and systematically while preserving genetic variation as the essential feedstock of its core business. Nevertheless, there's something to be said for keeping crop diversity alive in numerous local food cultures, preferably in the inherently diverse hands of millions of seed-raising small-scale farmers and gardeners, rather than relying overly on the professional sector, with its small number of seed banks and research centres supporting the wider needs of the modern global food system for crop uniformity, and therefore underlying genetic uniformity.

The cautionary tale of the Global Seed Vault springs to mind. Designed to preserve important crop varieties long term at a bespoke facility nestled in the permafrost of Spitsbergen, it was breached less than ten years after it opened by meltwater from unprecedentedly warm weather.[92] Although little damage was done on this particular occasion, it's another 'eggs in one basket' example that perhaps stands as a metaphor for the disadvantages of concentrating rather than distributing the responsibility for genetic stewardship.

Crisis #8: Health and Nutrition

Human health is the summary result of all our other activities, and nutrition – with its obvious link to farming – is basic to it. In that sense, health and nutrition are perhaps the key indicators of human well-being. I address them only cursorily here, partly because to treat them satisfactorily would take us far beyond the aims of this book and partly because to dwell on historical health data would be to miss the point that the major concern is now *future* health trends under the pressure of issues like climate change.

But at present on the face of it there's a good story to tell about human health based on crude summary measures like life expectancy, which increased from a global average of 52.6 years in 1960 to 72.4 years in 2017.[93] It's not quite so clear whose good story this is to tell, a point we'll come to in Crisis #9. But to anticipate that discussion, it's worth remarking that though the gap between the poorest and richest countries and world regions has narrowed over this time, it still stands at around 34 years of life between the top and bottom countries, and 19 years between the top and bottom global regions. The improvement is less impressive when we consider that global output has increased sevenfold over the same period. In the words of one expert, the world's poorer countries carry a 'huge additional burden' of infectious disease and infant and maternal health.[94]

It's tempting to think this additional burden results from the fact that poorer countries haven't yet modernised as the richer countries have. But the truth is that everybody in every country lives in the same modern world. It's just that modernisation has had different consequences for different people and different countries. These differential tracks of modernisation,

the economy isn't some determining thing in its own right, but is intrinsically a matter of politics. It also reminds us that economies change as politics changes, and that these changes are sometimes epochal. The last 500 years or so has been the epoch of the slowly emerging capitalist world system. It seems likely that we're now entering a new epoch in which that world system will be transformed. This is the crisis of our present political economy.

It's useful at this point to introduce the notion of what I'll call the 'symbolic economy' or 'symbolic goods'. People in all human societies operate with shared mental constructs about the nature of the physical things passing through their hands that aren't intrinsic to the things themselves. This would apply to rituals in premodern societies devoted to making game or crops abundant, perhaps by propitiating gods or distributing produce in special ways. It certainly applies to societies like our modern capitalist ones where we make numerical equivalences between unlike things (including land) on the basis of money and devote ourselves to the increase of money, using its fictional quantity to draw real work from other people that brings more physical things under our command.

I don't want to make great analytical claims for the concept of the symbolic economy. But I think it's a handy mental tool for our times given that we've created vast material architectures from the fictive construct of capital, resulting in non-symbolic problems like climate change and species loss. The concept is also a useful tonic for the tendency to assume that the way we construe our world, for example in our relationships with land or money, are just given in the nature of things.

The symbolic economy that virtually everyone in the world today has to reckon with is a capitalist one. To understand its present crisis and to project some possible futures that may arise from it, including a small farm future, it's necessary to understand something of its logic and its history. I lay this out in the next three subsections, with apologies for a lengthiness which I think is necessary, because here we get to the crux of several big issues on which both this book and the future of humanity hinge.

The Logic of Capital

In day-to-day life, most of us even in highly capitalist societies don't behave in especially 'capitalist' ways. Compared to many non-capitalist societies, it's necessary for us to get more of what we need by buying it in the form of commodities purchased for money, but in this situation our money isn't capital but just a means of exchange. Generally, as workers we produce and sell commodities – even if the commodity is only our labour power which we sell to an employer for wages, rather than being a physical object – and we use the money so obtained to buy other commodities produced by other workers, in this sequence:

$$C \rightarrow M \rightarrow C$$

where C is a commodity and M is money.[103] There's nothing especially 'capitalist' about buying commodities for money in markets, which has occurred in many different societies for millennia.

Capitalist logic starts to enter the picture when the production of commodities is used to generate profits. In this sequence, money is invested as capital to produce commodities whose sale generates more money than the initial investment:

$$M \rightarrow C \rightarrow M'$$

where M' > (is greater than) M.

Again, this needn't be especially 'capitalist'. For millennia, merchants have sought profits in this way through the fragmentation of markets, enabling them to buy cheap and sell dear. However, the producers and consumers of their trade goods rarely depended completely on these markets in order to furnish the necessities of life. Historically, a lot of effort was devoted to ensuring this was so. Merchants and other financial specialists didn't enjoy high reputations, and states regulated markets in order to limit profit-making opportunities.

Capitalism really gets going when those limits are removed and the logic of M → C → M' drives the economy at large. In English grain markets, for example, it was illegal to 'regrate' (buy in order to resell) or 'engross' (store until prices rise) before legislation was relaxed in the 1660s.[104] When the logic of M' > M is unleashed in this way, it has powerful consequences that can reorder the entire economic base of whole societies, and ultimately the world. But, for all that we tend to associate capitalism nowadays with 'the market', the logic of M' > M isn't fundamentally about actual market exchange. It's about using money to create extra money. One of the ways businesses do this is by creating political alliances to forge monopolies, making it easier for them to leverage M′ from their investments. This is why when you go to a Wednesday market in the average British 'market' town nowadays it's a fairly bedraggled affair, compared to large out-of-town stores – 'super'-markets – selling produce that mostly comes from wherever in the world it's cheapest to grow it, sold by staff in mostly low-paid jobs often topped up by government welfare benefits.

But supermarkets are still involved in the production of actual things, following the logic of the M → C → M′ loop, by turning money into tradeable commodities. If it's possible to make money without engaging in the onerous business of first turning money into commodities before earning an increase, then the logic of capital dictates that this course of action – the M → M′ loop – is preferable. And so it has proved. For example, by 2013 transactions on global exchange markets of a purely financial kind exceeded those involving trade and direct investment by a factor of 100. This circuit is especially favoured because in the contemporary deregulated financial sector, governments and banks combine to create money (M) by fiat out of nothing – a symbolic good – and then gain income (M′ minus M) by charging interest on it derived mostly from people's labour in the non-symbolic world.[105]

When it's unleashed across society, the logic of M′ generates economic growth. We're accustomed to hearing that economic growth is a good thing, but a more decisive point is that it's a *necessary* thing in a capitalist economy. The logic of M′ demands an excess of return over investment, and in a world where investors compete to find returns, there's a danger they'll bid the returns down against each other unless new ways of generating return are constantly found.

It's generally reckoned that economic growth of 3% per annum or more is necessary for a 'healthy' capitalist economy.[106] During the 1960s, global economic growth averaged 5.5% per annum, whereas over the last decade it's averaged 2.5% (with only two of the world's ten largest economies achieving average growth in excess of 1.8%).[107] But, exponential growth being what it is, the slowed growth over the last decade still added over US$19 trillion to the world economy at constant 2010 US dollars, whereas the fast growth of the 1960s added only US$7 trillion. Projecting just 2.5% annual growth forwards to 2050 suggests the global economy will have to add nearly US$40 trillion over the decade of the 2040s, meaning the new economic output it has to *add* in that decade will be about the size of the entire global economy in 1993 (and in view of Crisis #2, it'll have to do that while reducing carbon emissions pretty much to zero).

Many analysts have pointed out the improbable numbers of this sort that lurk beneath the face of exponential capitalist growth, without apparently shaking the conviction of the power brokers who matter that it's the best way to run the global economy. But one of the ways the problem manifests more immediately is in the difficulties investors experience in finding productive arenas to put up their money. This capital surplus absorption problem is one driver for the spread of capitalist profit-making into ever new arenas of social life that were previously organised in non-capitalist ways – from paying for extra online friends, to vast public–private infrastructure projects involving rents set long into the future.

Another way that capitalist enterprises seek to maximise returns on investment is by cutting input costs, among them the cost of labour. The competitive logic of the capitalist economy is such that if businesses don't do this they'll be crowded out by other businesses that do. However, workers are also consumers of capitalist products, so the more that gross labour income is trimmed, the less in aggregate consumers can spend on the products of capital investment. Such tensions are a part of the various crises that periodically rock capitalist economies, and which have been resolved, only ever temporarily, through various means: government stimulus packages, debt finance, new arenas of marketisation, going to war.

These problems of labour and capital have long exercised the minds of economic thinkers, almost from the outset of the modern capitalist economy itself. Here, I want to outline briefly some ideas of one such pioneer, David Ricardo (1772–1823), which are relevant to the latest, and possibly terminal, crisis of capitalism.

Ricardo is best known nowadays for his much-abused theory of comparative advantage, which he illustrated by a discussion of the mutual benefits accruing to England and Portugal from trading the former's cloth for the latter's wine. Ricardo showed that a country achieved a net income benefit by focusing on those goods it could produce most cheaply relative to other countries and importing other goods from abroad, even if it could also produce the import goods more cheaply itself. His theory is still routinely invoked as a justification for global free trade today – right down to the examples of English cloth and Portuguese wine.[108] But it only works given various assumptions. One of them is that there's no 'uneven development', giving one country technical advantages over another – not a sound assumption to make concerning 'free' trade between rich and poor countries today. Another is that capital investment is restricted to its country of origin, where it can only seek comparative advantage by investing in the most efficient domestic industries, rather than absolute advantage by investing wherever in the world it can earn the best return.

Ricardo affirmed 'most men of property to be satisfied with a low rate of profits in their own country, rather than seek a more advantageous employment for their wealth in foreign nations'.[109] But given the freedom of capital to seek advantageous employment wherever it wishes now written deeply into the structure of global economic governance, arguments for free trade on the basis of comparative advantage no longer hold water. With capital flow untethered, net returns to capital generally move from poorer regions or countries to richer ones, prompting many people to follow the flow of money in search of better employment. Here, the mismatch between immigration policies that seek to prevent flows of people in ways that no longer apply to flows of capital is a major force driving global inequality.[110]

But in the England of Ricardo's day, another problem seemed more pressing – economic rent. Prior to Ricardo, most economic thinkers in the agrarian societies of their time considered agriculture, and not manufacturing, to be the only truly productive economic activity. Ricardo reversed this. For him, the manufactures of capitalists pursuing the logic of M' created employment and consumer markets, driving a general progress of society and its productive forces.

But the capitalists were effectively held to ransom by landowners. As population and the demand for food grew, it became necessary to bring increasingly marginal land into cultivation, raising the price of grain and therefore the level of industrial wages necessary to cover workers' subsistence costs. In a capitalist society where a unit of like labour commands the same price universally, this monetary increase would eventually find its way back to the owners of the best agricultural land in the form of an economic rent in excess of the actual costs of grain production.

So the owners of land were pitted against the owners of capital. In Ricardo's view, the latter did the hard work, but it was the landlords who ultimately benefited by virtue of sheer ownership. No wonder he favoured international trade. In early 19th-century England, with its growing population and growing industry, this Ricardian view manifested in an argument for free trade in agricultural products against the domestic pro-tectionism of the Corn Laws passed by a landlord-dominated parliament, which imposed tariffs on imported grain.

The Corn Laws were repealed in 1846, allowing cheap imported grain to fund Britain's rise to economic dominance and helping the country enforce global 'free' trade, often from the barrel of a gun. In the words of economic historian Robert Heilbroner,

> *The dire implications of rent envisaged by Ricardo never came to pass. For the industrialists finally did break the power of the landlords and they did finally secure the importation of cheap food. The hillsides up which the wheatfields were ominously climbing in Ricardo's day were, within a few decades, returned to pasture. . . . But consider for a moment the situation if Britain today were forced to feed a population of, say, a hundred million entirely from the produce of home-grown crops. And suppose the old Corn Laws had never been repealed. Is there any doubt that Ricardo's picture of a landlord-dominated society would be a frightening reality?*[111]

Two centuries after Ricardo's death, it's worth contemplating whether that frightening reality may come back to haunt us, not just in Britain but across the world. The question arises for a variety of ecological and economic reasons. One is that, wherever we live, it's increasingly unwise to assume that other parts of the world will remain reliable exporters of cheap food, especially given the vulnerability of major breadbasket regions to climate change. This returns us to the issue of local production – and the dangers of unearned local Ricardian rent.

In fact, unearned Ricardian rent is widespread across the present capi-talist economy, especially in the case of land, which is a key commodity for absorbing surplus capital generated elsewhere. This is why increasingly few young adults in Britain today can afford to buy a house, and few farm-ers can service debt on the purchase of agricultural land just by growing food on it. And it's not only land. As we've seen, the logic of capital isn't fundamentally about production, but about earning as much money as possible on investment. With the M → M' loop fully unleashed by financial deregulation, nowadays we have a global rentier capitalism concerned with branding, intellectual property rights, data mining and financial speculation as much or more than delivering goods and services. One way or another, freeing people from the grip of Ricardian rent seems necessary to create a fair and genuinely productive economy. It's certainly a necessary step for creating a congenial small farm future.

The History of Capital

But let's take a step back historically, and briefly review how capitalism in its various forms has emerged. I begin with debates about the emergence of capitalism in England, which have wider relevance partly because England was supposedly the world's first capitalist power and partly because the debate bears on the role of small-scale farmers and is therefore central to the concerns of this book.

There's a view of English rural history and capitalist development that's commonly shared by conservatives and radicals alike, even if they emphasise different parts of it and evaluate it differently. Dubbed 'agrarian fundamentalism' by historian Robert Allen, its basic elements are the notion that in medieval times English peasants shared land and work routines, but this ended when landlords enclosed and fenced farmland for private use, turfing off the peasants. This improved the productivity of English agriculture, enabling the landlord class to accumulate capital, which they then deployed in industrial development, staffed by the erstwhile peasants who had become landless wage labourers or proletarians. In this way, England moved from a feudal, peasant-dominated economy to agrarian capitalism and then to a full-blown industrial capitalism that, with the assistance of its coal reserves, enabled it to establish itself as the first global capitalist power.

There are some grains of truth in this account, but it's misleading in its main details. Medieval England wasn't generally a world of shared peasant communism. The commons that were later enclosed only fully emerged in the late medieval and early modern periods – coming to fruition in the 17th century, the golden age of the English yeoman. Enclosure was a complex business that wasn't always imposed top-down by landlords but sometimes bottom-up by peasants themselves, but inasmuch as it *was* an elite project it didn't raise productivity so much as create Ricardian rent that manifested as upper-class opulence and working-class rural underemployment. Early

English industrialism was staffed by a working class that wasn't always fully proletarian, against the background of a highly commercialised agriculture that didn't lead directly into industrial capitalism, yet provided few opportunities for forms of peasant autonomy that might have been an attractive alternative to industrial labour.[112]

There are five general points to draw from this that I'll return to in various guises throughout the rest of the book. First, a more commercialised or capitalist farming isn't necessarily a more *productive* farming. Second, there's no hard-and-fast line between commercial farming and capitalist farming, and there's no simple evolutionary sequence from (a largely mythical) peasant communalism through agrarian capitalism to modern industrial capitalism. A good deal of modern thinking, both pro- and anti-capitalist, has been contemptuous of small-scale farmers on the grounds that they're not productive enough, or not capitalist enough, or too capitalist. Equally, a good deal of anti-capitalist thinking that favours peasant farming neglects the truth that peasants are often simply incorporated into capitalist economies as dependent producers. All these doctrines involve various false trails that a look at English agricultural history helps reveal.

Third, labour-saving developments in one part of the economy don't necessarily create the conditions for surplus labour to be absorbed elsewhere. Sometimes, they just create underemployment and economic misery – a point that applied to the 18th-century English countryside, and applies in much of the world, both rural and urban, today. So, fourth, if we try to avoid too much romantic fancy about the 17th-century age of the yeoman, it's worth asking if it and its parallels in other times and places might teach us something useful about the possibilities for a sustainable small farm future, a world in which rural capital (but not necessarily rural capitalism) is created at relatively local levels by commercial or semi-commercial farmers working alongside local industries and merchants in ways that serve a modest local prosperity – symbolic stocks that can create flows of local human benefit.

Fifth and finally, while many of us nowadays have ready-made positions favouring or opposing the capitalist political economy, working people throughout its history have usually just tried to build personal autonomy and resilience for themselves as best they can according to the available options. Sometimes this has involved working within the structures of the capitalist economy, sometimes working against it or stepping outside it.

The question is, what will be the most readily available options for working people in the future?

I explore these points further in Parts II–IV. But for now, back to some history. If industrial capitalism wasn't built out of a prior agrarian capitalism founded in rural class conflict, where did it come from? The other main explanation is that it emerged from the development of trading empires that slowly became globally interconnected, a view that now commands greater support among historians and social scientists than rural class conflict models. I can't do justice here to the depth of relevant scholarship, but a one-sentence summary might be that capitalism emerged out of a confluence where the great trading empires of Asia connected with the fiscal-military states of Europe and their seaborne empires that brought first precious metals and then plantation produce from the Americas into global circuits of exchange, much of it via the super-exploited labour of enslaved Amerindians and Africans.[113]

Again, a few points to draw from this to which we'll return. First, the 'world system' approach emphasises the importance of the state in the emergence of capitalism – particularly competitive, militarised and protectionist states in Europe that allied with merchant capital in overseas adventures. We've come to think of capitalist markets as somehow being opposed to the state, but in truth capitalist market dominance has only ever worked as a state-sponsored project.

Second, these state–capital alliances were usually monopolistic – an enduring feature of capitalist enterprises that's belied in our tendency to associate them with competitive 'free' markets. Capitalism, as we saw above, isn't fundamentally about creating free markets in goods, but about maximising financial returns in the easiest way, and the easiest way is often through creating large-scale monopolistic linkages.

Third, the burgeoning capitalist world economy both depended upon and exacerbated what historian Eric Hobsbawm called 'uneven development' within and between regions, creating unequal power relations between coloniser-capitalist 'cores' or centres and colonised 'peripheries' that we obscure when we talk about 'developed' and 'developing' countries. Anti-colonial historian Walter Rodney made this point memorably in his book *How Europe Underdeveloped Africa*, an early salvo in the battle to show that 'underdevelopment' is the flipside of 'development'. Part of this battle has involved the argument that there were emerging forms of capitalism in various parts of the early modern world, not just in England or Western Europe, but these were ultimately sawn off by Western Europe's successful colonial advance.[114]

Fourth and finally, capitalism isn't fundamentally about the creation of landless wage labour, as the rural class conflict model suggests. It also creates or co-opts other kinds of labour, depending on the circumstances – slaves, serfs, indentured servants, commercial farmers, peasants, and sometimes hybrid categories across them. Indeed, in some colonial situations it *created* peasants in the sense that it forced people to seek rural semi-independence by closing off other opportunities. Some analysts suggest that landless industrial wage labourers are the exception rather than the rule in the history of global capitalism.[115]

Nevertheless, industrial capitalism did emerge during the 19th century in the 'core' countries of the capitalist world system, furnishing a stereotype of capitalism that's endured to the present: the idea of a plucky individual entrepreneur who spots a market niche for some new good, puts up their capital in order to manufacture it, and either succeeds in the competitive capitalist marketplace or goes to the wall. That's certainly one strand of the capitalist story, and it's still in evidence, especially in emerging sectors, but generally less than in the early heyday of industrial capitalism. From the latter part of the 19th century, the familiar manifestation of capitalist industrialism came to be the vast horizontally and vertically integrated corporation, which in numerous ways was integrated with and not autonomous from centralised states and government.

Though farming and food production has never been as industrialisable as manufacturing, much the same occurred: corporate plantation agriculture in tropical colonised countries and agribusiness models of the kind pioneered in Chicago, where cowboys and small-scale prairie farmers were the initial feedstock for an increasingly mechanised global distribution system of meat and grain that ultimately dispensed with them in the Global North.[116] A common image we still have of capitalism is the innovative entrepreneur opening up a new and lucrative market niche (the alternative farming sector has its own versions of this) with the invisible hand of the market delivering public benefit (supply matching demand) out of private vice (profit-motivated self-interest).[117] The idea is still routinely invoked as a justification of modern capitalism, but it's out of date. A more apposite image nowadays for financialised, corporate capital is the visible – though sometimes velveted – fist, aimed at anyone who contests its logic, and many of those who don't. Arguments for efficiency through price competition lose their force in an era of monopoly capitalism when the competition has largely vanished, and the main ingenuity of the corporation lies in its strategies for offloading costs – an experience all too familiar to farmers on the receiving end of it, at all scales.

It remains for me to briefly track capitalist history up to the present. The term 'disaster capitalism' is often used to describe the march of private profit-making into the human miseries of war, climate-enhanced 'natural' disasters and the nexus of poverty, crime and policing at the start of the 21st century.[118] But the earlier part of the 20th century had disaster capitalisms of its own, cashing in on that period's miseries, for example when firms like IG Farben used slave labour during the Nazi period in Germany, another hint that the capitalist search for profit increase is none too fussy about the forms of labour it uses, given the opportunity. But in between these two eras of disaster capitalism came 30 years of strong postwar economic growth, rising working-class prosperity and the 'developmentalist' period in the postcolonial countries where an alliance of national industrial development, government welfare policies and pro-peasant land reform seemed to nurture the prospect of a capitalist catch-up in the poorer countries and rising prosperity for all.

These high hopes ended in the 1970s. Oil crisis and stagflation were the pretext for fiscal deregulation that tipped the balance away from the interests of citizens and workers within countries towards the interests of capital globally.[119] This prompted a crisis of public debt in the poor countries and later private debt in the rich countries, shaping a towering edifice of debt that can be happily deferred or sold in the world's symbolic economy for just so long as enough people remain confident in that symbolic economy, but that its non-symbolic ecology will ultimately have to pay.

In the poor countries, the developmentalist period of national, often pro-peasant, assertion gave way to doomed attempts at playing economic catch-up with the wealthy countries by opening markets to private capital, often at the insistence of multilateral institutions like the International Monetary Fund (IMF). The failure of these attempts drove a wedge between many governments and their citizenries who bore the brunt, prompting a 'catastrophic convergence' of poverty and violence, associated both with the rise of non-state 'entrepreneurs of violence' and with violent state-backed counterinsurgency, militarised resource extraction and border control sponsored by rich-country governments, now compounded by the effects of climate change.[120]

This latest iteration of capitalist history is often called neoliberalism. Enthusiasts of capitalism are apt to dismiss the term as merely a pejorative label adopted by its enemies, and it's true that it's applied rather indiscriminately. But even the IMF now invokes the term (with a degree of self-criticism, moreover), and it has a distinctive intellectual history, having been coined by the French industrialist Louis Marlio in the 1930s to describe the movement coalescing around the Austrian economists Ludwig Mises and Friedrich Hayek.[121]

The neoliberalism of Mises and Hayek wasn't simply an argument for rapacious, unfettered capitalism. They recognised the tendency of capital to form monopolies and extract Ricardian rent, and therefore emphasised the importance of the state in regulating markets to safeguard against it. But they were contemptuous about any claims of citizenries and electorates over the state or markets, taking the view that ordinary people would be adequately rewarded if they sat at the foot of the capitalist table, accepting the crumbs that came their way.

This elitist and idealised conception still has its adherents as an actual description of how the economy works. Sometimes, it's finessed with the view that electoral arithmetic enables skilled middle-class workers to vote themselves the lion's share of the rewards at the expense of the poor, making distribution a political, not an economic problem.[122]

Yet only in unusual historical circumstances such as the postwar boom do capitalist societies reward ordinary workers proportionately. In 2017, the average monthly income of the top 10% of earners worldwide was about $7,500, while the middle 40% averaged less than $700.[123] Since 1979 the middle 40% of households in the United States have seen only a 14% rise in their real income, while the poorest 20% have seen a 12% decline, and the richest 1%, a 185% increase. Globally, the share of income received by labour relative to capital has declined. These figures are symptomatic of the unsurprising fact that capital usually returns mostly to its owners. So globally, the 'middle' classes might be better off allying with the poor ones. This may happen as wage stagnation and rising poverty, inequality and work precarity, set against rising capitalist profits – increasingly common worldwide, especially in the richer countries – makes hopes of long-term prosperity for the majority of people ever more visibly blocked by a minority.[124]

Sociologist Wolfgang Streeck coined the term 'consolidation state' to describe the turning away of the contemporary state from the wider interests of its citizens towards the specific interests of global markets and the wealthy owners of capital. Naomi Klein calls it 'McGovernment', a 'happy meal of cutting taxes, privatizing services, liberalizing regulations, busting unions' to remove impediments to private markets.[125] In this way, the ideal of the creative and productive neoliberal market economy becomes the reality of rapacious and unfettered rent-seeking by global capital.

Can national states reclaim capitalism for their wider citizenries? Can Main Street hold its own over Wall Street? This is the claim of some reformist economic thinkers, but it seems unlikely without wider system change in view of the expansionary logic of the M → M' loop which now has few options but to abstract itself from bounded territory and 'dematerialise' from sites of actual production like farms and factories in favour of 'virtual' connections like computerised financial markets or distribution platforms – what's sometimes called a capitalist 'Empire' where the symbolic economy is further freed to overrun physical reality.[126] In that sense, many of the crises outlined earlier might be seen as warnings from the non-symbolic world not to get too dazzled by our symbolic goods.

In summary, I've traced the history of capitalism in seven broad and overlapping trends, all of which persist in the present world, or parts of it:

1. The formation of local agrarian capital, with an ambiguous relation to capitalism as such.
2. The emergence of rentier capitalism based on Ricardian landlordism, and then other forms of non-landed rent.
3. The formation of a capitalist world system through the connection of trading empires.
4. The emergence of entrepreneurial industrial capitalism.
5. The transformation of industrial capitalism into monopolistic corporate capitalism.
6. The development of neoliberalism, in practice if not in theory as the deregulated globalisation of capital.
7. The emergence of a de-materialised capitalist Empire.

With the possible exception of the first, all these forms of capital are effective generators of symbolic goods, with the result that it's hard to be a non-capitalist person or society in a capitalist world. The pioneering of modern capitalism in countries like Britain and the Netherlands created strong pressures for others to keep up, which countries like France, Germany, Japan and the United States (and, later, Taiwan, South Korea, Russia and China among others) did by various means.

Generally, the M → (C) → M' loop of capitalism acts as a powerful resource pump, and the severest penalty for a country that fails to keep up with it is that its resources get pumped out mostly to the benefit of people elsewhere, which is what's happened to colonised states. In this respect, capital accumulation initiates a kind of global ratchet effect, a high-stakes game of keeping up with the neighbours. Or, to coin another metaphor, perhaps it's like a virus that turns other economic 'cells' into replicators of its own signature codes. In their essence, those codes always involve making an increase on invested capital key to a whole society's mode of being, but in practice capitalism can be a plural and ever-changing beast that operates in some or all of the seven registers described above.

The Crisis of Capital

Many people today sense a terminal crisis bubbling up in the global capitalist political economy. It has two main components. The first is the material trace of capitalist growth which is manifested in Crises #1–#7. It's hard to imagine a realistic scenario in which the world can add around $40 trillion of new economic output in the 2040s alone while decarbonising by using low-EROI energy sources that require greater investment in unproductive intermediate stocks, and deal simultaneously with a raft of other crises related to soil, water and biodiversity loss.

But here I'm going to focus on a second form of crisis – the human inequalities within and between countries that seem both an ethical outrage and a political tinderbox. On this point, progress-literature (see 'Introduction', page 5) attempts to soothe us with a different view. Steven Pinker, for example, asserts that 'industrial capitalism launched the Great Escape from universal poverty in the 19th century and is rescuing the rest of humankind in a Great Convergence in the 21st'.[127] I'm reluctant to enter the statistical labyrinth through which such claims are defended or refuted because, unlike Pinker, I think summary statistics and grand historical claims make for uncomfortable bedfellows, but I'd like to take a cautious step inside, just to suggest that other views are possible.

Figure 1.2 shows the inflation-adjusted GDP from 1960 to 2018 for the world's countries aggregated into five population-weighted groups:[128]

Group 1: The 40 countries with the highest GDP per capita in 2017, of which 22 are West European, 4 were originally West European colonies (Australia, Canada, New Zealand and the United States) and the rest have their own histories of recent capitalist development (e.g. Japan, Kuwait, Singapore). Together, these countries account for 13% of the global population.

Group 2: Eleven countries of Eastern Europe that until 1989 were allied with Soviet Russia but are now part of the European Union. These countries account for 1% of the global population.

Group 3: The 40 countries with the highest GDP per capita in 2017, excepting the first two groups. These countries account for 11% of the global population.

Group 4: Five Asian countries with high rates of recent economic growth – China, Indonesia, Malaysia, South Korea and Thailand. These countries account for 24% of the total population.

Group 5: All other countries, 104 in total, accounting for 49% of the total population.

GDP has been persuasively criticised as a measure of well-being or of a society's total activities, but it's not such a bad proxy for assessing the performance of industrial capitalism and whether it's prompted the 'great convergence' that Pinker claims. And it strikes me that this convergence isn't the most obvious narrative to weave around Figure 1.2. A more obvious one is that while all groups show some growth, the wealthiest countries (comprising a minority of the world's people) have greatly pulled away from the rest over the last 60 years.

Some more specific world system dynamics are also visible in Figure 1.2. Eastern Europe did better once it quit being a dependent periphery of the Soviet Union, and better still once it attached itself to Group 1 by becoming a dependent periphery of the European Union (bear in mind that Figure 1.2 makes convergence look greater than it truly is because I've distinguished the Eastern European countries as a separate group, despite their small populations). The high-growth Asian countries of Group 4 are pulling away from the large pack of Group 5 countries to which they once belonged and may someday match the richer groups if they can avoid the 'middle-income trap', though they have a long way to go to reach the level of Group 1. So arguably there's a slight geographic drift in global economic power away from the northwest and towards the southeast.

But more than a 'great convergence', the data in Figure 1.2 seem suggestive of a 'great persistence' or even a 'great augmentation' of inequalities grounded historically in the colonial and world system dynamics of the capitalist political economy. The uneven development of global capitalism that I mentioned earlier continues to develop – unevenly – but it stays uneven. This is confirmed through more detailed studies that show patterns like those in Figure 1.2 result partly from global labour arbitrage, where multinational corporations headquartered in the wealthy countries find the cheapest global sources of industrial or agricultural labour, while realising most of the profits at home.[129] Simple dualities can always be made more complicated, but the idea that the originators of the capitalist-colonial world system centred around Europe remain rich, while the larger part of the rest remain relatively

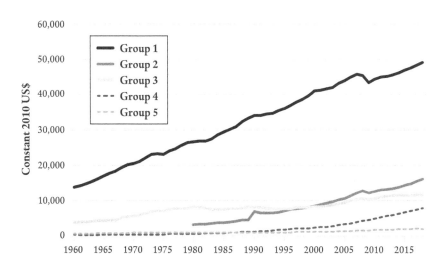

Figure 1.2. Grouped GDP per capita 1960–2017. *Source:* WDI n.d.

poor is a reasonable approximation to the truth, and I have few qualms in talking about 'rich' and 'poor' countries throughout the rest of this book.[130]

If we consider changes in life expectancy rather than GDP across the same five groups, a better case can be made for convergence. In 1960, average life expectancy in Group 1 was 70, compared to 45 in Group 5. By 2017, the gap had narrowed to respective figures of 81 and 68.[131] But is the narrowing due to the industrial capitalism that Pinker invokes? The most striking improvement in life expectancy occurred in Group 4 during the 1960s, and this was largely driven by developments in the China of Chairman Mao – an unlikely hero for industrial capitalism, perhaps a better one (albeit uncomfortably from my perspective) for small-scale or peasant farming.

Generally, improvements in life expectancy in the poorer countries have been achieved with scant industry or growth, mostly through improvements in education and infant/maternal well-being that have never really been a capitalist priority. It seems as plausible to argue that the rudiments of a decent life have been achieved in some places *despite* the dynamics of industrial capitalism rather than because of them. If that's true, then decent lives may be deliverable at a reasonably low cost, without the need for the untrammelled growth of capital – a happy conclusion for proponents of a small farm future and for opponents of the damage to Earth systems caused by capital growth.

At the end of an otherwise excellent book documenting the convergences between contemporary capitalism, poverty, violence and climate change, Christian Parenti writes that 'time has run out on the climate issue. Either capitalism solves the crisis, or it destroys civilization. . . . We cannot wait for a socialist, or communist, or anarchist, or deep-ecology, neoprimitive revolution; nor for a nostalgia-based *localista* conversion back to the mythical small-town economy of preindustrial America.' Invoking the conquest by city planning and middle-class do-gooderism of the water-borne illnesses that ravaged cities in the early years of modern urban-industrial capitalism, he adds 'capitalist society solved an environmental crisis through planning and public investment', expressing the hope that it can do the same with the far graver problem of climate change.[132]

Now, it's reasonable to say that the societies most of us live in today are capitalist societies, but it doesn't follow that everything those societies do is capitalist. In 19th-century London, water companies following a capitalist logic piped drinking water from the River Thames into people's homes and piped sewage back into the same source. Once the waterborne nature of the cholera epidemics afflicting the city was known, it took non-capitalist policy intervention to stop them.[133] I don't doubt that our present capitalist societies will have some successes in combating climate change, mostly arising out of actions taken by their non-capitalist parts. But for the reasons I've laid out in the book so far, I'm doubtful that these actions will outweigh the countervailing power of capitalism to create climate breakdown unless our societies largely stop being capitalist ones.

On current growth trends, it'll be well over a century before Group 5 GDP 'converges' on the *present* level of the capitalist pioneers in Group 1. Currently, Group 1 CO_2 emissions average 11.2 tonnes per capita (12.4 US tons), while Group 5's are 1.5 (1.7) – and these production-based measures underestimate the true discrepancy.[134] If the global capitalist political economy is enhancing human welfare, then it's been doing a much better job for the minority who are already rich than for most of the rest of the world's people, and the carbon cost of doing so makes it unlikely that it can continue for long in its present manner. Therefore, however implausible other candidates seem for organising the global political economy, I'd suggest that it's worth taking a good look at them. Of the ones Parenti mentions, the closest to what I'll be arguing for in this book is a *localista* conversion – but not a nostalgia-based conversion back to a mythical small-town economy of the past so much as a rational conversion to a small-scale economy of the future.

The data in Figure 1.2 are aggregated at country level, telling us nothing about the distribution of product or well-being *within* countries, or at the individual level globally. But I think my journey into the statistical labyrinth must end here. There are those who argue that the very poorest people have been getting better off in recent years, and that *poverty* is decreasing even if *inequality* is increasing. And there are those who argue otherwise.[135] Either way, I'd suggest the information I've presented here makes plausible the claim that global inequality and poverty are high, that they're not getting a whole lot better any time soon, that they have minimal prospects of doing so sustainably – and that if they are improving, it's probably not capitalism that's doing it.

Capitalism is about gaining the best return on capital invested, and since poor people and poor countries don't have much capital to invest, they don't get much of a return. Indeed, according to UN data there was a net transfer of US$500 billion out of 'developing' countries in 2016.[136] The basic geography of the global economy seems to be a footloose, extractive, rentier capitalism in most of the poorer countries, augmented by a rise in poorly paid manufacturing jobs serving corporations based in the wealthy countries, and a more grounded, monopolistic, skills-based capitalism of global corporations in the wealthier countries, albeit one that bestows its riches on increasingly few and is locked into a compounding spiral of debt, financialisation, industrial over-capacity, poorly paid service jobs and sluggish economic growth.[137]

So while there remain plenty of poor people who would undoubtedly love to have more buying capacity within the global industrial economy, that economy seems to have reached its limits. For the time being, the M → (C) → M' loop keeps turning, and the capitalist global political economy stays on the road. But it wouldn't take much of a system shock to bring the loop grinding to a halt through its own internal logic, quite apart from the larger biophysical crises in play. What happens when the non-symbolic world claims back the debt, when systemic political and economic crises start propagating, when increasing job precarity prompts political revolt or when cash stops being transferable is anybody's guess. But possibly the situation of the 2 billion or so, mostly poor, farmers of the world who currently seem destined not to find more lucrative jobs within the waged economy might brighten. Indeed, their numbers might swell.

Wolfgang Streeck argues that the combination of increasing inequality, debt and political stress with decreasing growth will probably end the era of capitalism – one that lasted longer than anyone could have expected on the basis of its strange socioeconomic ordering: an economy requiring limitless growth, and a society that, in his words: 'secures its collective reproduction as an unintended side-effect of individually rational, competitive profit maximization' that puts its productive capital into the hands of a minority, thereby largely abdicating political responsibility for human welfare. In Streeck's view, capitalism probably won't be replaced by some other functioning global order, but by macro-level *disorder* and indeterminacy.[138] It's a potentially frightening prospect, with numerous bad outcomes in the offing. But it does at least open up the tantalising possibility of a political economy that doesn't equate human development with economic growth, instead placing human health and well-being at the centre of an economy not dependent on quantitative growth. I'd argue it's time to make the most of that possibility and start building autonomies from capitalism again.

So the capitalist world system is mired in crises of justice, political legitimacy and its own self-reproduction. It's possible it'll survive them. It has survived numerous crises before, though not without human cost. But it's hard to see quite how it'll manage this time.

One possibility that's gained a head of steam lately is a 'green new deal' inspired by US president Franklin Roosevelt's Depression-busting New Deal of the 1930s. A green new deal promises to create many new jobs in low-carbon economic sectors – an excellent idea that I take up in these pages by advocating for a small farm future in which numerous people work agrarian holdings (in fact, this was also a somewhat forgotten part of Roosevelt's original New Deal). But there were major tensions in the 1930s between New Deal-type thinking and capitalist thinking, to which the neoliberalism of Mises and Hayek was one response. In the event, the massive shakedowns of global war, Cold War and rapid, fossil-fuelled postwar economic growth staved off the reckoning between capitalism and citizenries that was brewing in the 1930s. But it's now returned with a vengeance, and with an ecological reckoning thrown into the mix, too. If, as I hope, there's to be a successful green new deal, it's not clear that capitalism could survive it.

In relation to the idea of proximal and underlying causation introduced earlier, the dynamics of endless capitalist growth that we've examined here do seem to lie deep at the roots of many of the other crises we've considered. Critics of environmental breakdown and social injustice increasingly converge on the view that, to paraphrase Bill Clinton's campaign strategist: 'It's capitalism, stupid.' I think that's correct, but – as with Parenti, discussed above – we find numerous ways to avoid following through to the conclusion that localised rural capital formation based on small-scale farming is a promising alternative. I devote most of the rest of the book to examining what that might look like, but first I want to examine aspects of a crisis that possibly lies deeper still and that seems to prevent us from considering a small farm future – the last crisis on our list, that of culture.

Crisis #10: Culture

I argued above that the economy is political. It, and politics, too, are also cultural. It's tempting to think that our present culture of capital accumulation and profit-seeking are just modern versions of a universal human economic urge, but it's worth pondering the fact that other historic societies have considered the idea of making profit the basis of the social economy to be problematic and morally suspect, if not absurd. Indeed, this view is also widespread in our own capitalist culture. Other worlds are possible.

The 'capitalism is natural' way of thinking sees the economy as a demand-led process. Consumers want things, so once productive capacities have risen above insecure subsistence then entrepreneurs step in to supply them. In the previous section I emphasised an alternative way of thinking – profit wants more profit, so once profit-seekers have risen above the checks and balances that normally keep them down, they step in and reorder societies, or the world, to create it. The rising carbon emissions, fossil energy use, soil loss, species loss and human inequalities we examined earlier are the material trace or collateral damage of that process, even though most of us don't want these things to happen. You could argue that most of us also don't do enough to stop them, but the entrenched systemic logic of profit-making (not our weakness as individuals) seems more to the point in grasping the present crisis.

Even so, profit-making must ultimately be sustained by human cultures that embrace it. Sometimes the embrace might be unwilling or resentful, but if capitalism is a specific, bounded historical phenomenon rather than an inherent human trait, then it must have some kind of cultural resonance and genesis somewhere. Locating it might help us get a better handle on the other crises we've considered, and inform a view of alternatives, including a small farm future.

The prime candidate, I'd suggest, is 'modernity'. We often use the word as a synonym for 'nowadays', but I mean it here in the sense of a distinctive and bounded historical phenomenon – a self-consciousness of living in modern times that are different from the past in ways that are important for human life. The sense of modernity that's most relevant to the global capitalist political economy of today started emerging in Western Europe in the 16th century and came to full fruition in the 20th century.

One aspect of modernity is the idea that society inevitably changes, usually for the better, which was not a common notion in earlier epochs. Another was a coming into history of ordinary people or the working class. No longer just an amorphous mass like the peasantry who occasionally needed appeasing by their rulers, people slowly became citizens with a stake in society and an ongoing hand in the conduct of government. At the cultural level, this manifested in a rising sense of individualism and of life that was something to be lived or embroidered as a personal project, expressed in things like marriage for romantic love, consumer fashions, sports and leisure pursuits.[139]

Environmentalists sometimes identify mass consumerism as the root of the world's problems today, and it's hard to argue that consumerism doesn't have an environmental impact. But we need to tread carefully. The emergence of consumerism is related to capitalism but it's not the same thing, and the idea of striving to create one's individual life as a project is harder to criticise than the idea of striving to create the maximum return on investment. Arguably, modern mass self-creation requires the mass capital-creation that only maximising return on investment delivers, but it's worth at least considering whether we can separate them and find less capital-intensive ways of self-creation.

Historian Daniel Horowitz detects a recurrent historical pattern in modern times involving a moral critique of excessive and frivolous consumerism directed mostly at working-class people, by contrast with more authentic and immaterial forms of self-improvement associated either with the better-off or with people in the past.[140] This kind of moralism is surely best avoided, but without lapsing into a crass rejection of the genuine problems environmentalists pose as mere nostalgia or elitist disdain for working-class material culture. It seems clear though that if modern societies are to move towards less materialised forms of self-creation, it'll be necessary to share such capital as does exist more evenly. Currently some selves get an awful lot more capital to create with than others.

It's important to emphasise the liberating aspects of modernity as self-creation for ordinary people as I've done above, but equally important to note the ways modernity can be enslaving. I mean this literally. Just as it was becoming possible for at least some working-class people to embroider their individualism in Europe's emerging modernity of the 17th–19th centuries, so were the European powers shipping off other people as slaves to the Americas, creating a wholly different working-class experience of modernity for more than 10 million transported Africans and their descendants. The consequences still scar Europe, Africa and the Americas and suck the decency out of any attempt to weigh up the pros and cons of modernity. They also point up a characteristic method of modern self-justification: the betterment of some ordinary people often comes at the expense of immiserating other ordinary people – the slave-grown sugar in the tea drunk by the emerging consumers of 18th-century England, for example. But when the latter achieve betterment themselves, we tend to chalk it up as a benefit of modernisation while ignoring the original cost.

Few experiences of modernity stand comparison to the horrors of slavery in the Americas, but the story's not completely rosy even for those of us who are modernity's financial beneficiaries. The idea of ordinary people coming into history and creating themselves as individuals must be counterposed with the experience of modernism – the alienating, mass-scale, monolithic, rationalised, expert-led, bureaucratic grid through which much of modern life is lived. Even as this grid provides some of us with levels of material comfort unknown to most people in the past and to ever new ways of creating ourselves aesthetically, it seems to deny us ways to create ourselves materially and spiritually – no land to grow food for ourselves, no capacity to maintain or mend the machines upon which we increasingly rely and that come to us wreathed in layers of electronic sophistication that might as well be magic, no autonomy of action in the face of policies and procedures laid down minutely by the organs of state power.

This modernist phenomenon of well-paid and materially comfortable but meaningless and alienating work is increasingly apparent, and instead of labouring the point I'll simply mention the resonant titles of two recent books that explore the malaise: *Bullshit Jobs* and *The Case for Working with Your Hands*.[141] It's tempting to dismiss this as over-privileged moaning, what's sometimes sardonically described as a first-world problem. But I think we should take it more seriously, if only because first-world problems usually become whole-world problems.

The problem is a whole-world one for two reasons. First, it creates large numbers of people with a lot of money in their pockets to draw down on global resources but no capacity to restore the resource stocks they're depleting through their work, as – for example – farmers can. Second, it fosters a kind of morbid cultural psychology that invests feelings of alienation and incompetence or, worse, a narcissistic embrace of modernism's capacity to deliver endless personal service. There's something to be said for experiencing the objective resistance of the non-symbolic world to a narcissistic sense of mastery – a broken tractor, a hail-ravaged crop. Of course, such things are no joke for people living on the margins of subsistence. But the reason they're living on the margins of subsistence isn't usually because of the objective resistance of the non-symbolic world. Instead, it's because the narcissism of somebody else's symbolic economy has offloaded the risk onto them.

This, then, is the crisis of modernist culture – the ability to create ourselves as individuals and protect ourselves from the vicissitudes of the non-symbolic world, set against the ability to alienate ourselves as individuals and offload the consequences of our self-creation onto other people (including future people) and the non-symbolic world. In view of the other crises we face, the only convincing way I can see of transcending this crisis is to start making ourselves as individuals in less materialised ways that are more engaged with the Creation, the non-symbolic world, around us. The small farm future I describe in these pages is the most convincing form I can see that transcendence taking.

One reason the prospect of a small farm future sits awkwardly with modern culture is that it flouts a sense of progress. Small-scale agriculture was what people did in the past, but we've now progressed beyond it. It's hard to shake off this view because when we think about history through the lens of modernity we tend to use spatial metaphors with binary moral overtones. We move forwards, upwards or onwards, we lift people up out of poverty, we support progressive ideas and we don't look back – but when we do, we see backward societies where a lot of people farmed.

In one sense, such objections are easily dealt with. A small farm future needn't be the same as a small farm past. We don't have to go back. But that's not quite good enough, because the culture of modernity involves a sense of radical rupture with the past, and a wholly new destiny for humanity – a destiny that's regarded as better than everything that went before it, largely *because* people quit farming, left the countryside and got busy with their modernist life projects. So in order to make a case for a small farm future as modernity's follow-up act, it's necessary to probe a little at this idea of modernity as a historical upgrade.

Sociologist Göran Therborn defines being modern as being 'unbound by tradition, by the wisdom of our fathers, by the skills of our masters, by any ancient authority. To be modern is a *cultural time orientation* to the present and toward the future' (emphasis in the original).[142] It's a nice definition, one that I'm happy to identify with as a 'modern' myself. But note that being *unbound* by the past isn't the same as defying, ridiculing or measuring oneself against it. And yet this looms large in many writings that celebrate the virtues of the modern. For example, Rutger Bregman tells us that 'in the past, everything was worse. For roughly 99% of the world's history, 99% of humanity was poor, hungry, dirty, afraid, stupid, sick and ugly,' while Anthony Warner makes the bold and conveniently untestable assertion that 'every society that has ever existed would eagerly swap their lives with someone living in the developed world today'. Other writers I mentioned earlier – Steven Pinker and the authors of the *Ecomodernist Manifesto* among them – also weigh in on the theme that when all is said and counted, the evidence proves conclusively that modern lives are just better than premodern ones.[143]

You'd have thought a confident culture that was truly modern in the sense described by Therborn could let the dead lie, rather than indulging in shrill pronouncements of its superiority over them. In this respect, chest-thumping pronouncements about the virtues of our times seem self-undermining. Like the class bully whose tough-guy antics betray an inner sense of weakness, the anxiety leaks from them that for all our achievements we moderns are not the betters of our forebears, are not the heroes of our story that we'd like to be, and that our achievements in fact have put our civilisation under existential threat. It's not as if the only positive social changes that could possibly have happened to premodern societies were the ones that actually did happen thanks to modernity and capitalism. For my part, I see no virtue in trying to measure our superiority over past epochs, so the main point of interest in the flourishing sub-genre of progress-literature is that it obstructs the case for a small farm future as a modern response to our modern problems by creating bad associations with a deprecated past.

But if progress-literature does have a deeper idea worth wrestling with, perhaps it's the desire to transcend external constraint or limits. In an influential recent book Nick Srnicek and Alex Williams criticise what they call folk politics – the domain of the 'small-scale, the authentic, the traditional and the natural', its 'guiding intuition that immediacy is always better and often more authentic, with the corollary being a deep suspicion of abstraction and mediation'. For them, by contrast, there is 'no authentic human essence to be realised, no harmonious unity to be returned to, no unalienated humanity obscured by false mediations, no organic wholeness to be achieved'. Seeking a left-wing, post-capitalist alternative to the present neoliberal moment in global politics, they argue that 'given neoliberalism's inherently expansionary nature, only an alternative expansionary and inclusive universal of some kind will be able to combat and supersede capitalism on a global scale . . . . Whereas folk-political approaches lack an enticing vision of the future'. In this way, they embrace the present and the future:

> *The newest wave of automation is creating the possibility for huge swathes of boring and demeaning work to be permanently eliminated. Clean energy technologies make possible virtually limitless and environmentally sustainable forms of power production. And new medical technologies not only enable a longer, healthier life, but also make possible new experiments with gender and sexual identity. Many of the classic demands of the left – for less work, for an end to scarcity, for economic democracy, for the production of socially useful goods, and for the liberation of humanity – are materially more achievable than at any other point in history.*[144]

An obvious problem here is that, as we saw earlier, the idea that humanity is entering a future of limitless clean energy and material abundance isn't well founded. So it's possible that people may have to embrace the old human essences of being biological, labouring, suffering creatures after all, which isn't an unenticing vision for everyone. A less obvious problem is that Srnicek and Williams are themselves making a claim for a kind of authentic human essence – an expansive, universalist, self-overcoming one. Doubtless this appeals to some people – there are aspects of it that appeal to me – but it's not the only way of construing what it means to be human.

The fact that there isn't necessarily any authentic human essence behind small-scale, immediate or traditionally oriented work doesn't make it intrinsically less worthy than the transcendence sought by Srnicek and Williams. For many people, there does seem to be something quite intrinsically satisfying about working outdoors on practical problems thrown up by a material world of things and creatures that don't dance to our tune. But there's a lot of cultural processing behind every 'enticing vision', whether it's practical engagement with nature or Srnicek and Williams's 'world without work'.

The other feature of small-scale farming that people often single out as problematic is that it can involve hard physical work. This is strange inasmuch as a capacity for hard, disciplined work is a characteristic feature of modernity, and the supposed indolence of non-modern peoples has frequently prompted criticism from their modernist observers. It's not even as if we denigrate hard *physical* work. Consider our celebration of mountaineers, explorers, sportspeople, and gym members.

The difference, I think, is that these are people working hard physically in ways that make them stand out as exceptional individuals, or at least that dramatise an individual life project – thoroughly modernist pursuits. Small-scale farmers, on the other hand, merely work physically in order to create their daily livelihoods. I've noticed this even at alternative farming conferences, where much emphasis is placed on being innovative – in other words, celebrating one's individual exceptionalism. Of course, there's a lot to be said for innovation, so long as it's clear why we're innovating, who's benefiting and what the wider consequences are. But we seem loath to accept that working moderately hard to create a modest local livelihood using standard, well-established farming methods and spending the rest of our time creating ourselves through simple low-carbon activities like walking in the woods, visiting friends, reading a book, playing the guitar or making love constitutes a worthwhile form of modern life.

I'd argue that, ironically, we'll be making true progress – we'll be truly modern – when we let go of older modernist traditions that insist our lives must get more moneyed, automated, commodified, materialised, mediated, individually crafted and so on. It's not that there's nothing worth celebrating or defending in the traditions of modernity, but doing so requires a nuanced and creative response to changing times that acknowledges modernity's downsides. The heavy-handed nostalgia for a perfected vision of past modern achievements as the lodestar of human progress offered by figures like Steven Pinker is stuck in the past. It's time to move forwards to a small farm future.

CHAPTER TWO

Wicked Problems:
Of Progress and Other Utopias

As I charted the ten crises in Chapter 1, I intentionally sequenced them from physical and technological issues – our human numbers, the climate, energy availability, soils, water and so on – to deeper cultural, political and economic forces driving them. These deeper forces mean it's unlikely current problems can be solved by only technical means. In fact, it's possible that they can't be solved at all, since they correspond to what are sometimes called 'wicked' or 'super-wicked' problems[145] with these kinds of characteristics:

- There is no single definitive formulation of the problem.
- There are no 'right', 'wrong' or precisely enumerable solutions.
- Any solution is a one-shot operation, with no possibility of trial-and-error learning.
- Problems are symptomatic of other problems.
- No single authority is empowered to enact solutions.
- The problems are caused by the people who must solve them.
- The future consequences of the problem are excessively discounted.
- The time window for solutions is running out.

Some or all of these features plausibly apply to each of the ten crises, suggesting that the search for simple solutions will prove elusive, especially since many of them challenge the capacities or even the future existence of institutions like governments. But even if the problems we face are wicked, it still seems worth identifying orientations to them that might be more fruitful than others. The ones inspiring this book include such various and overlapping but not entirely congruent ideas as peasant or producer republicanism, political localism, degrowth, steady-state economics, deindustrialisation, bioregionalism, home economics and agrarian populism.

Even though a lot of people are receptive to these ideas and although there are important traditions of localist thinking in politics, economics and agriculture, there haven't been many attempts to describe how local agrarian producerism might be an adaptive response to these crises. One reason is that it invites ridicule. This isn't always unjustified given some of the more implausible agrarian visions in circulation, but a feature of the present global moment is that *all* visions of a sustainable, fair and prosperous future now seem implausible, most certainly including business-as-usual models of capitalist growth and political-economic globalisation. In the words of climate change activist Gail Bradbrook: 'This is not the time to be realistic.'[146] I agree, and I think this suggests the need for more utopian thinking, so long as we're careful about how we construe our utopias. One problem is that our inherited words for social and political change carry historical baggage that often obstructs a productive utopianism – I'm thinking particularly of 'progress', 'romanticism', 'growth', 'development', 'improvement' and indeed 'utopia'.

I discussed the issue of progress at the end of 'Crisis #10: Culture'. The problem isn't so much any specific example of progress – there's no question that there's been progress in globally falling infant mortality rates, for example – as in the temptation to generalise them inappropriately as exemplary of some wider, unitary and unstoppable trend like capitalism, modernity or progress itself.

The disadvantage of this kind of thinking is that it diverts attention from past complexities and future challenges into a monocausal narrative of progress conceived as what Steven Pinker calls an 'inexorable tectonic force'.[147] Nothing can resist a tectonic force – so people with alternative programmes are easily dismissed for 'standing in the way of progress' regardless of what they have to say, and people who lost past battles are considered wrong just because they lost. Political theorist Iseult Honohan suggests we might usefully think of history instead 'less as a straight line which makes our ancestors increasingly remote from us, and more as a winding procession, where our circumstances may bring us closer to some parts of the past than others'.[148] No doubt there are many good arguments against a future turn to small-scale, labour-intensive, locally oriented farming, but the idea that it stands against progress isn't one of them.

Still, romanticism is no less problematic. Where progressives see the past as a blighted lowland from which we must climb up to reach the light, romantics often see it as a lofty beacon from which we're stumbling down into the shadows. Both visions read history as an unfolding morality tale, the one projecting utopia into the future, the other into the past. I think it's better viewed as a kind of disorderly chapbook full of wisdom and folly, inspirations and cautions, but with no single take-home message. So while I've argued that the capitalist world system has caused many ills, this is not to say that we should unspool its history and try to restore some kind of past order.

Instead I'd espouse a historical openness that allows us to look at how past societies dealt with the issues they faced and forged a sense of meaning, without feeling the need to judge them against the present. The liberating thing about this is that we can then learn from past societies with neither an embarrassment at reviving old ways nor an urge to mimic them precisely. This applies particularly to issues of ecological or biophysical constraint, which we'll examine in more detail in Part II. The great difficulty is that modernist notions of progress cut the ground from beneath the feet of anyone who tries to articulate past solutions to present problems, indicting their efforts as romanticism. I've experienced this many times as I've tried to make the case for a small farm future. All I can do here is register my objection to this false equivalence. At the same time, it's worth highlighting modernism's own romanticism around touchstone concepts like money, market trade and cities.

Growth is another troublesome modern concept. Its essence is quantitative – to grow is to get bigger. Getting bigger isn't the same as getting better, but the main way that the contemporary capitalist global economy has found to make things better for the worst off without fundamental systemic change is to grow the economy, to the disproportionate benefit of the best off rather than the worst. In biological systems, growth is delimited – organisms grow up to a point, and then stop growing. Continued growth is no advantage, and in fact is disadvantageous and ultimately pathological. The growth of the human political economy is now disadvantageously affecting planetary systems and has become pathological. It can't and therefore won't continue, but there are different ways the discontinuance can happen – some better than others, as seen through different human eyes. There are those who argue that persistent economic growth can be enduringly decoupled from major negative Earth system impacts, but there's no evidence this is true. Therefore it seems prudent to disregard this 'utopianism of growth' for other utopias.

Unlike growth, *development* is qualitative, not quantitative. It's about things getting better, not bigger. Therefore, utopias of 'development' seem more fitted to our times than utopias of growth. The problem is, we tend to think of development as restricted and path-dependent. To invoke a biological metaphor again, a child 'develops' into an adult, but only in a limited set of 'correct' ways. We've got into an analogous mindset about economic development, considering there to be only a limited number of ways that an economy can properly develop, with 'developing' economies metaphorically occupying the position of a child at an earlier stage. In this view, an economy must follow a dynamic of capitalist growth, which reverts us to the problem of growth. The notion that developing economies are at earlier stages not only ducks the role of the developed economies in actively underdeveloping them, it also involves a colonising mindset that closes off the possibilities that people, countries or economies may wish to develop in other ways of their own choosing.

Improvement seems more value-neutral than development. Humans are restless innovators and are always looking to improve things. This seems positive, except that it's worth asking about the trade-offs that the improvement may involve. What's the impetus behind the improvement; who benefits, who loses? As we saw earlier, John Locke's vision for improving the 'uncultivated waste of America' involved replacing its indigenous peoples with European farmers. Agricultural improvement in 18th-century England involved expropriating land by various means from small-scale farmers and creating large landed estates, while Victorian reformers later sought to improve working-class people (in often worthy, if patronising, ways) without much conception that the scars of poverty they bore had resulted from the 'unimprovement' worked by their forebears. When farmers today talk of 'improved grassland' they often mean ryegrass monocultures nourished by synthetic fertiliser – an improvement in calorific production per acre, but not in many other ways. Improvements are rarely straightforward or universally agreed, and their genesis is usually complex and conflicted.

This lesson is written into our concept of utopia – an improved or perfected society of ideal well-being, which we correctly view as an impossibility (a 'no-place' in its Greek etymology). And yet we've come to think that the pursuit of private, individual self-interest creates ever-compounding public benefit through mystical concepts like Adam Smith's invisible hand of the market.[149] In service of such concepts we restrict the ability of our political communities to limit private accumulation through markets, instead combusting ever more fossil fuels that imperil the ability of Earth to sustain its current complement of life in order to produce mass consumer goods and possibilities for endless travel that we think will improve our happiness. We concentrate wealth into fewer hands and express a kind of millenarian hope that a priestly caste of scientists will create new marvels that allow us to continue acting in this way indefinitely without blowback from the social or natural worlds. And when we encounter criticisms of this behaviour we dare to call them utopian.

It's hard to think of anything much more utopian than this contemporary capitalist political economy. But that doesn't make it easy to replace with more plausible utopias, partly because of our strong cultural commitment to mythologies of progress and transformation. The deep institutional underpinnings of the global political economy on the ground also make it hard for alternative visions of the 'wouldn't it be nice if – ' variety to get much purchase.

Still, utopian thinkers have been writing 'wouldn't it be nice if – ' treatises for centuries, and sometimes they've had a big role in bringing a new politics into being. But when we look back at even the most far-sighted utopias of the past, the conventionalism of their assumptions about aspects of life that didn't endure is often as striking as the paths they illuminate into a new future. From Plato onwards most premodern utopias were written by high-ranking men, and in the margins of their main concerns you often see the hard work of their idealised societies being quietly done by women or low-status functionaries. Even feminist utopias like Charlotte Perkins Gilman's *Herland* (1915) replicated now outmoded thinking about racial and genetic hierarchies while presciently reconfiguring gender relations in more contemporary terms.

What leaden-footed assumptions of the present will our contemporary utopias turn out to have made? My punt is on human liberation through automation. I won't sidetrack here into a full-blown discussion of techno-logical futurism, but it strikes me that a post-capitalist world without work is unlikely to materialise soon, if ever. A slowing in the growth machine of global industrial output, challenging energy dynamics, declining rewards to global labour, perturbations to the global political economy from the crises we've examined and the difficulty of untethering technology from capitalist control all point to, at best, a much more limited liberation aris-ing from labour-saving technology than these utopias typically imagine.[150]

Besides, why the constant emphasis on saving labour in these high-tech utopias? Anyone who's worked on a farm surely appreciates the help that machinery can provide, but they don't necessarily seek a world without work. In fact, many people seek physical work in a garden, if not a farm, as a way of recuperating from alienating office work or plugged-in leisure. We slip too easily into overdrawn dualities that insist we must choose between endlessly revolutionising high-tech automation or primitivist anti-technology – a false opposition between industrial agriculture and digging sticks.[151] In the face of that dismal choice I respond with an element of indifference to the technologies of the future. I'm not advocating for a small farm future without mechanical devices, so much as de-emphasising the importance of machines in how we construe the future. There are more important things to focus on.

Perhaps this techno-obsessiveness is a clue that the vision of a world without work is less post-capitalist than simply a mirror of capitalism, with the same drive to improve technology, release labour and increase control. A more nuanced and less one-sidedly negative view of work is possible, which may be just as well, since present levels of agricultural mechanisation probably won't be feasible in the post-capitalist future. Nor, I suspect, will they be widely desired. The greater challenge will be to create congenial and equitable societies able to absorb a lot of human labour in low-carbon enterprises, in which farming (or, better, gardening) will loom large. Of course, with human rather than machine labour in play, this returns us to the problem of hidden female and low-status labour – also a problem in contemporary capitalist economies. That's why I emphasise equity and individual rights in Part III of this book.

A world of abundant, low-tech gardens nurtured by human hand may seem an attractive utopia to some, but I readily acknowledge it's not everyone's cup of tea. The truth is that *no* utopia is going to be everyone's cup of tea, which is one reason why attempts to implement utopias usually turn dystopian. As political philosopher Robert Nozick put it: 'The idea that there is one best composite answer . . . one best society for *everyone* to live in, seems to me to be an incredible one.' This points in turn to a view of utopia not as a single society that somehow resolves all human differences but as a possibility for people to form their own utopias: 'Utopia is a framework for utopias, a place where people are at liberty to join together voluntarily to pursue and attempt to realize their own vision of the good life in the ideal community but where no one can *impose* his own utopian vision upon others.'[152]

So now imagine your own utopia along those lines without the unwise assumption that there'll be some subordinated category of human or machine labour to furnish you with necessities of life like food and fibre. If there's no place in your utopia for providing these for yourself, you'll have to consider what you can offer people who are willing to provide them for you, and weigh the implications of your extreme dependence on their goodwill. Against that background, I'd suggest that Nozick's framework implicitly generates something like a small farm future of widespread material self-provision. This is especially so once we've jettisoned, as I think we must, all the fanciful metaphors – the downward trickles, rising tides and invisible hands – by which the global wealthy convince themselves that the pursuit of the wealth accruing mostly to themselves is actually a help to the poor.

Of course, in the real world nobody gets to sit down and choose their individual utopia. Small farm utopias have been thin on the ground historically because control of land and its agricultural potential has been monopolised by centralising elite power. But the likely future fraying of centralising power in its current global guise offers some possibilities for wresting local small farm futures from the crisis that are likely to be more nearly utopian for a lot of people than many of the alternatives. Part of my argument involves the need to retain concepts of individual rights, personal autonomy and choice bequeathed by modernity. It's an advantage of Nozick's framework for utopias that he also takes this modernist logic seriously.[153] You can give up on the logic and argue that life is unfair, so it's okay for some people to work as peons in the global political economy. But this seems hard to square with any kind of just or universalist political theory, and it doesn't give you much ground to stand on if circumstances turn *you* into the peon. I'd argue instead that it's worth accepting Nozick's modernist logic – and thereby probably accepting something like a small farm future.

CHAPTER THREE

The Return of the Peasant

A small farm future would obviously involve a lot of people working as small-scale farmers, who seem a threatened category in the world today. It's therefore worth reflecting a little on what a small-scale farmer is and the nature of the threats they face. In fact, the demise of the small-scale farmer has long been heralded without ever quite occurring. Farmers – most of them small in the scale of their operations – are still the single largest component of the global workforce, comprising over 20% of it.[154] As well as being a threatened category, small-scale farmers seem to be a tenacious one.

The difficulties of discussing small-scale farmers start with our very language for describing them. Words like peasant, homesteader, smallholder, agrarian, yeoman, subsistence farmer, family farmer, self-provisioner or makeshift farmer all capture some aspect of the idea without fully ringing true. Historian Steven Stoll writes: 'The paucity of language seems like an artifact of capitalism and its tendency to eliminate all competing economic forms', pointing out that our modern distinction between 'subsistence' and 'surplus' effaces what 'subsistence farmers' actually do, which is produce food and other necessities, ideally at a level that enables them to thrive rather than merely subsist, and without necessarily making sharp distinctions between what they produce for their own use and what they produce for exchange.[155] Scholars like Stoll have shown that while subsistence farmers are often poor and hungry, this isn't due to their farming style but to the way they're linked to wider networks of economic exchange.

A good deal of scholarly writing focuses on these wider networks of exchange, and therefore emphasises the differences within and across particular kinds of farming. But sometimes it's as well to emphasise similarities over differences. Small-scale farmers often farm directly to feed themselves and their families, while the work unit even on larger and more commercialised holdings is often family-based, suggesting possible affinities between different kinds of 'family farming' – a useful but problematic term that I examine further in Chapter 12. A family dairy farmer in the United Kingdom who rents an extra hundred acres for his cows is obviously different from a family dairy farmer in India who rents a small tract from an upper-caste landlord for a buffalo whose milk she uses to help feed her family. Nevertheless, the various types of small-scale or family farmer often share these three features.

1. Much of the farm work is done by unwaged family labour.
2. The capital assets of the farm (its fields, buildings, tools and livestock, as well as its store of human skills and knowledge) aren't just investments with costs on the debit side geared to producing a greater financial surplus, but a long-term resource base constituting both a local and a family 'patrimony'.
3. The economic life of the farm takes the unwaged labour input and the capital patrimony as givens, and then seeks to earn income at levels appropriate to supporting or extending them.

These qualities make the family farm fundamentally different in character from capitalist forms of agriculture pursuing the M → C → M′ loop, even if family farms can often appear quite capitalist, with high-tech modern machinery or global market dependencies through which they're often co-opted into the dynamics of global capital.[156] The crisis of the family farm in both rich and poor countries is often discussed, and rightly so given that in both cases farm incomes are usually below national averages and often below national poverty lines, with many farms hovering on the margins of ongoing viability. For example, in 2010 the Commission for Rural Communities found that a quarter of British farming households lived below the poverty line.[157] Worse, the two crises are connected, since world market competition and differential levels of mechanisation and subsidies (direct and indirect) push family farmers in rich countries to bid down the price of grain against each other to their own detriment, simultaneously forcing farmers in poor countries out of staple crop production and into economic precarity, including the growing of commodity crops like coffee sold on over-saturated and fluctuating world markets that pay only poverty wages. In this respect, a good deal of global poverty and hunger results counterintuitively from the *excess* production of cheap food, particularly mechanised production of grain from wealthy breadbasket areas such as the North American prairies. The notion that hunger can be ended by growing more cheap food globally is, currently, the opposite of the truth.[158]

But despite their different locations within the global political economy, family farmers in rich and poor countries alike generally share a commitment to farming as a strategy of household livelihood-making, possibly one strategy among several, which is different from the logic of capital increase. In fact, it's not only different but antithetical. What unites all those not-quite-satisfactory small-scale farmer words is their attempt to build autonomies at the individual, household or local level from wider forces seeking to restructure the economy and institutionalise people's dependence upon the M $\rightarrow$ (C) $\rightarrow$ M' loop.

Currently, mainstream economic thinking sees such autonomy-building efforts as futile, suggesting that small-scale farmers are better off fully embracing the capitalist economy, probably by quitting farming. To some extent, that seems to be what's happened in recent years. According to International Labour Organization figures, in 1990 1.4 billion people worked in farming globally, whereas by 2016 the number had decreased to 1.2 billion. China is a key part of that story, losing more than 300 million people from agriculture over that period while climbing the league table of global wealth. Elsewhere, there are now *more* people in farming. Indeed, in 84 of the 186 countries for which data are available the number of people in farming has been increasing, with around 200 million people added to its ranks over the same time period. More than 80% of these people live in Africa, where generally populations are growing, poverty remains prevalent and urban opportunities are limited.[159]

It's hard to get enthusiastic about the return of the peasant in this context, which looks like a strategy of last resort among people with few other options – an impoverished global peasantry as a kind of residuum of the world's capitalist political economy. If everywhere can 'lift' itself out of rural poverty in the way that China may possibly do eventually, and do it sustainably, then a return of the peasant would surely be unwelcome. But that's unlikely, so it's necessary to question the progress-literature and end of peasantries writings mentioned earlier, which fill a market niche in the wealthy countries for false reassurances that our comfort doesn't come at the expense of other people's misery, and that everyone will soon sit at the table of consumer plenty. Meanwhile, international agencies that don't have this aim to please keep producing reports that assume poor small-scale farmers in their multitudes will be a long-term fixture of the human world, and that it's necessary to address their situation rather than wishing them out of existence.[160] Indeed, fossil-fuelled mass industrialism has been the only engine for creating incomes large enough to buy most of us in the rich world out of farming in modern times. But with income stagnation or decline, manufacturing over-capacity, global labour arbitrage, stalled economic growth and other crises, this window now seems to be closing – perhaps it was always destined to be only a brief hiatus in humanity's general agrarian vocation.

Here, we need to revive an old debate. Wherever modern industrial capitalism has arisen, it's been tracked by discussions as to whether it's truly necessary or whether the advantages of a modern society can be built on a peasant base. William Thornton's *A Plea for Peasant Proprietors* (1848) was an opening salvo in early-industrialising England, with the debate moving to the United States, Russia and Eastern Europe at the end of the 19th century, and to Latin America, Asia and Africa in the 20th and 21st centuries. Though in some cases, especially in Asia, capitalism clearly *was* built on a peasant base, generally the local debate was overtaken by a voracious expansion of the capitalist economy that made its arguments academic. But that doesn't mean the question was wrongheaded. If industrial capitalism proves only a short-term interval in a longer history of agrarian localism – and at the expense of worldwide social and ecological crisis – this forces us to pose the question again in an urgent and now global form: can we build congenial modern societies on an ecologically sustainable local agrarian base?

Much of this book is taken up with a search for a plausible affirmative to that question, because to me the alternatives seem worse. But one aspect of arguments for development that's worth taking seriously is the idea that having access to small patches of productive land is a means for the owners of capital to lower their costs by offloading onto workers the responsibility to provide food for themselves – a strategy widely adopted historically, from slave provision grounds on the plantations of the Caribbean, mining camp gardens in 19th- and 20th-century Appalachia, homeland plots in apartheid South Africa and any number of peasant holdings around the world that provide an insufficient livelihood. There is no doubting this 'semi-proletarianisation', more poetically named by Steven Stoll as 'the captured garden'. But it can be a double-edged thing, providing a level of autonomy from serving capital as well, and current evidence suggests that people sometimes seek plots of land, however small, as a hedge against the extreme exploitation of urban or rural landless wage labour, or what might be termed the 'recaptured garden'.[161]

I don't have an axe to grind about the livelihood decisions that the rural poor make in the here-and-now of the global capitalist political economy. I don't suggest that the peasant way is always the right way for people in every circumstance. Plenty of studies suggest that under particular and current local constraints, a 'recaptured garden' of self-reliance and local marketing isn't optimal. A good deal of writing in peasant studies goes further, criticising the very idea of a peasant way for its 'essentialism' in supposing that there's some essence of peasantness or small farm identity that transcends local history or geography.[162]

I plead both guilty and not guilty to this charge of peasant essentialism. I accept that small-scale farmers are always fully implicated in the historical circumstances of their times, are rarely a unified group, and are not necessarily more in touch with some authentic essence of nature or the earth than anyone else. In that sense, I plead not guilty – and this book offers no prescriptions as to how particular small-scale farmers or peasants ought to behave in their own historical circumstances. It's not a book about the specific politics of peasant agriculture in the world today.

But I do argue that in the general circumstances likely to face many people in the future as various crises unfold, a recaptured garden is more likely to commend itself than it does now – not just for today's rural poor, but much more widely – and that this is because there are recurrent possibilities for solving ecological and social problems available to people engaged in small-scale agricultures oriented to their local ecological base that are scarcely available to those otherwise engaged.

In that sense, I plead guilty to small farm essentialism. Sometimes we get so engrossed fossicking in the rock pools of local particularity and fine-grained history we fail to notice that the tide's about to come in. So whereas mainstream ideology generally advocates for poor people to increase their autonomy by getting a bigger wage, I argue that increasing autonomy by getting a bigger garden will probably soon be more to the point.

As we saw earlier, the 'global garden' is not that big – currently, only 0.65 hectares (1.6 acres) per person on average. That implies the necessity for small-scale intensive agriculture, defined by Robert Netting as,

> *producing relatively high annual or multicrop yields from permanent fields that are seldom or never rested, with fertility restored and sustained by practices such as thorough tillage, crop diversification and rotation, animal husbandry, fertilization, irrigation, drainage and terracing. I am not talking here about amber waves of grain but about gardens and orchards, about rice paddies, dairy farms and* chinampas. . . . *Land is objectively a scarce good, agrarian production per unit area is relatively high and sustainable, fields are permanent, work takes skill and relatively long periods of time, decisions must be made frequently, and the farm family has some continuing rights to the land and its fruits.*[163]

I'll wrap up here by suggesting why recapturing the garden through intensive small-scale agriculture of this sort commends itself over growing the wage. Earlier we examined Ricardian rent, which is a problem facing many rural dwellers trying to produce a material livelihood for themselves in the face of landlord pressures towards monetisation. But in the current phase of rentier capitalism Ricardian rent is increasingly a problem for urban dwellers trying to buy a material livelihood with their wages. We might also speak of an 'ecological rent' levied by the Earth on our present global political economy in currencies of climate stability, soil renewability, water availability and crop resilience, with payments overdue. I find it hard to see how the interlocking crises we face won't be augmented, leading ultimately to breakdown in social systems and planetary systems, if we continue down these present paths of economic and ecological rent-seeking. But there's an outside chance that recapturing the garden and turning to intensive small-holder agriculture may avert that outcome and restore well-being.

Small-scale farming has persisted to the present often in hostile policy environments. If political institutions and scientific research were devoted to actively supporting it, there's a good chance it could produce higher returns acre for acre than existing forms of capitalist farming (in fact, as we'll see in Part II, sometimes it already does), while producing copious low-carbon, labour-intensive employment of the kind that green new dealers and ecological economists argue is necessary for sustainable prosperity. Pro-peasant land reform has successfully tackled hunger and poverty before, and there's a good chance it can do so again in the future.[164] It's in this rather generic sense of recapturing the garden that I use terms such as 'peasant', 'small-scale farmer', 'homesteader', 'self-reliant farmer' and the like fairly interchangeably in this book without too many apologies about upsetting hair-splitting academic categories, and perhaps indeed with the somewhat mischievous intent of endorsing a small farm or peasant essentialism in the very particular sense described above.

Still, those writers who are critical of a generic 'peasant' category are right inasmuch as a post-capitalist small farm future won't just happen by default outside of history, and peasantries are fractured by other identifications, agendas and internal differentiations that intersect with the wider political economy. Jan Douwe van der Ploeg, one of the foremost thinkers about contemporary peasantries, writes that positions on the peasantry are polarised between uncritical support and outright aversion, with no critical position between the two.[165] In the rest of the book, I try to develop such a critical position that's fit for the crises of our time. But it has to start with the recognition that some people do actually want to be peasants. They want to recapture the garden. And their numbers are likely to increase.

PART II
Small Farm Ecology

If all the land in England was divided up quite fair
There would be work for everyone to earn an honest share
Well some have thousand-acre farms which they have got somehow
But I'll be satisfied to get three acres and a cow.

19TH-CENTURY ENGLISH
LAND REFORM SONG[1]

CHAPTER FOUR

The Farm as Ecosystem

The ten crises I described in Part I comprise a deep set of challenges to the present global order. Agriculture is at the heart of many of them, a major force driving the environment beyond planetary boundaries.[2]

Historically, most parts of the world have developed agricultures that were less drastically compromising of ecological integrity. Typically, they were low in GHG emissions and external energy use, conserved or sustainably cycled resources like soil and water, and often involved distributed, land-sharing models of settlement. Faced with our present crises, people are rightly looking to historical models to inspire a more promising future for farming. This book fits within that mould.

But traditional agricultures aren't a panacea. The question is whether it's possible to retain some of the benefits of modernity while pursuing the kind of low-energy, distributed agriculture that characterised historical models. There are difficult ecological trade-offs that agricultures of all kinds must struggle to balance. Even low-energy traditional agricultures haven't always balanced them well. Here, I examine agriculture's core ecological dilemmas and from there try to reconstruct the aspects of traditional agricultures that give us the best chance of tackling present crises.

'Ecological agriculture' is a term often used to refer to farming methods seen as more environmentally benign than 'conventional' agriculture. But every kind of farming is 'ecological' in the sense that it's part of a matrix of relationships between numerous organisms and the geophysical systems sustaining them. In fact, whether a farm is described as 'ecological' or 'conventional', it usually has a similar ecological structure.

Ecologist Phil Grime provides a useful way of thinking about this. He describes a framework for the evolutionary strategies shaping organisms and ecosystems according to habitat disturbance and resources:[3]

1. High disturbance, low productivity: no strategy
2. Low disturbance, low productivity: stress-tolerator dominance
3. Low disturbance, high productivity: competitor dominance
4. High disturbance, high productivity: ruderal dominance

'Disturbance' refers to events that endanger an organism's well-being, such as fire, flood, frost, trampling or predation. 'Productivity' refers to the inputs and nutrients necessary for the organism's growth and well-being. Grime suggests that high-disturbance, low-productivity situations aren't propitious for life. For example, our farm track comprises a ten-inch layer of crushed rock containing few useful plant nutrients, and it's frequently disturbed by vehicles driving over it. Consequently, nothing grows where the wheels pass.

But in low-nutrient situations that are relatively undisturbed, some organisms can get by. In between the wheelings on our track, untouched by passing vehicles, low- and slow-growing herbaceous perennials such as yarrow and white clover have established. Such 'stress tolerators' adapted to low-nutrient situations are commonly found in wild habitats.

High-nutrient, low-disturbance situations produce organisms adapted to quickly grabbing the available nutrients before other organisms can get to the prize, often in the case of plants by investing in rapid, spreading growth at the expense of long-term survival. Where I live, for example, extensive stands of nettles with their large, tangled root systems quickly take hold in old compost heaps or field margins absorbing fertiliser runoff. Woodland edges sport thickets of blackthorn, a wild relative of the plum. These 'competitor' organisms proliferate and reproduce quickly, beating other organisms to the nutrients. Once the nutrient source is exhausted, the competitors lose their advantage and stress-tolerating organisms overtake them.

High-nutrient, high-disturbance situations are dominated by ruderal — literally 'growing out of rubbish' — organisms that corner nutrients even better than competitors. There's only so much time before the next lethal disturbance, so these ruderals draw down on the nutrient riches to invest in rapid growth in order to complete their life cycles as quickly as possible, usually by producing seeds that can disperse or weather disturbance better than a growing plant. For example, annual meadow grass, which lives, reproduces and dies in a single season, is often found on ground trampled (disturbed) and dunged (nourished) by grazing animals.

Let's pause to consider what plants, both wild and domesticated, need to do to survive, and the trade-offs they must resolve. They have relatively constant annual sunlight with which to turn atmospheric CO_2 into the carbohydrates that build their bodies and fuel their metabolisms. From this basic input, they must create leaves and supporting structures like stems to fuel their metabolism and keep up with surrounding plants that might otherwise outcompete them for light. They also have to create roots to anchor them in the soil and find nutrients and water, and they may have to invest in defensive structures or substances that protect them from the climate, predators or diseases – bark, wood, thorns, waxy coatings and poisons. On top of all this, they have to create resource-demanding reproductive structures that enable them to survive winter, fire or drought and to produce new offspring. And they must balance these trade-offs at all times throughout their lives, which sometimes last hundreds or thousands of years.

Evolutionary processes favour the three strategies Grime describes, depending on circumstances. For example, the ruderal strategy is typically followed by pioneer plants occupying bare and fertile ground, like annual meadow grass. It simplifies the trade-offs we've considered by maximising allocation to fast reproduction at the expense of roots and defensive structures that would boost long-term resilience. The plant is essentially wagering that it will produce seeds before its vulnerabilities are exposed. In this sense, seeds *are* its strategy of resilience, as well as its vehicle for reproduction. They're better able to ride out disturbances likely to be lethal to living plants, and face fewer critical trade-offs.

At the other extreme, stress tolerators are often long-lived perennial plants in mature and undisturbed ecosystems. Although they have to allocate more carbon than ruderals to non-reproductive structures, the advantage of their longevity is that reproduction isn't so all-or-nothing. For a perennial plant, there's always next year. In seasonal climates with cycles of growth and dormancy, perennials also have the advantage of starting from a more established structure rather than needing to grow a whole new plant from seed. This gives them a head start in capturing sunlight and fixing carbon.

Of course, nature is complex. It doesn't allocate every living thing into one of three boxes. Every species is unique. Still, Grime's framework helps elucidate higher-order patterns, emerging from real constraints, without getting lost in details. In his words, evolutionary outcomes are restricted to a 'rather narrow range of basic alternatives'[4] – and this is what both human designers of ecosystems and inhuman processes of natural selection have to work with.

Indeed, although Grime's framework is intended to explain adaptations among wild organisms, it also applies to human provisioning. In low-productivity situations, humans at low population densities have tended to employ the stress-tolerator strategy of foraging and hunting. Throughout history, however, people have also gravitated towards high-productivity 'competitor' strategies, either by seeking out the more productive environments or by developing strategies that *make* environments more productive, by controlling fire and water, or plants and animals.

Yet in the continuum from foraging to farming, the most productive strategy of all has been to embrace the super-productivity of ruderal plants, which is what we've done with our key staples of wheat, rice and maize. In fact, most of the world's cropland nowadays is devoted to a handful of ruderal super-crops: the ten most widely grown crops – which occupy 75% of global herbaceous cropland – are, with the exception of cotton, all essentially annual, ruderal food crops whose main product is a nutrient-rich seed. Six of the ten are cereals.[5]

Historically, farming has largely been a strategy to shift the landscape into the 'ruderal space' of high productivity and high disturbance, and keep it there. Farmers have increased productivity by irrigating with nutrient-rich river water, adding compost or manure, tilling in fallows, or applying synthetic fertilisers. Agricultural societies have also enhanced productivity with plant breeding to augment ruderal characteristics, such as increasing a crop's allocation to seed by reducing its allocation to stem. These enhancements, together with domestication traits like non-shattering seed heads, make these crops uncompetitive with wild plants that favour the same habitats (weeds), requiring large inputs of human labour to protect and propagate them.

The cultivation involved in farming mimics the disturbance that selects for ruderal plants. This cultivation prevents succession by perennial weeds and creates the conditions favoured by ruderal, quick-seeding crops. Plants that employ the stress-tolerator or competitor strategies do find a place agriculturally, but in terms of overall contribution to human nutrition, the plants that employ the ruderal strategy dominate.

High-yielding crop production therefore holds up the tendencies of ecological succession towards low-nutrient, undisturbed states through labour-demanding inputs that disturb the agroecosystem and increase its nutrients. This is true whether the labour is performed directly by humans, by domestic animals, or by machines and pesticides, though one reason for the widespread adoption of arable 'super-crops' is that it's easier to substitute animal or machine for human labour in their cultivation. Several of the crises I described in Part I – water drawdown, soil loss, eutrophication, land-take, nutritional stress and, to a degree, climate change and economic crisis – largely stem from these practicalities of the ruderal agroecosystem. The rollcall of past societies that have failed to deal with these issues is lengthy, but so, too, is the list of adaptations traditional agricultures have developed to stave off that outcome.

Perhaps the most obvious path of adaptation is to embrace rather than resist natural ecological succession, which in many parts of the world tends towards wooded landscapes of stress-tolerant trees. At low population density, it's possible for people to make a low-impact livelihood from woodlands. That livelihood can be stretched in more productive early-succession directions through practices such as swidden (slash-and-burn) agriculture, which was once thought to be environmentally destructive but has undergone a reevaluation in recent years.[6] Forest gardening, popular in alternative agricultural circles, is a latter-day adaptation of such practices. Unfortunately, as with hunting or foraging, which grades into forest gardening, it's only possible to intensify productivity through these low-input and low-impact methods up to a certain point – a point that falls far short of feeding the world's current population.

A different path of adaptation has occurred historically in grassland ecosystems. Humans can't eat grass, but ruminant mammals can and domestic ruminants like cattle, sheep and goats provide meat, milk and fibre for pastoralist farmers. We often see natural grasslands in regions where it is too arid for trees. Historically, these have been relatively low-productivity places dominated by stress-tolerant plants and home to nomadic pastoralists who – like their swidden woodland counterparts – have been criticised for their environmentally destructive ways, but have often been exonerated by more recent scholarship that recognises the value of their adaptive engagement with the land.[7]

The fundamental problem with pastoralism, however, is that like woodland and swidden it's a land-hungry way of producing food – in this case because it jumps a trophic level – that is, we eat the animal that eats the plant instead of eating the plant. Almost 70% of global agricultural land is grassland, predominantly for grazing ruminants that provide at best only about 9% of humanity's total calorific consumption and 17% of its protein.[8] This poor productivity prompts a vegan-environmentalist critique of pastoralism: all that land devoted to the production of a little milk and meat when we could grow plants for direct human consumption much more efficiently!

It's a fair point but it has some hidden complexities, which become obvious if you think about farming without high (fossil) energy inputs. First, the flip side of livestock's land inefficiency – from a farmer's point of view – is its labour efficiency. With a little livestock it's possible to control large areas of grass or brush, keep it in a relatively high-productivity or early-successional state without reverting to low-productivity woodland, and produce high-quality foodstuffs and other products with less hard work than is necessary for tending ruderal-dominated cropland.

Second, an essential task in tending such cropland is keeping fertility high. The fertility has to come from somewhere. In modern industrial agriculture it comes mostly from energy-intensive fertilisers synthesised using fossil fuels or mined from mineral deposits. It's possible nowadays to synthesise fertiliser with renewable energy, but in low-energy societies this would be a last resort. The first resort would be generating fertility on-farm, primarily by using grass and leguminous cover crops as fallows or as permanent pasture, with ruminants then acting as low-input grass managers and vectors for moving fertility around the farm. This is a key point: when cheap and abundant energy isn't available and people have to rely on their local landscape to provide the necessities of life, including crop fertilisers, grass-ruminant symbioses are a vital and efficient tool for maintaining cropland productivity. A mixed-farming strategy that combines grassland with cropland (and sometimes woodland) optimises the advantages of its constituent parts.

So there are some trade-offs between labour, energy input and environmental impact with which farmers of the future are going to have to wrestle, just as farmers of the past did. The easiest path involves husbanding or mimicking low-productivity and low-disturbance ecosystems like woodlands and grasslands, which in the wild are dominated by long-lived, stress-tolerating plants (and their animal predators, like cattle). Following this path has the added benefit of keeping habitat disturbance and human environmental impact low. The problem with mimicking nature in this way is that nature puts a low priority on gifting humans an easy meal. This problem is a conundrum on our now densely populated planet because in order to produce enough food we need to push the agricultural ecosystem in a more high-input, high-output direction like the early-succession, post-disturbance situation of a ruderal ecosystem. But this solution involves more human labour input, and higher environmental impact.

Ruderal cropping is harder work than foraging or pastoralism, a point that's somewhat lost to us nowadays – at least in wealthy countries – because a lot of the work is either done by machines or by people in places we don't much see. From a farmer's point of view, the stress-tolerator strategy – manifested as, for example, foraging, swidden or pastoralism – commends itself for the easy life when energy availability is low.

Unfortunately, in today's world of 7.7 billion people, with our per capita land allocation of 1.6 acres, the stress-tolerator strategy is not an option for most of us. Ruderal-heavy cropping is the reality we must confront, a path of intensification where we trade off greater labour or energy input for greater productivity. We could think of this as a 'tight' farming situation, in contrast to 'loose' situations where lower population density enables more extensive strategies like swidden or full-blown pastoralism. A problem in tight situations is that high-productivity ruderal crops are heavy demanders of fertility, so in the absence of cheap and abundant energy, farms have to supply the fertility as well as grow the crops. Whether that involves a livestock component like grass-ruminant symbioses or not, this fertility-making aspect of tight farming invariably requires more human labour than is necessary in looser situations.

Table 4.1 summarises these points.

Table 4.1. Labour input and food productivity in the agroecosystem

INTENSITY OF LABOUR INPUT	PRODUCTIVITY		
	Low	Medium	High
High	No sensible strategy		Arable farming Gardening
Medium		Forest garden Swidden Pastoralism	
Low	Woodland		No viable strategy

Sustainability and labour input considerations push towards the bottom left of the table, whereas food output considerations push towards the top right. Most farmers and gardeners will probably reflect ruefully on spending more time in the top left corner of high inputs for low outputs than they'd care to admit; obviously this is something that a thoughtful farmer tries to avoid. The best place to be in the table is the bottom right. Who wouldn't want a low-input, high-output farm? Down the ages, people have always searched for a Jack-and-the-beanstalk, trade-off free cornucopia. Claims to have found it are a dime a dozen, and they're widespread in both the mainstream and alternative farm sectors today. True, it's usually possible for every individual farmer to edge their practice a little closer to this ideal, but I'd argue that the dream of genuinely low-input, high-output farming is ultimately illusory. Instead, Table 4.1 presents us with some insurmountable dilemmas that in the future will probably be best addressed, but not fully solved, by labour-intensive small farm strategies operating around the middle to top-right reaches of the table. The rest of Part II is largely devoted to elaborating that suggestion.

CHAPTER FIVE

The Arable Corner

H istorically, the productivity advantages of ruderal cereal crops like
wheat have tempted many farmers, including small-scale, low-
impact, locally oriented peasant farmers. But such farmers often combine
the cultivation of cereals with many other foodstuffs to create a healthy,
balanced diet. This often includes non-cereal staples like potatoes, yams,
taro, plantains or cassava.

However, stretching back into antiquity, the main development of cereal
farming has come from centralised states, for whom cereals' nutrient density,
transportability and storability conferred political advantage.[9] Ancient states
were often associated with a specific cereal, such as wheat in Mesopotamia or
maize in Meso-America, and we're no less reliant upon them today.

This is shown in Table 5.1, which indicates changes in global per capita
production of various staple crops between 1961 and 1964, and 2014 and
2017. As you look across the rows, you get a sense of changes over time,
which include a growing reliance on the three big cereal crops of maize,
rice and wheat.[10] Whereas past civilisations often arose relatively locally on
the basis of a key cereal crop, Table 5.1 suggests that we've now created a
single, truly global civilisation that deploys all three crops to the detriment
of local alternatives.

No doubt there are some things to celebrate about this modern global
cereal civilisation. But it also has its downsides, which in some ways are a
product of its success in readily furnishing humanity with our basic nutritional needs. A high-productivity, ruderal-arable strategy boxes us into
an ecological corner by amplifying human population, amplifying input
intensification for the key cereal crops – more energy-intensive fertilisers
and pesticides, more irrigation water, more high-yielding but genetically

Table 5.1. Changes in global staple crop production

	1961–1964	2014–2017	RATIO
Average production, kg per capita			
Maize	66	148	2.2
Rice	75	101	1.4
Wheat	77	101	1.3
Barley	27	20	0.7
Cassava	24	39	1.6
Millet	8	4	0.5
Oats	15	3	0.2
Plantains	4	5	1.2
Potatoes	85	49	0.6
Quinoa	0.01	0.02	2.1
Rye	10	2	0.2
Sorghum	14	9	0.6
Sweet potato	31	12	0.4
Taro	2	1	0.9
Yams	3	10	3.4
% Total production traded internationally			
Maize	9.1	13.7	
Rice	3.1	5.5	
Wheat	17.5	24.3	

Source: FAO n.d.

uniform crops – and amplifying crises of soil, water and human health associated with over-reliance on cereal-based nutrition. It also boxes us into socioeconomic corners: agricultural depressions, rural dispossession and slum urbanisation, along with amplifying pressure to 'feed the world' – a world that seems mired in chronic poverty, not in spite of our cereal-fuelled wealth, but largely because of it.

The trends shown in Table 5.1 can be partly explained by the Green Revolution, when high-yielding cereal varieties were introduced in the 1960s following international plant-breeding initiatives promoted by the US government. Ecologically, the Green Revolution involved pushing the ruderal characteristics of annual cereals, breeding them to emphasise allocation to seed over stem and to achieve higher yields through increased responsiveness to large inputs of nitrogenous fertilisers and pesticides. The Green Revolution's legacy is hotly contested between those who argue that it fed the hungry and 'spared' land for wildlife rather than cropping, and those who argue that it was detrimental to peasant farming, increased dependence on polluting and unsustainable fertilisers and pesticides, undermined agrarian radicalism that favoured a more equal distribution of resources – a 'green' revolution engineered to prevent a 'red' one – and generally suited the interests of cash-poor governments more than cash-poor people.[11] On this latter view, which I largely share, the long-term consequence has been a global economy that's more dependent on global cereal exports, and more reliant on highly mechanised cereal farming on vulnerable semi-arid continental grassland at high risk from climate change and water stress, with corresponding trade policies that favour wealthy countries.[12]

The precariousness of that increased dependence is one aspect of our boxed arable corner today. There is also the precarious situation of the global poor who, lacking secure access to land, must rely on the uncertain path of national economic 'development' to put enough money in their pockets to buy food. If the Green Revolution and the models of economic development associated with it had been truly successful in improving life and livelihoods around the world then maybe getting boxed into an arable corner wouldn't be so bad. But its success is debatable at best.

Basically, there's a danger that the arable corner locks in injustice. The latest iteration of this is in 'pro-poor' genetically modified crops like golden rice, which is engineered to produce vitamin A so that people who can't afford to eat much besides rice don't suffer vitamin A deficiency. Many people argue that enabling a balanced diet would be more successful than the genetically modified fortification of staple foods – a view that golden rice advocate Mark Lynas, among others, terms the 'let them eat broccoli' argument.[13] In this view, it's unrealistic to expect that poor people should be able to access enough fresh vegetables or wholefoods to secure a basic level of biological well-being – in other words that we're so deeply boxed into the arable corner that the aspiration to eat a substantially more diverse diet than a single cereal crop is a luxury.

That's hardly the case even in our present situation of advanced cereal dependence. The fact that it seems plausible to suggest it at all shows how mentally trapped we are in cereal-state thinking and its casual inequalities: wealth for the few, poverty for the many; fresh fruit and vegetables for the few, cereals for the many. Perhaps there's a shorthand way of saying all this. Civilisations that produce a lot of ruderal crops also tend to produce a lot of effectively ruderal people – people who have to subsist on rubbish, who lack the opportunity to build a rounded and resilient existence, who are condemned to be servants rather than beneficiaries of 'civilisation' and who, all too often, have few choices but to follow the 'live fast, die young' pattern of ruderal organisms.

The advantage of ruderal plants in the wild is that they produce an abundance of seeds that can weather inevitable disturbances, and then regenerate. Domesticated ruderals produce a lot of seeds, but they can't regenerate unaided. Is our domesticated, ruderal civilisation – so overwhelmingly reliant on just three cereal crops – courting the same risk? Nobody can say for sure, but archaeologist Jennifer Pournelle strikes an appropriate note of caution: 'Reckless transformations of entire agronomic systems into production of *any* single, easily divisible, transportable, marketable and transformable crop is not the hallmark of statehood: rather the tocsin of impending collapse. States resilient over millennia do not convert all available biomass into one risible foodstuff.'[14]

One approach that might overcome problems of the arable corner is the breeding of high-yielding but longer-lived perennial grain crops. Unlike golden rice, perennial grains have been heralded in alternative farming circles. But perennial grain breeding risks landing us back in the same arable corner because it still approaches the complex problems of human ecology and society with a path of single arable crop development.

The core logic of perennial grain breeding seems compelling. As we saw earlier, the annual, ruderal habit of the major cereal crops demands a lot of soil disturbance, crop nutrition, and often irrigation, which underly some of the crises we examined in Part I – soil erosion, loss of soil organic matter, fertiliser runoff and water drawdown among them. Wild grasslands like the original prairies of North America experience none of these problems, essentially because they involve a continuous groundcover of perennial grasses and nutrient-cycling broadleaf plants. Wouldn't it be great, the logic goes, if human agriculture could mimic the prairie? That is, could we create a 'domestic prairie' of highly nutritious and seed-yielding – but perennial – grasses to feed us?

It *would* be great, but there's a catch – the one that we examined in Table 4.1. Wild prairies produce plenty of leafy biomass that can feed ruminants like bison, but they don't produce much that can feed people the way annual wheat or maize can. We could raise ruminants on the prairies and eat their meat or milk, but the jump in trophic levels means that our per acre food production would be low. Perennial grain breeding attempts to overcome the problem by developing new crops selected for high seed yield while retaining perennial traits to deliver the environmental benefits of wild perennial grassland. But it hasn't yet succeeded, and it probably never will.

Crop breeders who espouse what I call the 'strong perennial vision' take the view that there's no intrinsic trade-off between the perennial habit and seed yield. For them, the problem of developing high-yielding perennial grains is purely a problem of plant genetics that will eventually be overcome with sophisticated modern genetic knowledge and (non-genetically modified) plant-breeding techniques. Plus, they argue that the head start in spring growth that perennial plants enjoy over their annual counterparts gives them a larger carbon budget to play with in allocating to both seeds and other structures. In the words of one prominent team of perennial grain breeders: 'Plants can pay the energetic cost of perennation by harvesting a much larger fraction of the seasonally available photosynthetic energy.'[15]

But the idea of paying energetic costs is a human metaphor, not a description of ecological reality. Plants aren't accountants shifting carbon between budget lines in order to maximise overall returns. They're complex organisms whose main concern is to fulfil the destiny of their ecologically constrained life history, which in the case of stress-tolerant perennial plants is to live long and reproduce cautiously. It's likely there are hard ecological trade-offs between the perennial habit and edible seed allocation that aren't easily, and haven't yet been, surmounted by human designs.[16]

An important and in many ways inspiring figure in both the alternative agriculture movement and in perennial grain breeding is Wes Jackson, founder of the Land Institute in Kansas, probably the most well-known and important organisation advocating this strong perennial vision. Jackson has argued that sustainable agriculture should look more to nature's wisdom than to human cleverness and create a natural systems agriculture based on nature's ecosystems.[17] Yet in making the case for perennial grains, he implicitly advocates for the use of human cleverness to create an agro-ecosystem without natural precedent, and apparently without the trade-offs that usually confront organisms within nature's ecosystems.

The problem isn't in creating unprecedented ecosystems. Humans have already had great success breeding for traits that were never selected for in nature – notably by pushing hard at the ruderal traits of annual cereals, which culminated in the Green Revolution. But the trade-off for this increased productivity is crops that can't take care of themselves without major human inputs and with potentially severe environmental costs. Still, I suspect that pushing the arable envelope with annual cereals in the Green Revolution will prove to have been a more realistic example of working with nature and accepting the trade-offs nature imposes than current attempts to pull off the trade-off free hat trick of high yield and minimal input by breeding perennial grains against the powerful inherent tendencies of their life histories.

Despite these reservations, once we move past the hype, efforts to breed perennial grains may prove worthwhile. It's possible there's enough genetic variability to produce high-yielding perennial grains. Already, there's some evidence of this in rice, even though it has a different ecology to crops of the dry prairie. But I still question the insistence on not only the possibility but also the desirability of matching perennial yields to current annual yields. It doesn't necessarily matter if perennial grain yields are lower than annual ones, so long as they're adequate to purpose. The bigger question is: What *is* the purpose?

The torrent of cheap grain pouring out from industrial-scale mechanised agriculture in breadbasket regions like the North American plains has undermined more sustainable and labour-intensive agriculture in other parts of the world and entrenched poverty in them. Perennial grain advocates sometimes emphasise the compatibility of their programme with capital-intensive, labour-light, mechanised agriculture.[18] If our goal is to match current yields of export-oriented, environmentally unsustainable annual cereals with sustainable perennial analogues there's a danger of creating a permanent arable corner that makes the entrenchment of global poverty almost eternal.

An alternative to this strong perennial vision – one that stands a chance of backing us out of the arable corner rather than pushing us further into it – is diversified local husbandry that uses as little annual cropping as possible and mitigates the environmental costs of that cropping through the thoughtful integration with perennials – trees, shrubs, pasture, cover crops and so on. The types of husbandry that most commend themselves in the light of present crises are at garden or small farm scales. Even Land Institute authors have conceded that 'in sparsely distributed garden-sized patches, annual grains would have limited negative impact', adding 'however, the human population's demand for cereal grains combined with social and economic pressures will make such an arrangement extremely unlikely in most situations'.[19]

More recently, they seem to have largely recanted the position that annuals could have a place in sustainable agriculture, indicting most historical small-scale agricultures involving annual crops for their inherent unsustainability. This chimes with other recent writings that present the cultivation of annuals as an irredeemable vice – not always on firm historical grounds. It may be that over the long evolutionary haul human agricultures that use annual crops in any way whatsoever will be incapable of reconciling the trade-offs involved and will drive us to destruction. But it seems premature and counterproductive right now to argue for perennial-only agriculture that replicates the arable corner by emphasising high-yielding grains, while dismissing the careful, long-term calibration of many traditional small-scale annual-based agricultures to local environmental conditions.[20]

Golden rice and perennial grains both dramatise a choice humanity now faces. The option they represent supposes we can develop high-tech plant-breeding solutions to ecological and socioeconomic problems while either avoiding or managing global economic inequalities long term. A second option focuses on the development of thriving, socially just small farm societies while embracing both the possibilities and pitfalls of annual crops and annual grains, and managing those possibilities and pitfalls by growing annual grains mostly in sparsely distributed garden-sized patches along with perennial crops – what I think of as a 'weak perennial vision'. Our chances of fully solving present crises may be 'extremely unlikely' either way, to invoke the Land Institute authors' words. But my case for a small farm future rests on the view that the second option in its myriad local forms is *less* unlikely (and *more* appealing). It does, however, require that we confront the social and economic pressures of which the Land Institute authors speak, and which is an aim of this book.

Nothing I've said here is meant to suggest that pushing the arable envelope through high-tech plant breeding like perennial grain development is always the wrong thing to do. But I do suggest it's problematic to reduce human social problems to arable crop-breeding problems. Instead of grand strategies for 'feeding the world', we could use some smaller strategies to feed ourselves and our locales, without neglecting how these play more widely. We could try to escape the arable corner in favour of a more diversified local farming. We could, in short, eat broccoli, along with a wide range of other foodstuffs, and treat cereal crops as supplementary to more diverse and local provisioning strategies.

CHAPTER SIX

A Note on Alternative Agriculture

People have practised diverse, local and low-energy agricultural strategies, probably starting long before the supposed origins of agriculture around 10,000 years ago.[21] These strategies haven't *solved* the ecological trade-offs and dilemmas that we see in all forms of agriculture, but they've often *resolved* them in ways that endured historically because they were satisfactory and sustainable.

It's a historical irony that when we talk about 'conventional' farming we're actually referring to highly specialised modern forms of production that break these long-established mixed-farming strategies into their constituent parts – grain or arable farming, dairying, meat production, commercial horticulture or orcharding, fish farming, forestry – producing cheap product via heavy fossil energy inputs in the form of synthetic fertilisers and pesticides, purchased fodders, mechanical farm traction and global cold-chain food distribution networks. Barely more than a century old, this conventional agriculture is already playing a role in each of the crises I outlined in Part I and to Earth systems breakdown, more generally.

So we badly need to switch to something less conventional. Combining the strategies of arable and horticulture, pasture and woodland, and seeking synergies between them, the world's mixed-farming traditions offer the best practical examples of the low-energy, resource-conserving, locally resilient agriculture that's now needed. These traditions have been taken up by various modern movements that apply traditional agrarian thinking to contemporary problems, movements that – irony upon irony – often go by the name of 'alternative agriculture'. It's worth exploring how modern alternative agriculture might enable us to back out of the arable corner and feed the world's people – but also exploring the difficulties it encounters in doing so and the trade-offs it must accept. By way of examples, I'll look at two important aspects of alternative agriculture – intensification and bio-mimicry – before touching on how the solutions and difficulties faced by the movement play out in three specific approaches: organics, regenerative agriculture and permaculture.

Alternative Agriculture as (Bio)Intensification

Sceptics of alternative agriculture sometimes say that if it worked there'd be no need for the word 'alternative' – it would just be called 'agriculture'. But beyond the charmed circle of fossil-fuelled industrial agriculture a good deal of the world's food – possibly most of it across much of the 'developing' world – *is* grown 'alternatively' by relatively small-scale farmers using more labour-intensive and less capital- and carbon-intensive techniques, though it's hard to assemble robust global data to establish this indubitably.[22]

The late Joan Thirsk, doyenne of English agricultural historians, describes a cyclical pattern through 750 years of English farming between a mainstream agriculture based on cereals and beef, and phases of 'alternative agriculture' when disjunctions in the agricultural economy forced farmers to pursue other options.[23] The alternatives they chose were mostly higher-value and more labour-intensive enterprises such as dairying and market gardening.

Thirsk's work suggests that, like everyone, farmers usually take the easy option. But sometimes the easy option is no longer an option. When this happens, a dynamic of *intensification* usually results. To intensify farming is to increase the productivity of a given area of land, and this can be measured in various ways – the yield of a single major crop, the aggregate yield of several crops, or the amount of money earned, for example. To achieve this, a farmer will increase the inputs devoted to the crop – applying more labour or mechanical energy, more fertility or crop nutrition, more irrigation water or drainage, more complex cropping regimens or treatments, more terraforming of soil and so on.

The modernisation of agriculture in Europe and its colonial offshoots involved a particular form of both intensification and extensification that we've come to think of as exemplary of 'conventional' farming. Intensification pushed the yield for a handful of super-crops – mostly grains and grain legumes, but also livestock – fertilisation, intensive pest management, irrigation and apparently labour-saving mechanisation both on the farm and in the wider food distribution system. The extensification side enlarged the geographic bounds of agricultural production, by removing people from the land via enclosure, farm engrossment and colonial expropriation, and by turning other landscapes such as forests or grasslands into farmland. The result is the curious intensive-extensive landscape typical of the modernised farm, especially in the Global North – an unpeopled prairie of high-productivity cereals or grass worked by machines that represent huge embodiments of external fossil energy.

This kind of agriculture isn't the only one possible, however. In Europe and its settler colonies, the typical situation was one of scarce labour and abundant land, leading to a path of intensification in which mechanisation substituted for labour, though it must be said that another approach to the labour problem widely followed in the history of European colonialism was slavery, a point too easily glossed over when we speak of modern development as a story of technological progress that ended human toil. But elsewhere in the world – the rice ecologies of Eastern and Southern Asia, for example – the typical situation was of scarce land and abundant labour, impelling a path of intensification that included both increased land productivity and increased labour demand. The notion that agricultural 'development' must involve labour substitution and not labour intensification is a prejudice that arises out of European history, despite apparently open-and-shut arguments about farm drudgery or the benefits of economic modernisation that prevail these days in arguments about how best to feed and provision the world.[24]

The path of intensification that Joan Thirsk describes in premodern England mostly involved farmers changing to more labour-intensive practices to shore up falling incomes. That's still relevant, but the most pressing need nowadays is to intensify farming to shore up productivity of food and fibre while minimising GHG emissions, soil loss, water drawdown and other negative impacts.

There are some effective ways of minimising such impacts that have been pioneered in alternative-farming circles, such as the use of natural pest predators instead of pesticides, and the cultivation of cover crops to protect soil. Generally, these approaches involve replacing high-environmental-impact fossil fuel and agri-chemical methods with lower-impact biological ones. That is, they're forms of *biointensification*. But it's hard to get away from the fact that, as with Thirsk's historical forms of alternative agriculture, the main form of intensification – and indeed of biointensification – is the application of more human labour per acre of land.

We tend to bristle at the idea of human labour intensification because of associations between farm work and drudgery – drudgery that has historically been borne hardest by women, slaves and others disproportionately subjected to labour coercion. We need to confront those historical associations (see Chapter 2, 'Wicked Problems', page 81, Chapter 12, 'Households, Families and Beyond', page 165, and Chapter 20, 'Dispossessions', page 262). But we also need to disentangle them from labour intensification per se, which is not inescapably exploitative, and indeed need not necessarily be drudgery, for anyone.

One way of lightening the load is to focus on small scale. Growing 20 cabbages biointensively with your own labour to help provide for yourself through the winter is more of a pleasure than a chore. Not so with growing 20,000 cabbages biointensively to sell to a wholesaler. In other words, biointensification has affinities with the garden, and not so much with the farm. Or at least, not so much with the big farm. Of course, a world where most people grow their own cabbages and other produce would look very different from our present one, with huge knock-on implications for economic productivity, property relations and residence patterns. But that may be the bullet we have to bite to create a just, peaceful and sustainable future, which wouldn't be without its compensations.

Alternative Agriculture as Biomimicry

Another way of thinking about alternative agriculture is biomimicry – especially the notion that alternative agriculture seeks inspiration from nature and works 'with' it, whereas conventional agriculture works 'against' it. But agriculture of almost any kind involves working against the ecological tendency to revert to a low-disturbance, low-input, low-productivity state, and it's not always clear that 'alternative' approaches like perennial grain breeding are more 'natural' than their conventional counterparts. So before we establish a useful vision of biomimicry's role in a viable small farm future, we must probe critically at over-simplified notions of alternative agriculture as 'natural agriculture'. Even if we're not always working with nature in alternative agriculture any more than we are in its conventional counterpart, can we nevertheless better attend to the natural world through it, while simultaneously meeting human needs?

The notion of alternative agriculture as natural agriculture often finds expression in the idea that well-raised crops bursting with natural health can better resist pests and diseases than those artificially propped up with fertilisers and pesticides – the manifestation of a common metaphor: 'the balance of nature'. There's probably a grain of truth to the idea of naturally healthy crops, but 'the balance of nature' is an inert and problematic metaphor suggesting two weights at a standstill on lever scales. If there's any balance in the natural world it's not like this. Rather, it's a temporary equilibrium representing the aggregate outcome of innumerable organisms pursuing their destinies and reacting back on one another.

At best, 'the balance of nature' can work as a rule of thumb. For example, there's wisdom in encouraging the natural predators of a crop pest rather than using a broad-spectrum pesticide that kills pests and their predators alike. But the idea can also mislead. A field-scale monoculture of leafy brassicas may be susceptible to attack by ruderal pests such as aphids that are able to multiply quickly in order to take advantage of the huge meal provided. That same field-scale monoculture will be largely unaffected by more stress-tolerant pests that are unable to multiply so fast, like pigeons. Those pigeons, however, could quickly destroy a few brassicas planted in a backyard plot, as many gardeners can ruefully attest. That is to say, generally speaking, there's no single, golden point of 'balance' in the agroecosystem. There is, rather, a series of dynamic games between farmer, crop, pest and other wild species constantly acting, and reacting, upon one another to create the complex system we call a farm.

Ecologist R. Ford Denison argues that we shouldn't necessarily model agroecosystems after wild ecosystems, since the two systems are pursuing different aims. In fact, he suggests, ecosystems aren't really pursuing aims at all, and that individual organisms are competitively tested by evolutionary processes in ways that ecosystems aren't. As Denison puts it: 'Evolution has improved trees much more consistently than it has improved forests. In other words, nature's wisdom is to be found more in the adaptation of individual plants and animals than in the overall organization of the natural communities and ecosystems . . . where they live.'[25]

In this view, even long-established ecosystems such as prairies or forests haven't been tested competitively, and there's no reason to think that copying them will lead to better agriculture. Channelling this logic, agronomist Andrew McGuire enjoins: 'Don't mimic nature on the farm, improve it.' And Denison ventures this *coup de grâce*: 'Local sourcing of nutrients in natural ecosystems . . . is a constraint imposed by the lack of external inputs, not an example of "nature's wisdom".'[26]

These criticisms of simplistic biomimicry in the alternative agriculture movement are compelling, within reason. A diverse forest garden isn't necessarily a better agroecosystem than a cornfield just because it looks more natural. Even so, something seems amiss with the critique, because too many cornfields and too many non-local sources of nutrients and energy are creating the arable corners and biophysical crises that are driving the human ecology beyond planetary boundaries. Nature doesn't care about this; evolution isn't oriented to long-term goals or ideas like the good of the planet. But there are long-term energy dynamics in ecosystems towards stress-tolerant and structurally complex states to which all organisms, including humans, are evolutionarily adapted through deep time, and which for all our technical prowess humans haven't yet managed to transcend. This is why our non-local sourcing of nutrients has got us into our present mess.

We've now created a truly planet-wide ruderal civilisation, largely by using fossil fuels to break local resource constraints and drive ecological dynamics against their normal successional direction on a vast scale. Whether this transgresses 'nature's wisdom' seems less to the point than whether it's actually wise. What are we trying to gain from such a state, and what are the risks? Certainly, this planet wide ruderal civilisation has no natural precedents and it's fundamentally reliant on the external energy inputs of fossil fuels. The tragedy of agriculture – 'tragedy' in the classic sense of a dilemma between two compelling but incompatible options – is that in view of our large human populations we now have little choice but to continue at least some way down this high-yielding, ruderal path even though the benefits of lower-yielding, stress-tolerant, locally diverse agriculture are increasingly obvious. The alternative agricultures that are worth their salt are the ones that embrace this tragedy and wrestle with it, rather than promoting trade-off-free solutionism.

Many alternative agriculture proponents and practitioners commonly emphasise another aspect of biomimicry, namely, crop diversity. Its banner headline is that second only to a vacuum, nature abhors a monoculture. This isn't entirely true. Particularly in early-successional states, nature can be quite tolerant of monocultures typified by competitor or ruderal organisms; think of blackthorn thickets and nettle stands. Nature can even tolerate more persistently dominant species, especially in grassland ecosystems where evidence suggests that the wild ancestors of many of our domesticated grass crops originally grew in monocultural stands.[27] Since agriculture mostly involves recreating high-productivity, post-disturbance conditions favouring ruderals and competitors, and has a special fondness for grasses, it's not surprising that it's also inclined towards monoculture – though we should bear in mind that these wild monocultures are likely to have much greater underlying genetic diversity than their domestic counterparts. Attempts to prove that diverse crop polycultures yield more biomass, calories or other nutrients than monocultures acre for acre haven't been conspicuously successful, except in the special and non-generalisable case of legume mixes.[28]

But the strongest arguments for crop diversity aren't about total productivity. They're about growing an appealing and balanced diet, security against the failure of single crops, supporting wild biodiversity, establishing beneficial interactions at the farm or farmscape level and producing a full range of products for local needs without assuming that global infrastructures based on cheap fossil energy can import them from afar in perpetuity. So while it's probably wise not to be too dogmatic about crop diversity as an ecological essential, there is a good case for building it in on the farm. At small scales, there are usually arguments both for and against multi-cropping, reflecting various trade-offs. The two-acre garden on my farm, for example, mostly involves monocultures when you look at it one square foot at a time, but it's more diverse than most of the surrounding cropland when you zoom out to look at it acre by acre.

If you zoom out further to encompass my entire farm, the mix of annual and perennial food crops, orchards, pasture and woodland works as a reasonably integrated whole with complementarities that support human livelihoods on the farm and in the nearby town, while lowering external dependencies for energy and other inputs. Its diversity stands out in the landscape from larger, more specialised farms serving larger, more distant markets, and it replicates long-established local patterns of low-energy mixed farming. It's not the only sensible way we could have developed the farm, and its structure isn't biomimetic in the sense that its diverse elements necessarily resemble what would be there if it wasn't being farmed for human purposes. But it has an ecological logic based on biological dynamics that goes way beyond the biomimicry of the arable corner where the super-productivity of individual species is emphasised above all else. At the farmscape level, the argument for a happy medium of diversity is strong.

Some Alternative Agriculture Movements

When people talk about alternative agriculture, they often home in on specific approaches such as organics, regenerative agriculture and permaculture rather than underlying principles such as intensification or biomimicry. I'd now like to turn to specific approaches, using these three as examples, but rather than describing them in depth the aim is to probe further into some key underlying ideas that could inform a small farm future. As ever, I stress the dilemmas the movements face and the trade-offs they must balance. This puts me in the role of a sympathetic sceptic. In case there's any doubt, I'd emphasise that my sympathy outweighs my scepticism. The issues these movements confront, and the ways they confront them, unquestionably paves the way for the small farm future I'd like to see.

Organics

'Organic' has two distinct agricultural meanings. It refers, first, to farming that fertilises crops from organic (living) sources, such as human or animal manures and cover crops. It also refers, more problematically, to farming that protects crops from weeds or pests through organic or 'living' methods, as opposed to conventional agriculture that uses nitrogenous fertiliser synthesised primarily from fossil fuel combustion, mined phosphates and manufactured pesticides.

The second meaning refers to a formal certification process in which farmers pay for audits confirming that their methods correspond to organic methods broadly in the first sense, but as laid down in detail by national certifying bodies. They're then entitled to market their produce as 'organic' at premium prices.

Organic farming in this second sense is sometimes criticised for its buy-in to the existing labour-shedding capitalist political economy of food, a path to conventionalisation: expansion of farm scale, reliance on fossil fuel-intensive practices, and excessive use of organically certified – but still questionable – pesticides. Meanwhile, just as organic farming has undergone conventionalisation, conventional farming has undergone 'organici-sation'. From the high-water mark of synthetic agri-chemical farming in the 1950s and 1960s, it's now widely agreed by organic and conventional farmers alike that using organic fertility where possible, promoting soil health and soil life and avoiding excessive tillage and biocides makes sense. This trend is accentuated by proliferating concerns about the consequences of 'conventional' agri-chemicals for human and ecosystem health.

Probably the most vexed issue concerning conventional versus organic practices is tillage, which usually increases soil erosion and CO_2 emissions while reducing soil carbon, water infiltration and the soil life that promotes healthy crop growth. Many large-scale conventional arable farmers are adopting a chemical no-till approach, using herbicides to create a clean seedbed, special seed drills to sow the crop without overly disturbing the soil and synthetic fertilisers to promote growth. Organic arable farmers can't use these methods, and have traditionally relied on growing nitrogen-fixing cover crops to build soil fertility. These cover crops are then ploughed in prior to planting the cash crop, invoking the downsides of tillage.

Recent developments in organic no-till methods include roller-crimpers that knock back the cover crop sufficiently to establish the cash crop without the need for more than occasional tillage. I'm not sure they'd work well in the cool, moist climate and heavy soils where I live – but tillage is less problematic here than in places with warmer climes and lighter soils that are more vulnerable to erosion. Therein lies a universal rule: in agriculture, there are no universal rules. The same goes for no-till and regenerative agriculture, which isn't optimal in every possible situation.[29]

The other way to go, organically, is to collect sources of organic fertility and apply them as a mulch or compost to the soil without tilling it. The sources can include animal and human manures, crop residues, food waste and any other organic matter obtainable from settlements, fields or watercourses. This more laborious method was identified by soil scientist Franklin King as the secret to East Asian societies' long-term ability to feed themselves at high population densities over the course of centuries.[30] Many no-till gardeners in the Global North do much the same thing today, but a good deal of the fertility they use can be traced back to the synthetic nitrogen or mined phosphates used in conventional agriculture, and a good deal of the heavy lifting involved is still done by fossil fuel-powered machines. Take a look around your neighbourhood and imagine how you'd get fertility into your garden from it without a fossil-fuelled infrastructure in the background. This gives a firmer sense of the centuries-long efforts King described, and possibly the work of centuries to come.

Here, then, is a major trade-off for future farmers to reckon with. In order to keep farm fertility and crop productivity high we could use synthetic fertiliser, but it comes at a high energy cost that may be hard for most farmers to pay in a post-fossil-fuel future, as well as causing other downstream pollution. Or, we could grow fertility-boosting cover crops and till them in, but in many places this comes at a cost to soil integrity. Or we could close the fertility loop, collecting all available organic fertility and cycling it back into crops with minimal tillage, but this imposes labour costs and points to a largely distributed and ruralised population, which some may consider disadvantageous. Probably all three will occur, but in an energy-, climate- and soil-challenged future it seems likely the third will gain greater relevance, and will point to a future of smaller-scale, more labour-intensive farming.

Another area of debate around organics concerns land sparing. In wealthy countries, organic yields per acre tend to be lower than conventional ones, and this is compounded by the need to build fertility through low-productivity livestock husbandry or fallowing rather than by purchasing industrially synthesised fertiliser. A greater turn to organic agriculture could therefore also lead to land-hungry extensification.

The two different meanings of 'organic' further compound the nuance – and confusion – as well. Conventionalised, labour-minimising, organically certified farming may involve extensification, but that wouldn't necessarily be true of the labour-intensive husbanding of organic fertility of the kind described by King. Organic farmers also make the plausible argument that they're disadvantaged by the choice of modern crop varieties, which have overwhelmingly been developed to suit the needs of conventional rather than organic husbandry. Meanwhile, some studies suggest that organic agriculture among poor farmers in poor countries can be *higher* yielding than its conventional counterpart, essentially because farmers use organic fertility-intensifying methods, including their own carefully deployed labour, rather than no fertility inputs at all. Various organic or organic-ish methods have been developed to improve the output/input equation in these situations, such as Zero Budget Natural Farming in India. Evaluating them goes beyond my remit, but it's possible that thoughtful application of low-cost organic techniques could increase yields at the global level.[31]

A final point on yields: though it may be true that conventional yields are sometimes higher than organic ones on a crop-for-crop or field-for-field basis, the essence of good organic farming is creating an agroecosystem where total productivity is fitted to the capacities of the farm or farmscape. So whereas conventionally raised pigs, for example, might be fed on soy grown from anywhere, including cleared tropical rainforests at high carbon cost, in an ideal scenario, organically raised pigs would only be raised on the capacities of the local farmscape to feed them. Developing local food systems that give people a clear sense of what those capacities are is critical if humanity is to steer beyond its present crises. This is one of the strongest arguments for a small farm future.

Regenerative Agriculture

Regenerative agriculture is a more recent and less formally organised movement than organics. It shares organics' concern with soil health but deepens it via an emphasis in contemporary soil science on the symbiotic relationships between plants and other organisms living in their root zones. The basic idea is that plants exude sugars from their roots containing carbon fixed from the atmosphere by photosynthesis, which become food for a plethora of soil life, particularly fungi. These in turn tap various nutrients in the soil and make them more available to plants, while storing much of the donated carbon. This cycle is disturbed by tillage but enhanced by growing a diversity of plants that develop symbiotic relationships with soil organisms. Therefore, proponents of regenerative agriculture emphasise the first three practices listed in the left-hand column of Table 6.1.

Table 6.1. Regenerative agriculture practices and projected outcomes

Practices	Projected outcomes	
1. Minimum or no tillage	1. Soil building/soil protection	4. In-field crop nutrition
2. Continuous cover of living plants	2. Improved water infiltration	5. Sequestration of human-origin GHG emissions
3. Diverse rotations	3. Few or no weeds/pests	6. Higher yields
4. Use of perennial plants		7. Increased farm income
5. Use of grazing livestock		8. Increased global food availability
6. Inoculation of soil fungi		9. Improved human health
7. Elimination of synthetic fertilisers and pesticides		

Other regenerative agriculture proponents emphasise some, but not always all, of the other practices listed in the left-hand column of the table. Here, I'll just mention (4) and (5) in passing. An easy way to keep a continuous cover of living plants is by using perennials, and the easiest form of broadscale perennial agriculture involves maintaining pastures for livestock. Therefore, it's no surprise that some of the best-known regenerative farmers focus mainly on pasture and livestock.[32]

On the upside, when ruminants feed on and trample the grass – under careful grazing management – it prompts the grass to regenerate. In doing so it enhances carbon cycling from the atmosphere through the plant and its root exudates, and into the soil. But, as we saw earlier, the drop in trophic levels involved in pastoralism makes it a low-productivity agriculture acre for acre, and not widely generalisable for feeding humanity. There are alternatives to managed grazing of perennial grasses, such as intercropping annual cash crops with perennial groundcovers, but this is trickier, less reliable and less feasible worldwide because it depends on climate, local conditions and the vagaries of the weather year to year.

It's likely that the regenerative practices in Table 6.1 will become more widespread in the future because of the promise they hold to deliver the outcomes listed. What's less certain is the extent to which they can fully deliver on those outcomes. The least controversial claims are those listed in the centre column of Table 6.1, namely that regenerative practices protect and build soil (though how much is debatable), often improve water infiltration, and reduce pest and disease problems. The more controversial claims are listed in the right-hand column of Table 6.1. I comment briefly below on the first two.[33] The case for outcomes (7)–(9) is unproven, at best.

In-field nutrition: The idea is that crops under a regenerative regimen require no external fertilisation because the symbiotic relationships they have with soil organisms provide complete crop nutrition. This may be plausible in the case of nitrogen, since soil bacteria are able to fix it in plant-available form from the atmosphere where it's abundant, but most of the other key plant nutrients are a fixed stock in the soil. The argument is that these nutrients in fact are copiously available in the mineral fractions of the soil but inaccessible to crops in that form, and that regenerative practices make them biologically available.

Ultimately, though, if crops are sold off the holding then the stocks are depleted, and this seems likely to be an unavoidable long-term constraint.[34] Regenerative agriculture proponents typically emphasise the higher nutrient values in their soils, while ignoring or dismissing long-term drawdown. Perhaps this is the alternative farming movement's version of the Ehrlich-Simon wager, in which it's assumed that human cleverness eliminates resource limits (see Chapter 1, 'Crisis #5: Stuff', page 39). A more cautious approach commends itself, however: humans spreading out in the landscape, skimming its productivity and returning their wastes to the soil.

Carbon sequestration: Plants remove CO_2 from the atmosphere and build carbohydrates from it, some of which they exude into the soil. Some of that exudate stays long term, thereby sequestering a portion of the carbon humans are adding to the atmosphere by burning fossil fuels.

There's no doubt that soil can act as a carbon sink in this way. Where things get murky is determining how much of the carbon that humans are adding to the atmosphere soils can absorb if we turn them over to regenerative practices, how long the carbon will stay absorbed, and whether these practices can adequately feed humanity – all areas in which strongly held opinions currently seem to outweigh firm evidence. There are numerous complexities here, and trying to plumb their depths to estimate how much agricultural soil management can remove carbon from the atmosphere is a pit of despair from which few who enter it ever return with their sanity intact.

Of those who have plumbed it and returned, the most generous reputable estimations suggest that 15% of carbon emissions from fossil fuels, at most, can be sequestered in the soil by using regenerative practices. This is quite a lot, but not enough to be a climate saviour. At something like 4.1 trillion tonnes (4.6 trillion US tons), the carbon pool in remaining fossil fuel reserves is large; so is its potential to catastrophically disturb the Earth's climate.[35] So it may be wiser to leave it stably sequestered deep underground than to burn it and hope it can then be sequestered in farm soils. Leaving it in the ground has its own radical implications for a fossil fuel-free agriculture, pointing (again) towards traditional mixed-farming approaches. In the long run, variants of these traditional approaches are probably going to be our best bet for regenerating human ecologies and economies.

Permaculture

Permaculture – a contraction of the words 'permanent' and 'agriculture' – originated in the work of two Australian agrarian thinkers, Bill Mollison and David Holmgren.[36] Its emphasis is on design-rich, whole-systems or whole-landscape thinking as a way of devising sustainable human lifeways, and on biomimicry as a key design principle. Although permaculture design can be applied at any scale, its main elaboration has been in small-scale domestic or homestead settings. Unlike organics, it has developed as a more grassroots and to some degree countercultural movement.

At its best, permaculture represents exemplary alternative agricultural intensification in the form of highly productive, carefully optimised, labour-intensive, usually small-scale land husbandry. Indeed, historic smallholder land husbandry of this kind, such as the East Asian systems described by Franklin King, was one of Mollison and Holmgren's inspirations. A strength of permaculture in theory is that it emphasises design solutions that are specific to each unique situation, rather than one-size-fits-all solutionism.

My experiences within the movement as a permaculturist somewhat inclined to heresy suggest to me that in practice a certain amount of received wisdom and off-the-peg solutionism does get recycled within it around issues like perennial cropping (the strong perennial vision), tillage and water management, along with a tendency to downplay the unavoidable human labour that goes into producing a homestead living, however smart the design.[37] Still, the emphasis within permaculture on the labour-intensive personal producerism of the homesteader probably makes it closer to the vision for a small farm future outlined in this book than any other strand of agrarian thinking.

Conclusion – Only (Bio)Intensify

To draw together the strands of this chapter, I'd suggest it has established four broad themes that must inform any plausible vision for a sustainable, low-energy, agricultural future:

1. Most importantly, future farming will be *biointensive*, using low-impact biological inputs to ensure adequate farm outputs. The key biointensive input is probably human labour. Deploying it primarily for self-provisioning over small scales makes the work demand less daunting.
2. Future farming will involve *biomimicry*, but since farmers seek different outcomes to wild ecosystems the mimicry will only be partial. Generally, farmscapes will mix cropland, pasture and woodland in ways that correspond to local traditions of low-energy mixed farming and that don't necessarily look much like wilderness. But they'll be inspired by the structural complexity and local resource cycling of wild ecosystems.
3. Future farming will face various trade-offs. The trade-offs that balance crop output with labour input, crop nutrition, soil health and GHG emissions will loom largest. These trade-offs will probably resist wholly satisfactory solutions.
4. Future farming will probably involve a lot of small farms distributed widely across farmable space. The rural population will be large, and farmers will make a larger proportion of the population than they do in wealthy countries today.

The three chapters to follow expand on the implications of this future farmscape by looking in more detail at some of the issues surrounding its gardens, livestock and woodlands.

CHAPTER SEVEN

The Apothecary's Garden

The untenable problems of the arable corner combined with the forms of intensification in various methods of alternative agriculture suggest that the labour-intensive garden is probably the optimum unit for sustainable agrarianism. Where population pressure on land is high and external (fossil) energy availability is low, this intensive, horticultural smallholder-householder 'tight' adaptation has historically been key to food production. That holds true in certain places today as well.[38]

Today's permaculture movement is an aspirational take on this historic pattern of intensive smallholder gardening, with its emphasis on thorough cycling of human, animal and plant wastes within the holding and imaginative optimisation of available space to meet multiple human needs using skilfully applied manual labour. In a populous world increasingly plagued by crises that are likely to disrupt the flow of non-local resources, it's likely this may change from aspirational to essential in the future.

That's a far from rosy prospect in many ways, but I've called this section 'the apothecary's garden' to emphasise that it could pay dividends in human well-being if done well. This is partly because garden as opposed to field cultures are more heavily accented towards producing healthy fresh fruit and vegetables. Physical and mental well-being are also enhanced by the outdoor exercise and connectedness of garden work. And the garden can be the source of medicinal plants and other non-food crops that allow their curators to address other needs. While I don't commend total self-sufficiency – I'd hope for medical professionals, peacemakers and other such specialists in a small farm future – the ability of the gardener to self-provision widely, acting in part as their own grocer, apothecary, personal trainer and builder's merchant, seems health-promoting in many senses of the term. There's evidence to suggest that access to gardens and garden crops – even to tiny areas for poor people in large cities – and to outdoor spaces in general is beneficial in various, and sometimes surprising, ways.[39]

Of course, our modern arable civilisation also furnishes garden crops, at least for the wealthy. Most supermarkets have an aisle or two devoted to perfect-looking fruit and vegetables, often grown far from the point of sale. But it seems fair to say that their real forte lies in presenting oil, fat, starch and protein derived from a handful of global commodity super-crops grown on mass scales in endlessly tempting but unhealthy combinations, which is one reason why obesity and other diet-related health problems are a growing global issue.

So there's a case for emphasising garden produce, grown locally on garden scales. As Robert Netting put it: 'The economies of scale that apparently rule manufacturing do not really apply to any sustainable kind of food production – when you count all the costs, it is cheaper to raise a zucchini in your garden than on your megafarm.'[40] This raises an issue that often surprises people: not only is small-scale farming theoretically competitive with large-scale agriculture economically when hidden costs like environmental degradation are factored in, it's also often economically competitive in practice even when they're not. Indeed, sometimes small-scale farming produces *more* output per acre than large-scale production. In farming, there aren't always economies of scale. And sometimes there are diseconomies of large scale.

The reasons for this inverse productivity relationship have been hotly debated. Some people dismiss it as a fallacy of the 'captured garden' whereby impoverished farmers unreasonably exploit their own labour in order to make ends meet. That does sometimes seem to be the case, but it can't account for all instances of the inverse productivity relationship. In fact, no single explanation suffices, but the main factor seems to be the lower transaction costs of small farms employing their own labour and growing produce for their own consumption. Big farms, on the other hand, have lower transaction costs in obtaining finance or purchased farm equipment and selling their produce, which is why there isn't usually an inverse productivity relationship in wealthy countries.[41] Human attention and ingenuity always addresses itself most keenly to the key limiting factor it faces, and when you're working to produce food for your household from a small area, rather than paying someone to produce it for a market, that limiting factor is usually the productivity of your land.

There are various reasons why small farms have outlasted their long-predicted demise and fared better through the most recent period of economic globalisation than, say, small factories. The inverse productivity relationship and the factors underlying it is one of them. Particularly in poor countries, higher land productivity and greater use of labour relative to capital means they make more socially efficient use of land than big farms do.[42] The ratcheting of global crises is likely to make those factors a wider global reality.

The case I'm building for a small farm future is a multi-stranded one that's independent of the inverse productivity relationship, but that relationship is certainly part of the overall tapestry. Generally, if rural small-holders can operate without too many top-down distortions, they respond by producing food abundantly,[43] and there's a good case for building that abundance from small-scale, garden-based strategies geared to household self-production for both ecological and social reasons.

There can never be a single right answer to the question of how much a society's food should be self-produced and how much should be for market sale. The same is true for the balance between garden produce (fruit and vegetables) and field produce (cereals or other staples – which can, of course, also be grown in the garden). But perhaps the onus of explanation should shift from why you would bother raising a zucchini in your garden, to why you don't. One good reason a lot of people don't is because they don't have access to a garden. For a small farm future, that will need to change.

CHAPTER EIGHT

Beasts of the Field (and Garden): Beyond Shopping Aisle Ethics

I s there a place for livestock in the low-energy small farm future?

We know that livestock require more farmland than vegetables or cereal crops do to produce a comparable amount of human nutrition. The same applies to other resources as well, such as water and energy. And livestock farming produces relatively more environmental negatives, such as GHGs, soil acidification and eutrophication of watercourses. Current livestock numbers are such that an 'average' global family of 4.45 people is accompanied by almost one whole cow, 70% of a sheep, 60% of both a pig and a goat, and 15 poultry. This is a lot of livestock when you imagine the land and fodder devoted to such a menagerie for the world's 1.7 billion families.[44] One recent study suggests that livestock products from even the best-performing commercial farms have higher impacts across key environmental indicators than their vegetable counterparts.[45]

There's no question that the ecological impact of livestock farming, as currently practised, is severe. But it's worth remembering that each type of farm animal has a role that slots into the ecology of traditional, low-energy mixed farming, essentially as tappers, cyclers and providers of inputs and nutrients that are harder for people to access unaided. This is the concept of 'default' livestock: animals that are raised as part of long-term human ecological adaptations and whose use of resources complements human self-provisioning rather than competing with it – as is often the case with modern commercial livestock farming. It's noteworthy in this respect that the research just cited pointing to the heavy environmental impacts of livestock farming was based on what are called 'commercially viable farms', a loaded term, all things considered.

In his fine book *Meat: A Benign Extravagance*, Simon Fairlie analyses various benefits of default livestock.[46] Fairlie asserts that, among other things, default livestock can:

1. Cycle fertility efficiently within the agroecosystem
2. Consume waste fodders that would otherwise be lost to the agroecosystem or less efficiently incorporated into it
3. Provide a hedge against food scarcity
4. Provide traction and other work on the farm, and transport off it
5. Act as crop pest controllers
6. Furnish non-food by-products often superior to plant substitutes (wool, leather, feathers, horn, gut, bone)
7. Provide superior sources of food, fibre and income for poor or landless farmers
8. In higher-latitude countries, efficiently provide oil and fat that's otherwise locally unavailable

These benefits point to the difference between what I call 'shopping aisle ethics' and 'peasant ethics'. If you take the existing global political economy and the food system associated with it as a given, then when you're standing in the supermarket aisle trying to decide which ready-meal to buy it's almost certainly 'better for the environment' to choose a bean dinner over a beef one. But it's 'better for the environment' still to choose a local, low-energy farming system, and that system will raise livestock for the reasons listed above.

Livestock as Farmhands

I won't discuss Fairlie's list point by point, but it's worth expanding on his first four points at least in general terms because they contribute to the vision of the small farm agroecosystem wherein livestock contribute as proximal farmhands, thereby increasing the labour inputs, as well as the food and fibre outputs on a farm.

The inefficiency of livestock looms large in the modern case against meat, but it's actually their *efficiency* as farmhands that justifies their presence on the traditional low-energy holding. The two narratives aren't contradictory. Default livestock on the peasant farm fit into the farm's ongoing ecological needs, with products like meat or milk skimmed sparingly from the surface of this larger ecological labour. The inefficiency kicks in when commercial livestock farming attempts to maximise this bounty, leading to the dilemmas of the shopping aisle – dilemmas that are different from those of the peasant farm.

Fertility management is livestock's most important job on the low-energy farm. Livestock don't *create* fertility; they derive it from their food. But premodern farmers devised numerous ingenious ways to use livestock efficiently as fertility vectors and managers, particularly in the alternation between grassland and cropland to maintain the farm's fertility in the absence of high-energy synthetic fertilisers. Grazing ruminants can manage nutrient cycling on temporary grassland before it's tilled for crops, or transfer nutrients from permanent grassland to cropland through their manure.

It's possible to grow crops without livestock, but they still require fertility. In the absence of synthetic fertiliser, the stockless farmer has to generate fertility by growing fallows, which need to be cut regularly by hand or machine and then probably tilled, a process that doesn't furnish any other useful product. In this scenario, the stockless farm would be less productive and require more human or mechanical labour than the mixed-livestock farm.

There are many other historical examples of livestock as fertility vectors in low-energy farming systems. A few from the region where I live include grazing sheep on wild downland by day and bringing them onto the fields at night to dung them, using geese to graze the aftermath of wheat fields, pigs to turn food waste and woodland gleanings into high-quality meat and fat, even doves to bring phosphates to the farm from the woods. From another part of the world: the intensive horticultural systems of the Jiaxing region of 17th-century China supported nearly eight people per hectare of farmland (over three people per acre) using about a tonne of manure by dry-weight annually per hectare (about half a US ton per acre), of which 34% came from humans, 47% from pigs or sheep and 19% from silkworms.[47]

Not all this livestock labour is necessarily appropriate on the modern low-energy farm, but the examples give a flavour of the possibilities. Some of the examples also suggest another livestock function, as cyclers of food and crop wastes, readily turning organic material into high-grade products like eggs, meat and – crucially – fat.

Livestock can also be a hedge against scarcity. They provide predictable winter food in seasonal climates, and can be a kind of early warning system for less predictable climate fluctuations or other factors that might lead to scarcity. The flip side of livestock's land-hungry ways is that it provides a margin of error. When times are tough, a farmer can trim back livestock numbers and extend the intensity of cultivation or, in some circumstances, even diversify *into* livestock as a hedge against scarcity.[48] In practice, there are always oscillations between grassland and cropland, farm by farm and region by region, year by year and decade by decade. It's as well to build them into the farming system and to use livestock to keep marginal lands in a healthy, early-successional state that's easy to make more productive if and when the need arises.

Maybe so, the vegan-environmentalist counterargument runs, but that scarcely justifies the vast global extent of land-inefficient ruminant grazing today. And that, I think, is true. It's hard to defend the present extent of the world's agricultural grassland purely as a hedge against potential scarcity. In fact, its extent arises mostly for the exact opposite reason – not a hedge against scarcity, but demand for land-hungry meat from the world's wealthier people, while the poor have to make do with arable corner solutions like (golden) rice.

It's possible that in the future farmland will be more equitably distributed. Imagine if each of us had our 1.6-acre global land allowance. In such a tight farming situation, it would be hard to keep a herd of large ruminants like cows. Backyard poultry or a pig would better lend themselves as waste cyclers, but the lack of ruminants might make fertility maintenance more laborious, perhaps something akin to the human labour-intensive farming of East Asia described by Franklin King. Historically, however, people have been inventive at fitting ruminants and fertility-cycling livestock into tight farming situations, through use of commons and wastelands, but it's hard to escape the fact that in the heavily populated, low-energy, tight farming situations that are likely in the future, it will be difficult to keep ruminants in today's numbers. The consequence is that people, rather than animals or machines, will perform a larger share of farm work. This takes us back to the case for small farm biointensification (see Chapter 6, 'Alternative Agriculture as (Bio)Intensification', page 116).

Still, moving on to Fairlie's fourth point, there are ways of getting useful work out of livestock even on small horticultural holdings with space only for a pig or a few poultry. Typically, they involve using natural livestock behaviour to get a job done. For example, pigs on a bigger scale and poultry on a smaller scale will turn over a field or garden bed (plough it), spread their dung on it (fertilise it) and eat a good many of its weeds and pests prior to planting (apply pesticides) – a process mischievously called a pig or chicken 'tractor' in the permaculture movement, since it achieves the same various outcomes as farm machinery.

Integrating animals in this way is not only an effective way of getting a job done; it also promotes animal welfare by allowing for, and nurturing, their normal behaviours. It requires some skilled human management, and the results are often patchier than those of high-input mechanised agriculture, but in a low-input small farm situation there's no substitute for the work and welfare that thoughtful integration of default livestock can achieve.

On larger holdings that nevertheless operate outside the fossil fuel nexus, animal labour is often performed by draught teams of horses or oxen. Horse agriculture might seem almost laughably quaint in a world that also includes industrial mega-agriculture, but it's enjoying a mini revival in wealthy countries. Yet for many poor small-scale farmers in poor countries, a draught team, let alone a tractor, is aspirational. In a future with less energy, more egalitarianism, and more emphasis on low-carbon jobs, it's likely we'd see many more draught animals in global agriculture than we do today.

Animal teams are more compatible with the grassland-cropland rotation of the self-sustaining farm than modern farm machinery, even when it's renewably powered, and are competitive with it in output per acre. They're not so competitive in terms of output per worker, but in a low-energy, low-carbon, more egalitarian future this isn't such a problem.[49]

In summary, default livestock play important roles on the low-energy holding, among which farm work of various kinds is the most important, while products like meat, eggs and milk are something of a bonus. In low-energy situations where synthetic fertilisers are scarce, people have yet to devise agroecosystems that dispense with livestock, except by loading more work onto humans themselves as stock-free gardeners.

Livestock as Climate Villains

As well as the land-take of non-default livestock, livestock farming is also often criticised for its contribution to climate change. This is another area of bafflingly intricate science, which I touch on only lightly here in order to get a handle on whether default livestock might still be feasible on low-energy, peasant holdings in a climate-challenged future.

There are three main aspects of livestock farming that contribute to climate change:

1. Emissions of methane, principally from the digestive processes of ruminants, and from livestock manures
2. Emissions of nitrous oxide from livestock manures
3. The climate effects of land use associated with livestock farming

Methane

Estimates of methane emissions from livestock suggest it comprises about 6% of total GHG emissions from human activities, mostly from ruminant digestion.[50] This is a significant contribution to climate breakdown, but not the most fearful among them.

There are some underlying complexities to these estimates, however. Although methane has strong climate-forcing effects, it's short-lived in the atmosphere, whereas CO_2 persists long term. To compare the effects of different GHGs, scientists calculate a 'CO$_2$ equivalent'. But since different GHGs have different persistence periods, CO_2 equivalence is only meaningful within a given time frame. The shorter the chosen time frame, the larger methane emissions will loom. The 6% figure is based on a 100-year time frame.

But because CO_2 accumulates in the atmosphere long term whereas methane doesn't, the two gases have different properties, as a stock and a flow, respectively. This means they're not strictly comparable, despite the magic worked by the CO_2 equivalence method. Arguably, the implication is that efforts to reduce short-term methane emissions from sources like livestock make limited sense as climate change mitigation strategies unless they are part of a larger strategy to reduce long-lasting CO_2 emissions, primarily from fossil fuels. In fact, emissions of methane from fossil fuels are similar to those from the global livestock herd, but whereas the fossil fuel industry adds to the stock of GHGs in the atmosphere in the form of CO_2, livestock-based methane emissions are not climate forcing unless the herd size grows.[51]

Nitrous Oxide

In addition to methane emissions, livestock farming contributes about 2% of total human GHG emissions with nitrous oxide arising from manure. It is another small but significant contribution to climate change. The complexity in this case is that manure is used to fertilise crops. If we dispensed with livestock, we'd need to replace the manure with other sources of nitrogen-rich fertiliser, and these sources emit nitrous oxide at similar rates to manure.

This argument doesn't justify keeping livestock at existing global levels. Around a third of global cropland is devoted to growing livestock fodders,[52] so that proportion of crop fertilisation is arguably unnecessary. And most livestock manure remains on pastures; it's not fully cycled back into crop production for humans. Default livestock tightly bound to nutrient cycling on farms geared primarily to growing crops for human consumption would reduce nitrous oxide emissions.

Land Use

The debate about livestock and land use centres on the opportunities for climate change mitigation that are lost by devoting land to livestock, rather than emissions that are directly attributable to it. Using cropland to grow livestock fodders, for example, directly adds to human climate impacts. So does clearing forests, particularly tropical forests, to create pastures. These are climate-forcing activities that are hard to justify, but they're not the same as raising default livestock on existing, un-treed farmland.

Still, since climate change mitigation requires not only ending emissions but the sequestration of existing atmospheric carbon, there's a good converse case for turning farmland into woodland rather than just avoiding turning woodland into farmland. In other words, raising less livestock would free a lot of land for other uses. And then if we grew trees on this land, the argument goes, they'd sequester atmospheric carbon by turning it into wood.

Re-forestation as a climate mitigation strategy has been in the news recently, partly because of scientific controversies over how effective it is.[53] I won't probe the complexities of the issue here, but it seems fair to say that – as with soil carbon sequestration and reduction of livestock methane emissions – thoughtful forestation has some (limited) potential for removing carbon from the atmosphere in the short term. But, as with livestock reduction, it only makes sense as a climate change mitigation strategy if it's accompanied simultaneously with a radical reduction in fossil fuel combustion. There's a strong case for trimming the global livestock herd and restructuring it into a default one, which would create opportunities for forestation, but the main benefits wouldn't be climate change mitigation, and indiscriminate tree-planting on pastureland would be counterproductive.

Livestock and the Small Farm

Fossil fuels are the key enabler for the world's current vast menagerie of farm animals. Without them, we'd need to look to our local farmlands and woodlands to provide much of our energy, fibre and crop fertilisers and we'd have to trade off our liking for meat and dairy with these other necessities. As it is, we can provide most of these necessities, at least for the time being, from fossil fuels. This enables demand for meat to push the envelope of land-hungry livestock husbandry to the extent that about a quarter of the world's entire land surface is now devoted to permanent meadows and pastures. A lower-energy, post-fossil fuel world would hand us a less meaty world on a plate.

Or it might, unless current economic inequalities persist. In that scenario, the human liking for meat and low-cost energy backed by the economic power of the wealthy to obtain it – regardless of its land efficiency or environmental and social costs – would probably ensure that large swathes of the Earth remained pasturelands for farmed ruminants, other large swathes were devoted to intensive biofuel production, while the rest of humanity made do with the arable corner, possibly with tweaks, like golden rice, to its dysfunctions.

So one problem with the narrative that livestock are climate villains is the way it displaces attention from both fossil fuels and economic inequality, with its tall tales that cows are worse than cars, that trees can offset power stations, that judicious tweaks to the fossil-fuelled political economy can make it sustainable, and that the global wealthy can remedy their outsize carbon footprints through lifestyle changes like turning vegan. The argument that we should tackle environmental crises by avoiding meat is like saying we should tackle economic inequality by boycotting luxury cars.

I suggest an alternative: small-scale farming, based on the careful husbanding of overwhelmingly local resources, which must be normalised in the political economy as something that's widely supported and that most people actively practise. In that relatively egalitarian world of distributed, low-energy farmsteading, people wouldn't avoid eating meat because it was bad for the environment. They'd produce as much meat as they could to improve land use efficiency and the tastiness of their food. By today's standards, that amount would be little, and its environmental impact slight. Essentially, the climate crisis is a crisis of fossil energy combustion and wealth concentration, which will be mitigated when people spread out and skim local resources with sustainable, low-energy methods as small-scale farmers of broadly equal social status. If we do that efficiently, we'll be sure to raise some livestock.

CHAPTER NINE

The Fruited Thorn: Agroforestry

Futurology nowadays involves a lot of utopian visions of centralised (and often vegan) urban civilisation pursuing high-tech, high-yielding grain-based agriculture that 'spares' a lot of land for re-wilding. I'm trying to build a case for something different: a distributed, omnivorous, de-centralised agricultural order in which re-wilding applies not only to other plants and animals but also to some degree to ourselves. We'd share land with wild organisms and keep grain farming to a minimum in favour of labour-intensive vegetable gardens, default livestock and woodland produce. The part of this that I've yet barely described is the woodland produce.

In loose situations people can sometimes exist largely from the bounty of natural woodland, like the pioneer colonists of Appalachia who made use of the wildwood's fuel, nuts, berries, herbs, mushrooms, fish and game, while pushing its productivity through gardens and rye fields in the clearings and with cattle wandering ferally in the woods.[54] They landed on a productive transition point in the continuum between foraging and farming, like many other forest peoples and swidden agriculturalists. In tighter situations, there's a need to push productivity further with fields, gardens and livestock, but also with some reconstruction of natural woodland according to human priorities.

Woodland usually comprises mostly perennial plants, so in theory a woodland agriculture might deliver that strong perennial vision I described earlier. Trees and shrubs indeed have much to commend them for human ecology, including fuel, construction material, shelter, nitrogen fixation, water management, livestock fodder, a resource for biodiversity and pest management, and objects of beauty. They also provide human food, though with limitations. Their leaves are unlikely to provide more than a marginal contribution to the human plate, although their reproductive tissues (fruit and nuts) are more promising. As with the grass seeds on which most human agricultures are based, and for similar biological reasons, nuts from certain tree species come with a large protein and energy package. Often, they also come with strong defences such as poison or shells, but animals with powerful jaws and stomachs, or with ingenious tools and fire, are sometimes able to cash in.

Fruit yields its gifts more easily – at least in energy-rich sugars, not so much in fat or protein – since it's essentially a bribe from trees to animals to spread their seed. Even then trees often have their defences: fruit borne aloft from ground-dwelling animals on a sometimes thorny trunk. The larger problem is that, as long-lived perennials, trees are sparing with these gifts. It takes them a long time to reach sexual maturity and start providing them, and ultimately their interest, unlike an annual grass, is not to over-invest in risky reproduction.

Temperate-climate commercial fruit orchardists address this limitation by breeding against the biological advantages of woody perennials. That is, they breed for smaller, shorter-lived trees on dwarfing rootstocks with higher nutrient requirements and such minimal allocation to stems and defence that they need artificial support and heavy pest protection. So again we encounter a trade-off between productivity and perenniality/sustainability. I call this trade-off 'the fruited thorn'.

Still, there's a lot to be said for reconstructing woodlands for human priorities through the intentional integration of tree crops into gardens and farms, a practice sometimes known as agroforestry or forest gardening. The upright woody growth of fruiting canopy trees is used to create additional three-dimensional space, maximising productivity through complex, multilayered polycultures encompassing below-ground tuberous perennials, perennial groundcover plants, shrubs, trees and vining climbers. This can be a beautifully productive horticultural strategy. In moist, low-latitude biomes to which cereals are not well suited and where perennial crops rich in fat, protein and energy are available it can provide all the food that people need.

Places where this is possible have produced garden cultures of great antiquity, but even tropical garden cultures usually grow staples like yams, sweet potatoes or rice as annuals. And the further you travel from the equator the more the level of incident sunlight and the miserly reproductive habits of perennial plants limit the avoidance of annual cropping. At low latitudes, perennial crops like nuts can more or less hold their own with cereals in terms of per acre yields of protein and energy, but at higher latitudes this ceases to be true. For example, per acre yields of these macronutrients from wheat are more than double those from walnuts in France, which is about the northern limit for sustaining viable commercial nut production.[55] Temperate forest gardening with perennial plants has recently become popular, but the example of low-latitude agroforestry suggests it's probably best developed with a mix of annual and perennial plants. These mixed annual–perennial horticultures have long persisted without fomenting global crises. We could do worse than learning from their example.

Indeed, the potential is high for combining annual crops with perennial grassland and woodland crops in mixed agroforestry systems. In addition to forest gardens, these systems often involve 'alleys' of annual crops or pasture between rows of trees, possibly akin to the cultivation of 'sparsely distributed garden-sized patches' of annual crops between perennial ones (see Chapter 5, 'The Arable Corner', page 113). Most of these ideas are far from new, but recent research and practice is validating their contemporary relevance.[56] Despite my scepticism about unguarded cheerleading for perennial crops in alternative agriculture, moving towards small-scale, labour-intensive forms of husbandry that are slanted towards perennials – especially tree crops – seems a positive and necessary agricultural trend.

We've now discussed, however briefly, the human ecology of field crops, gardens, livestock and wood crops with a view to constructing more sustainable farm systems for the future out of this raw material. Earlier, I mentioned the idea of people re-wilding themselves in the context of that future – spreading out across the landscape like other organisms do to skim its flows sustainably rather than concentrating so as to mine its stocks, practising the arts of self-reliance, knowing how to fill the larder, and knowing how to stop when the larder is full rather than pursuing an economy of endless accumulation.

There are dangers in using the language of 'wildness' to characterise this way of being. Maybe it recalls racist and colonial histories of 'wild people' living more 'natural' and less accumulative lives who were obliterated by their contraries: grain-based urban peoples invoking their own 'civility' against the 'wildness' of the colonised. This has applied among colonisers as well as the colonised – for example the mountaineers of Appalachia I mentioned at the beginning of this chapter, whose public image in the early years of the independent United States quickly sank from that of resourceful pioneers to semi-racialised and degenerate hillbillies.[57] I invoke the language of 'wildness' here only cautiously because of the contemporary re-wilding movement, which often misses the point that if we're to successfully re-wild the Earth's habitats we need to re-wild human cultures as well, including our agricultures. In view of the tight farming situations we face in the present world, self-provisioning through agroforestry is probably about as wild as we can get.

The most troubling counterarguments against this case for human re-wilding are, first, that it's a path of economic insecurity, dearth and potential starvation and, second, that it's impractical in today's vastly populated world. So in the last two chapters of Part II I turn away from the general ecological dynamics of agriculture to address these wider points of human ecology.

CHAPTER TEN

Dearth

Is there a danger of food shortages or famine in societies that aren't integrated into a wider economy able to smooth out the inevitable peaks and troughs of local production, or increase food availability through high-tech means, especially during an emergency? The image of desperate, starving peasant farmers haunts popular consciousness. As do the words of historian Richard Tawney: 'the position of the rural population is that of a man standing permanently up to the neck in water so that even a ripple is sufficient to drown him'.[58] Language like 'subsistence farming' doesn't really help, since the distance from subsistence to bare subsistence and thence to hunger seems short. The decline in major famines since the 1960s is often attributed to globalisation, diversification out of agriculture, and economic development.[59] Surely nobody can conscionably argue we should reverse all that?

But there's a more complex story to tell, and it turns on what we mean by 'integration into a wider economy'. The starting point is a degree of uncertainty about premodern hunger and famines – how widespread were they, who suffered from them, and why? Solid data are hard to come by, but there are plausible grounds to think they were less widespread than we might think – and that their victims were often poor people caught in the arable corners of their day, people who struggled mostly because the powerful didn't much care about their fate. Modern famines are similar. When we see a man up to his neck in water, it's worth checking if someone is pressing down on his head. Evidence from various times and places suggests that independent smallholders with secure access to enough land haven't usually suffered from catastrophic hunger.[60]

In fact, modernisation has often been a driver of hunger. England's last serious famine was in the 1620s, striking commercial livestock farmers, not autonomous peasants, who were 'victims of premature specialisation', unable to sell their produce at sufficiently high prices to afford the grain they needed to survive.[61] The completion of the first era of globalisation in the 19th century prompted major famines in Asia and Latin America as peasants were forcibly incorporated as colonial subjects into the world economy, while the turn to commercial production of staple foods for global markets in some cases worsened inequality, hunger and disease. Integrated global markets and their speculative structures can actively fuel hunger, which occurred, for example, in the 2008 food-price spike.[62]

Tawney's metaphor is often applied indiscriminately to all historic peasant societies, but he was actually addressing his comments to parts of 1930s China after the modernising convulsions of the 19th century. The same occurred with 20th-century modernisation in Africa – and indeed in the 20th century more widely. The decades around the two world wars were, in the words of famine expert Alex de Waal, 'the most dreadful period of famine in world history' caused by modern governments fomenting famines or acting indifferently to their occurrence.[63]

De Waal imputes the decline of famines over the last 50 years or so in large part to the rise of democracies and international humanitarianism that consider famine unacceptable. Indeed, humanitarianism is essential to a small farm future, too, in order to prevent any number of possible bad outcomes (see Part IV). De Waal likewise fears a return of famines with the breakdown of global multilateralism and the 'prospect of unending war fought with diminishing respect for humanitarian norms by militant insurgents, regional powers and western counter-terrorists'.[64]

It's noteworthy that this take on hunger is fundamentally political, attaching little importance to the practicalities of food production to the genesis of hunger. In fact, a lot of experts are critical of what de Waal calls the 'alimentary economics' that relates hunger directly to the production or availability of food.[65] The argument that we need a huge increase in food production only achievable through high-tech methods falls squarely into this position – that feeding the world necessarily comes down to the quantity of food we produce. I'm less optimistic than de Waal that a confluence of climate, soil, water and biodiversity crises won't, in fact, usher in a future of production-squeezed hunger, but that's not the situation the world currently faces. The forms that food production takes – big-scale, small-scale, corporate, peasant – are not in themselves the issue.

The role of markets and economic 'development' in episodes of hunger is ambiguous. Research suggests that giving rein to private markets sometimes mitigates hunger by preventing monopolists from pushing food prices beyond the reach of poor people or preventing traders from withholding food due to low fixed prices. On the other hand, the pure logic of the market isn't in itself geared to helping people get food if they can't afford it, and poor people sometimes starve among relative plenty because they have no money to buy food – a situation for which efficient private markets give no relief.[66]

That kind of privation almost never happens to smallholders with adequate land access, because they can grow food for themselves. Except in times of major dislocation, they usually develop resilient, multi-stranded farming strategies that enable them to cope with problems such as flood or drought. What's clear from famine history is that the people at highest risk aren't farmers with good land access, or people (usually urban) with strong citizenship entitlements, but those caught in between: poor (usually rural) people exposed to local or global market fluctuations who possess neither good land access nor good political leverage.

What kinds of 'economic development' really free people from hunger? The kinds that help poor, small-scale farmers get secure access to land; better produce food for themselves and others by building a robust farm enterprise; participate more easily in markets (by which I mostly mean actual, physical markets where they can sell actual physical, produce); and ensure financial or in-kind returns that enable them to get other needed goods and services.[67] The kinds of economic development, on the other hand, that propel such farmers off the land and into insecure rural or urban wage labour as part of wider GDP-boosting strategies for national or international economic development are as likely to push them into greater food vulnerability.

This is why the more hidden issue of chronic hunger remains so widespread, even if the incidence of dramatic famines has declined. Estimates for the number of people globally who currently suffer chronic hunger vary from about 800 million to 2.5 billion – possibly more than 30% of the entire world's population.[68] This is in a world where the average real

GDP per capita has increased almost threefold in the last 60 years, suggesting that economic development as such isn't the issue. But global wealth concentration might be.

Meanwhile, the majority of international land sales in Africa, now the most food-insecure continent, are biofuel concessions, while land reallocation to export agriculture in the famine-prone Horn of Africa fuels conflict and resulting food insecurity in the region.[69] All this surely upends the supposed dangers of food insecurity in a small farm future. A more likely culprit behind contemporary food insecurity is the march of economic modernisation, and its tendency to capture the gardens of rural people in poor countries while offering little in return.

So there's a case for bringing forwards *more* localised, small-scale farming to *mitigate* hunger and food insecurity. But this isn't how things always play out. Poor harvests and high food prices often benefit larger-scale farmers, while pushing small-scale farmers into distress. It's a historical fact that many poor, small-scale farmers have been propelled wholly or partly out of farming into rural precariats who swell the numbers of global hungry. However, this isn't some inherent disadvantage of small scale. Generally, it occurs where small-scale farmers are dependent on monetised markets for basic subsistence, and where larger-scale farmers have advantages in relative input costs – circumstances which have more to do with political leverage than any disinterested market dynamics.[70]

So, global market dynamics aside, there are advantages to the small farm as a safeguard against hunger, especially the small subsistence farm with limited market dependencies. Likewise, economic development can be a good hedge against hunger and dearth – but the kind that supports small-scale farmers and their communities to engage in productive activities rather than the kind that drains them of autonomy in favour of wider national or international goals. Perhaps the trend-spotting urban billionaires who are parlaying their inedible wealth into remote tracts of farmland to safeguard against future uncertainties help underline this point.[71]

CHAPTER ELEVEN

Can Alternative Agriculture Feed Us?

C an small-scale farming feed a world approaching 8 billion people, and rising? Given the interlocking crises we face, can *any* form of agriculture – small-scale, alternative or mainstream – feed such numbers, now and into the future?

Some models based on current and expected trends in climate change, food production and economic development suggest that it's feasible to feed the world at least in the immediate decades to come, albeit with numerous provisos about climate and energy futures, economic prospects, crop choices and levels of meat and biofuel production. Other models warn of interactive challenges to food security that may include multiple breadbasket failure and food shortage.[72] Global projections for *alternative* agriculture futures specifically have focused mostly on the feasibility of feeding the world with only organic sources of fertility, which is possible, arguably.[73]

The United Nations' Food and Agriculture Organization (FAO) published a major report in 2016 suggesting that the capacity to adapt food systems to climate disruption would vary regionally, with larger impacts in the low-latitude countries of the Global South.[74] Unlike the end-of-peasantry language widely deployed in progress-literature, the more technical analyses of the FAO report acknowledge there will still be billions of impoverished small-scale farmers over the coming decades, and it emphasises the need to support them.

But even if the criticism of alimentary economics is vindicated and present capacities for feeding humanity adequately persist, there's a wrinkle in this position. While it rightly emphasises that food shortages are mostly a function of *social* dynamics rather than biophysical carrying capacity, it's clear that social dynamics are in crisis and this isn't adequately incorporated into most modelling.

These social dynamics aren't minor factors and can't be externalised from future food modelling. They include the tendency of the global political economy to concentrate wealth and misery, the fracturing of political legitimacy, chronic economic crisis, and social reactions like religious and political fundamentalisms, war, counterinsurgency, border militarisation, and mass population movements away from crisis zones. Throw in challenging paths of energy descent and it seems possible there'll be even fewer options in the future for off-farm diversification to mitigate poverty and hunger in the Global South and possibly in the Global North. This brings me back to the question with which I opened this book: What if the familiar story of an urban-industrial route to prosperity loses any remaining plausibility?

With that in mind, I think it's worth asking whether your locality can feed its population. The answer will partly depend on how you define your locality, but that's an aim of the exercise. For many people the answer will be no, because you live in a city where population density is too high to produce enough food, although some spaces could still be identified for meeting a proportion of the city's needs. For people whose localities can't meet their needs, the question is which other localities might fill the breach – and why.

This question demands attention to the relationship between cities and their rural hinterlands, which in the present historical moment extend across the world, but may have to narrow in the future. It also demands attention to political power. If rural people outside your city are generating your food, what are you or your city generating for them in return? Saying that cities generate wealth isn't good enough if it's wealth that rural people can't tap. Of course, cities do contribute to general human well-being and it would be foolish to insist that everyone must provide all their own food and other resources. But it's not a bad starting place for testing one's assumptions. To put it another way, asking if your locality can feed its population starts posing questions about power and the geography of colonialism, both local and global.

It may turn out that there's plenty of land locally to grow enough food, in theory, but not enough other resources – chief among them, water – to do it in practice. People from Australia and Spain, for example, have told me this about their locales. That may be true, but to put it into context, Australia exports a million tonnes of wine and 23 million tonnes of wheat annually, and Spain exports over two million tonnes of wine and nearly a million tonnes of tomatoes, with all the embodied water that implies. But Australia and Spain are big places, with varied water and other endowments across their national spaces. If we break them up into regions and localities we can start asking the same questions about the flows of money and resources within and between them that we can ask about cities and the countryside.

In Australia particularly, we might also ask questions about how indigenous people dealt with these issues through deep human time – perhaps, for some of us, with an overdue dose of postcolonial humility. But we could use some humility about local self-provisioning wherever we are. In the United Kingdom, where I live, criticism of local food's footprint is often exemplified by the argument – wearily familiar to small-scale market growers – that early-season tomatoes imported from Spain have a lower carbon footprint than ones grown with indoor heat locally. That may be true (though no small local grower I know uses indoor heat), while the water footprint points the other way. A more important question is why we need early-season tomatoes, rather than growing them seasonally without heat and whetting our appetite by going without when they can't be easily grown, and eating other things instead.

This becomes an argument for nurturing local food cultures and accepting their potentialities and limitations. No doubt it's an argument that shouldn't be pushed too far; tomatoes are native to neither Spain nor the United Kingdom, after all. But if by some plausible definition of 'the locality' it turns out that the way you eat is too costly in terms of energy, GHG emissions, soil health, water or somebody else's well-being, there's a good case for trimming it back to what your locality can sustain. And if it's impossible to trim it back to a sustainable level, that may suggest a need to re-sort human populations more sustainably across agricultural space.

It seems likely that the coming years will see a major re-sorting along these lines due to climate change, energy descent, water stress and economic crisis, generally from cities to countrysides, from coasts to interiors and from lower latitudes to higher latitudes. The potential for human conflict in this process is high; in Parts III and IV of this book I address how it might be minimised socially and politically. Here, it remains for me to sketch what that could look like agriculturally in terms of a self-reliant local food culture that minimises its colonial exactions upon others.

By way of an example, I've chosen Britain, mostly because I'm British and British agriculture (as well as British agricultural statistics) is the one I know best. This is important because even though my modelling is quite crude it involves reimagining a local agriculture rather than simply tweaking the parameters of existing agricultural yields, as many modelling exercises do. And it's hard to reimagine a local agriculture in this way with global data, or even for large single countries with multiple biomes such as the United States.

The danger is that the results are unrepresentative of wider global trends, but I'd argue the British case isn't *so* unrepresentative. I model for a considerably larger population than currently exists on the assumption that Britain will be hosting climate change refugees in multitudes, in a country that's already quite densely populated (currently it's ranked 128th out of 209 countries in per capita farmland availability[75]). And although Britain has some high-quality agricultural land with good grain yields, it's also a high-latitude country with relatively challenging seasonality and a lot of low-quality grassland in its agricultural makeup. In other words, it's a reasonable model for the challenge faced by many countries in the transition to a low-impact, steady-state agriculture.

My conceit is to project a British farmscape in the year 2050 that's feeding its entire population from its own resources with minimal fossil fuel inputs. This involves numerous assumptions and data choices that will try the reader's patience if they're all laid out, so I'm restricting myself to explaining only the key parameters.

Population: I assume a 2050 population of about 83 million people – a challenging increase of 25% from the present, mostly comprising Britain's share of an anticipated 250 million climate refugees globally.

Low yield: I assume low crop yields. These are based on the lowest bounds of the ranges for current organic crop yields, with a 10% yield penalty further applied to accommodate for possible climate change impacts.[76] UK wheat yields in the last three years have averaged 8.4 tonnes per cropped hectare (125 bushels per acre), whereas I'm assuming 2.3 tonnes per cropped hectare, excluding fallows or leys – just 27% of current yields.

Doubtless many proponents of alternative agriculture would argue that I'm greatly underestimating what it's possible to provide. This is undoubtedly true, but my approach provides a worst-case scenario baseline to establish the lower productive limits of the system.

Nutrition: What do we eat when we 'feed ourselves'? The measure adopted in most studies is food energy, or calories. But people need more than just energy. It's easy to max out on nutrition defined in narrowly energetic terms by growing only cereals or other starchy crops, but this doesn't make for a nutritious diet. In my modelling I examined a range of nutritional indicators, such as energy, protein and various vitamins and trace minerals. It turned out that getting enough energy was the key limiting factor; providing for other dietary needs was relatively easy. For simplicity, I'm reporting only the returns of food energy, but it's important to note that the farmscapes I project aren't geared only to maximising food energy returns. I've modelled for national energy demands on the basis of existing government recommendations, but with a slightly higher allocation – 3,000 calories a day – for everyone involved in the sweaty business of farming.

Who is a farmer?: the model identifies eight types of farmer, food producer or land user:

1. Home gardeners, engaging in backyard production
2. City farmers or community gardeners, producing food in small urban green spaces
3. Market gardeners producing fruit and vegetables intensively on small, probably peri-urban, plots
4. Smallholders, producing all their own food, along with small surpluses, on small rural holdings
5. Mixed-arable farmers, producing a mixture of animal and staple plant products (with an emphasis on the latter) for commercial sale from larger rural holdings
6. Dairy farmers, producing milk from dairy cows with some beef as a by-product

7. Fisherfolk, producing wild seafood from inshore fisheries
8. Re-wilders and re-provisioners

The model doesn't provide for specialist beef or sheep farming, although that's an additional margin that could be exploited. Instead I leave room for people who want to turn some of the country's pastureland over to wilderness (the re-wilders) and for people whose operations service the wider farm economy, for example by producing timber, seeds, hay or bloodstock (the re-provisioners). Here I assume that these two categories produce no directly usable food, though this assumption is over-restrictive.

Cropping and rotations: These eight categories of people would produce a huge variety of foodstuffs, but I decided not to fully simulate this diversity and micro-specify exactly what they would produce. Instead I've restricted production in each category to a limited number of indicator crops that give an idea of how the producer might go about his or her business; in most cases, this is in the form of standard organic crop rotations. While the actual food produced would be more diverse than I've modelled, it doesn't make a great deal of difference to overall nutritional outcomes.

Non-food needs: In addition to food, the land would need to support textile and medicinal crops, as well as timber for construction and fuel. I've made some provision in the modelling for textile crops, but not medicinal ones – in both cases, the land-take is likely to be low relative to food, but the land-take for constructional timber and firewood is potentially high and the margin for producing it in the United Kingdom is tight. Still, my model leaves 46% of total UK land available for non-food uses. Most of this would probably be managed woodland, which could probably furnish the country's wood needs if we weaned ourselves off our presently profligate ways.[77]

Table 11.1 summarises the key inputs and outputs associated with the different types of farmer and my assumptions about them in the modelling. A few additional notes are necessary:

- I include full-time productive farm labour in the model but not domestic or volunteer labour, in keeping with the way agricultural statistics are usually compiled. Granted there would be more spare-time labour devoted to producing food in this scenario than at present.

Table 11.1. Alternative agriculture Britain 2050 – land use, inputs and products

	LAND USE	LABOUR AND OTHER INPUTS	MAIN PRODUCTS
Home gardeners	90% of current home garden space	Spare-time labour not included in model. Organic cover-cropping (closed loop fertility)	Potatoes, vegetables, fruit, eggs
City farmers	90% of urban green space	One full-time worker per hectare in model, plus volunteer labour not included. Organic cover-cropping and in situ forage (closed loop fertility)	Potatoes, vegetables, fruit, pork
Market gardeners	Double existing area	Two full-time workers per hectare (including fallows) on veg farms, 1.25 on fruit farms included in model. Organic cover-cropping and in situ forage (closed loop fertility)	Vegetables, fruit, sheep-meat
Smallholders	1.3-hectare 'family' holdings on existing permanent grassland	1.25 full-time workers per holding. Organic cover-cropping and in situ forage (closed loop fertility)	Potatoes, wheat, vegetables, fruit, eggs, milk, beef
Mixed-arable farmers	16-hectare holdings on existing cropland and permanent pasture	6 full-time workers per holding. Biofuel grown for horse or mechanical traction. Organic cover-cropping (leys/fallows) and in situ forage (closed loop fertility)	Wheat, potatoes, beans, field veg, fibre for textiles, dairy and beef from fallows
Dairy farmers	Small number of specialist dairy holdings on existing permanent pasture	0.2 full-time workers per hectare. In situ forage (closed loop fertility)	Milk, beef
Fisherfolk	Inshore fishery	No labour inputs included in model	Crab, herring, mackerel, whelks
Re-wilders/ re-provisioners	On existing rough grazing area	No labour inputs included in model	n/a

- Currently, like most wealthy countries, Britain imports most of its fruit and vegetables by cost, and since horticulture is especially labour-intensive this is also an implicit import of labour. (British food production isn't quite as labour-efficient as we often suppose.) I've doubled the area of commercial horticulture in the model, and also increased the amount of fruit and vegetables grown in other parts of the farmscape.

- I've put a lot of emphasis on relatively low-intensity smallholding, where each household gets 1.3 hectares (3.2 acres) to grow a garden and an orchard while keeping most land down to permanent pasture for feeding a low-productivity house cow furnishing about 3,000 litres (800 gallons) of milk annually. This is a basically 'peasant' vision corresponding with historic aspirations for 'three acres and a cow'.

- Fertility is generally provided in situ via cover crops, leys or fallows, often grazed by default livestock to increase efficiency and productivity. I also assume that 90% of human sewage is returned to the land, similar to present levels, but with greater than present energy efficiency. These provisions can take care of crop nutrition while fitting within the projected land-take.

- Farm traction is undertaken on small scales by hand and on larger scales either by machines or horses using biofuels (grass and oats in the latter case). The mixed-arable model is basically geared to horse agriculture, with two horses assumed to cultivate 10 hectares (25 acres) over a year while eating one hectare's worth of oats.

- Rough grazing is excluded from the model. I leave it to the foresters, re-wilders, re-provisioners and stock farmers to figure out how best to use it, while assuming no food productivity outturn from it. This means that my model effectively reduces the agricultural land-take to only 70% of the present amount, albeit by removing the least productive part.

There's a lot of potential for creating a farmscape with much higher productivity and diversity than I've modelled here. Some of the more obvious possibilities include: incorporating rough grazing; improved fertility management, organic crop improvement and micro-husbandry to increase crop yields; increasing cropland relative to grassland on the smallholdings; mushroom farming; shellfish farming; and collaborative small-scale enterprises such as neighbourhood pig clubs to raise pork from food waste.[78] But as I said before, the advantage of my approach is that it underestimates the possibilities, therefore providing a baseline minimum.

Now let's put some numbers to this model: Table 11.2 shows existing and projected land use. Table 11.3 shows the energy productivities of the land and labour devoted to the different kinds of farming.[79] And Table 11.4 gives an indication of the diet the proposed farmscape would provide for each of Britain's projected 83 million residents, as well as a comparison with recent dietary recommendations for human health and environmental sustainability.[80]

Bearing in mind the stringent parameters of the model – high population, low yields, no imports, reduced farmland, no synthetic fertility or fossil-fuelled farm traction, little farm intensification – the data suggest that it would be possible for 'alternative agriculture' to provide a nutritious home-grown diet for a population such as Britain's – including climate refugees – in the year 2050. In other words, yes, alternative agriculture can probably feed us. I'd like to underline that conclusion, because people often point out that Britain has been a net food importer for two centuries, as if that proves it couldn't feed itself in the future. It *has* been a net food importer, but this is a matter of political choice rather than ecological necessity. I've shown here that it could easily feed itself if it chose to, and I suspect this is true of many other importing countries.

Although it's consistent with recent dietary recommendations, some people might consider this diet austere. It's short on meat and, more importantly, fat. The 3.6 litres of whole milk turns into less than 200 grams of butter per week, plus skimmed milk and buttermilk. In this respect, the number of specialist dairy farms in the model is probably too low, an artefact of modelling that required many mixed-arable farms to meet calorific requirements. In reality a larger dairy sector is likely, with more intensification in other sectors to accommodate it. This is feasible because there's a large margin in the figures for increasing yields, along with potential for greater home or smallholder fat production from livestock, such as backyard chickens, pigs, dairy goats or house cows. Oilseed crops are another possibility, though in a northerly climate like Britain the main possibility is restricted to canola, a largely industrialised crop.

In place of sugar, oils and meat in quantity, the diet relies heavily on vegetables and potatoes to meet calorific requirements. Six hundred grams (1.3

pounds) of potatoes per day is doubtless more than most people would wish to eat, though it's less than the 2500 grams (5.5 pounds) consumed by Irish peasants of the early 19th century, who ate little else.[81] In cool temperate climates the potato is the most productive calorific crop per acre, exceeding wheat by a factor of between 1.5 and 2, so when land is under heavy population pressure (of the sort I'm modelling here) it's hard to avoid a potato-heavy diet. Disdain for the potato has a long pedigree, perhaps pioneered by William Cobbett (1763–1835), who called it the root of 'slovenliness, filth,

Table 11.2. Existing and projected Britain land use

	EXISTING UK LAND AREA (ha)	ALTERNATIVE AGRICULTURE UK 2050 (ha)		RATIO OF CROPLAND TO FALLOW/GRASS/LEY (%/%)
Home gardens	433,000		390,000	75/25
Urban green space	607,000	City farms	546,000	75/25
Arable cropland	5,963,000	Mixed-arable farms	8,977,000	62/38
Permanent pasture	6,135,000	Market gardens	336,000	60/40
Outdoor pigs	10,000	Smallholdings	2,846,000	5/95
Market gardens	168,000	Specialist dairy	116,000	0/100
Rough grazing	5,201,000	Re-wilding/ re-provisioning	5,201,000	–
Non-agricultural farmland	321,000		321,000	–
Farm woodland	1,037,000		1,037,000	–
Other woodland	2,136,000		2,136,000	–
All other UK land	2,261,000		2,365,000	–
Total UK land	24,272,000		24,272,000	

Table 11.3. Alternative agriculture Britain 2050, energy productivities

	AREA (ha)	% FARMED AREA	TOTAL WORKERS	% OF TOTAL LABOUR FORCE
Home gardens	390,000	3	—	—
City farms	546,000	4	546,000	1
Mixed-arable	8,977,000	68	3,367,000	7
Market gardens	336,000	3	546,000	1
Smallholders	2,846,000	22	2,737,000	6
Specialist dairy	116,000	1	23,000	>0
Fishing	—	—	—	—
Total	13,211,000	100	7,219,000	15

Table 11.4. Alternative agriculture Britain 2050, diet

	G PER PERSON PER DAY	COMPARED TO 'PLANETARY HEALTH DIET'
Cereals	220	230
Potatoes	620	50
Legumes	20	75
Other vegetables	520	300
Fruit	180	200
Milk	460	250
Meat	20	40
Eggs	10	10
Nuts	20	50
Fish	10	30
Honey/sugar	>0	30
Oils	—	50

FOOD ENERGY PRODUCED AS % OF NATIONAL REQUIREMENT	FOOD ENERGY PRODUCED (MJ/ FARMED HA)	FOOD ENERGY PRODUCED PER WORKER
5	33,300	–
4	23,900	17,200
76	22,700	57,600
2	29,600	7,300
12	11,600	11,500
0.3	6,900	32,900
0.5	–	–
100		

misery and slavery', imputing the 'misery and degradation of the Irish' to its use.[82] He got the causality the wrong way around, however: over-reliance on potatoes is the consequence and not the cause of miserable land poverty, the solution to which – in Cobbett's era – was import of overseas food for England and export of people overseas for Ireland.

Neither importing food nor exporting people is likely to be a reliable option in the challenged world to come. Still, the potato's 19th-century success as a food for the poor arguably allowed the persistence of great poverty and inequality by enabling people to survive in spite of it,[83] so a pro-peasant writer like Cobbett had a point in extolling the virtues of a wheat-based cottage economy as a rebuke to the economic stranglehold of the wealthy. It may be harder to reduce potato-dependence in the 21st century than it was in the 19th, but if government support for smallholding and food self-reliance were forthcoming it could help people increase other sources of nutrition and cut back reliance on that 'root of wretchedness'.

The figure of 15% of the labour force employed in agriculture would put Britain mid-table in current rankings of agricultural labour force participation, in the company of countries like Mexico, Tunisia and Ukraine.[84] That would be a profound change from the present, but not an unimaginable one in global perspective. It would also be a source of fulfilling, low-carbon employment in a crisis-wracked society. Farm employment could be lower with greater fossil energy availability, but I haven't assumed this in the model. On-farm energy is covered in the model, but not the off-farm energy that would be required to transport food to distant consumers. With seven million direct food producers, plus home gardeners, the model implies considerable ruralisation and localisation of food production. In a low-energy future, this may need to be carried further.

One way of doing so would be to extend home gardening and smallholding, but it would be hard to meet nutritional demands in this way without increasing the amount of cropland relative to grass. With the high population modelled here we're boxed a long way into the arable corner of relying on a few key high-energy crops – wheat and potatoes, principally – even if it's small-scale farmers and gardeners who are doing much of the 'arable' farming. With some loosening of the stringent assumptions I've made, the reality I'm suggesting would probably be more diverse and congenial. Nevertheless, as Table 11.2 shows, there's a need for considerable expansion of cropland at the expense of permanent pasture in the model – though it's worth recalling that oscillations between cropland and grassland have a long history.

As with any modelling exercise, the findings I've presented are only suggestive. But what I hope people will take from them is that, consistent with global studies, there's a margin of safety for agricultural productivity in terms of the bald 'carrying capacity' of Britain's agricultural land even with stringent assumptions about populations, yields, climate change and the availability of energy and plant nutrients. In this sense, critiques of alimentary economics seem vindicated. Expanding current mainstream business models, production methods and energy profiles in agriculture is not the only way to feed the world.

It seems possible that climate refugeeism, energy descent and other crises might impel something like the small farm future I've modelled. The modelling suggests that the capacities of the land itself probably aren't an insurmountable obstacle for people to thrive in such a future. The major obstacles seem political, economic and social. One danger is that this future might resemble the Ricardian world I described in Part I, where pressure on farmland helps to line the pockets of a narrow landlord caste. Therefore, we must consider how such a future can be averted, and what a more congenial small farm society might look like.

PART III

Small Farm Society

*Smallholding intensive cultivators have clung to their individu-
alized properties for dear life. While insisting on their rights of
tenure and exchange, they have resisted land concentration by
estate owners, state or corporate appropriation, and forced col-
lectivization. The possession of established private and common
property rights in a market economy of productive smallholdings
is a protection, though not a perfect one, against alienated, subservient and degraded work.*

ROBERT NETTING[1]

CHAPTER TWELVE

Households, Families and Beyond

In Part I, I showed that the world faces numerous interlocking crises that are probably insoluble through business-as-usual politics, economics and technology. In Part II, I suggested that traditional small-scale labour-intensive farming and gardening offer promising possibilities for responding to and mitigating these crises. These methods emphasise skimming the resources necessary for human flourishing from flows of renewable local resources, rather than feeding off depletable, concentrated stocks like fossil fuels. They point to distributed rural cultures dominated by self-reliant farmers.

When centralised, stock-concentrating civilisations have faltered in the past, people have often responded by switching to rural self-reliance.[2] There's a good chance that a large part of humanity faces another such episode in the near future. With climate change and water and soil scarcity, among other factors, population concentration in areas that remain agriculturally productive will be high and likely to lead to the kind of tight farming situation I modelled for 2050 Britain at the end of Part II.

An advantage of this tight, smallholding way of life is that the intimate relation between household and garden or farmland promotes biological and energetic efficiency. Low-energy, low-carbon farming requires a constant, timely and vigilant attention best delivered by people who are always on the spot, where the material and energy flows of the house and garden are complementary. The food and human wastes from the house feed the garden without inefficient transport and processing costs, and the garden's diverse abundance nourishes the household without the need to restrict its consumption to transport-friendly commodity crops. There are numerous creative ways of saving household energy and waste due to the closeness of house and garden unavailable to the farmer serving distant fields or markets. Another advantage is that damaging depletion of local resources is more obvious and remediable in settlements where day-to-day life is intimately associated with husbanding local resources.

A potential disadvantage of the smallholder-householder adaptation is inequality, both between households and within them. Between households, peasant cultivators have been endlessly prey to exploitation by aristocracies, bandits, local potentates or big men and entrepreneurs of violence who, quite apart from moral considerations, threaten to undermine the sustainability of the adaptation by drawing off surplus to wider, non-local ends. And yet, as Robert Netting makes plain, in tight farming situations of intensive, labour-demanding agriculture, the smallholder-householder adaptation has also recurred widely throughout global history precisely as a bulwark against greater miseries. This is my starting point in Part III. Intensive smallholding is a likely future adaptation to present crises. How can we make the best of it?

This is a critical question when we look *within* the smallholding household. Here, the potential for disparities of work and reward between its members is large, and historically women have borne this burden hardest. So it's understandable that many people have welcomed the coming of modernity, with its emphasis on individualism and the individual life project, as an improvement on the inequalities seemingly typical of various small farm societies.

In the face of the crises we're confronting, it's increasingly clear that the high-energy, high-consumption lifestyles associated with modernity in the rich countries can't continue, let alone further spread to poorer ones. But can we preserve more immaterial aspects of modernity like individual rights and the democratic accountability of governments in a future of renewable-resource-skimming localism? Nobody can say for sure, but it's worth considering how we might try. To do so, we need to lay aside romantic views of how small-scale, face-to-face, self-reliant farm communities operate. We also need to lay aside romantic views of how modern large-scale, market-oriented, urbanised societies operate, and the directions in which they're heading. How might small farm societies of the future plausibly combine the best features of each form while avoiding the worst of their drawbacks?

That's roughly the task I set myself in Part III. In this first chapter, I focus on the household farm and its gender relations, before looking at some other aspects in the later chapters.

Ecological efficiency and ecological restraint point to a type of small-scale farming intimately connected to the household and its needs. Often called 'family farming' – we'll take a critical look at the family part of it in a moment – this has been a common way of organising agriculture histori-cally, and it still is.

A defining feature of household or family farming is that the labour of its members doesn't earn a wage. The household can, however, pay itself in various ways: in its own subsistence, in money from crop sales, in leisure from work it decides to avoid, and in the pleasure of developing new and interesting farm projects. This payment comes to its members in the form of a share in the farm's total activities, not as an hourly wage. Wage labour is inimical to the household farm if it becomes too dominant because it introduces a monetised maxi-min logic – maximising financial income and minimising human labour – that undermines the farm's other priorities and ties it subserviently into the wider fiscal economy.

One explanation for household farming's long persistence is its capac-ity to protect its members from the worst effects of that wider economy (see Chapter 3, 'The Return of the Peasant', page 89), although it can only ever partially succeed at that. It's likely that the wider economy in the present global capitalist form that's alienated so many of us from the ecological capacities of our localities will suffer increasing shrinkage and disarray. So it's a fair bet that in many places household farming will grow in importance as people seek alternative forms of economic security to the faltering capacities of global markets to provide for their needs. Therefore, it's worth looking at how the household operates in existing and historical situations to see what might be in store, to herald its advantages and, if necessary, to prepare against its disadvantages.

The broadest way of thinking about how to organise household farms distinguishes between those whose members are related as family or kin and those whose aren't. Despite the obstinate myth of pre-capitalist com-munal society, small households comprising closely related kin have been the commonest basis of farm societies (and in parallel ways, of hunter-gatherer societies). When we celebrate more communal, village-level farm societies of the past, such as the open field villages of England prior to enclosure and privatisation, we often neglect the fact that day-to-day work was still undertaken mainly by individual farmers and their families.

Historian Andro Linklater hints at one reason why farming households of kin might be so common historically:

> *At one period in my life, I believed passionately in . . . egalitarian ideals, and lived for longer than was sensible on communes in the United States and Europe, farming unproductive, steeply sloping fields locked away in the mountains unwanted by their original owner. The experience offered a salutary lesson in understanding how ownership of the earth shapes the way society is organized. The most attractive qualities of a primitive commune, sharing the labor and the rewards, turned out to be its most destructive. It was not the group but an individual who actually plowed the field, dug the ditch, milked the goats, and made the granola. Over time, it became obvious that some performed these tasks better, or more slowly, or more lazily, than others, and so the tasks either had to be organized with rigid efficiency to spread the burden fairly, or . . . dissensions . . . boiled up and tore the community apart . . . Far from being able to dispense with government, equal ownership entailed a surprising intensity of organization and policing of personal foibles.[3]*

Indeed, getting things done with other people can certainly nourish the soul but it's also hard work, often involving extensive negotiations that probably count against it unless the task really can't be achieved alone. A lot of farm work doesn't tick that box. It's easier to sow and harvest a bed of carrots by yourself than by committee. True, it's often hard for one person to achieve the *totality* of work even on a small farm, but the nature of much farm work is unusual – it's skilled but often mundane, with a temptation to cut corners that's exacerbated by the fact that it's dispersed in space and therefore hard to supervise, unlike factory work. And the payoff is often delayed by months or years, sometimes whole lifetimes.

For these reasons, agrarian societies have found that kin usually make the best farmworkers, because they have skills and temperament born of intimate residence, and have a shared long-term stake in the well-being of the farm that requires no day-to-day supervisory reinforcement. In Robert Netting's pithy summation: 'The household as a small, enduring, self-reproducing kinship unit can mobilize disciplined and responsible labor for intensive agriculture in a way the wage-labor farm cannot match.'[4] We could also reasonably say that intentional communities of non-kin-based farm households probably cannot match it either.

I don't want to suggest there's no role for non-kin household farming in the future. There are plenty of enduring examples of it historically, among which religious communities loom large. Non-kin household farming seems to work best when members are brought together by a wider common purpose of the kind supplied by religious commitment, together with a vocation for farming, rather than when they resort to it by default as a way of escaping the rat race. On these grounds it seems likely to grow in the future, and I happily welcome it.

Nevertheless, it also seems likely that family-based household farming will predominate. Even in wealthy, urbanised countries today, where the case for basing households on economically co-operating kinfolk is at its weakest historically, households remain dominated by kin.[5] The question is whether the dissensions that Linklater describes bubbling up in communities of unrelated individuals are genuinely avoided in family farming situations or merely repressed through forms of coercion that autonomous individuals can't usually apply to one another. Generally, the evidence points to the latter: family farming typically benefits some members of the family more than others, such as seniors over juniors and men over women.

Let's be clear: this is a major dilemma for my argument and one of the most serious trade-offs discussed in this book. Ecologically, socially and politically there's a strong case for building human livelihoods around small, substantially self-reliant, family households, but if the result is patriarchal domination by senior males – as has often been the case in family farming historically – then maybe the case collapses. To sustain it, we need to examine the possibility of family farming without coercion or domination within families.

Let's start by acknowledging that the majority of the world's family subsistence farmers – the majority of the people who are farming to feed their families – are women.[6] And let's recognise the enormity of the often thankless labour that women (and men, too, but more often women) devote to that task globally. Out of this recognition proceeds a common argument that to liberate women from this thanklessness it's necessary to liberate them from subsistence farm labour into the wage-earning economy, following the route of modernisation, economic development and increasing female equality pursued by the wealthy countries of the Global North.

This argument isn't completely straightforward. Sometimes the commercialisation of farming drains women's economic autonomy, industrial wage labour has its own forms of patriarchy and gender division, and there are forms of feminist assertion in traditional family farming situations that can go unrecognised if it's assumed that the Western path of economic development is the only route for female liberation. While I acknowledge that off-farm wage labour can deliver female autonomy, if the larger arguments of this book are correct the opportunities for that kind of work are likely to narrow in the future, so it may be necessary to follow a harder road: seeking resources for female autonomy on the farm, in the absence of economic salvation from without.

In her book *A Field of One's Own*, Bina Agarwal anticipates this argument in an analysis of women's land rights in South Asia. She suggests that most rural women in the region have few prospects for quitting the farm and finding secure paid employment, so the best way to enhance gender equality is by improving women's access to farm property, building on customary rights and contemporary property laws. Elsewhere, Agarwal uses this point to criticise the emphasis on family farming in contemporary peasant and alternative farming movements, suggesting it's often desirable for women to farm co-operatively with other women to produce cash crops.[7] The argument can be generalised as a way of safeguarding all manner of people's autonomy in a global small farm future, perhaps more so than under the present capitalist political economy, which has its own forms of exclusion. It's an argument not for consumer choice, but for producer choice, to farm as one pleases, with whom one pleases.

But here's the crux of the dilemma. Inasmuch as producers can farm as they please and monetise their products, so the viability of the self-limiting farm household oriented to the local ecological base and its flows comes under threat. In practice, there's often a lot of scope to improve women's access to local markets, credit and other resources without fundamentally threatening the basis of local farm society in existing small farm societies. But the wider problem of how to balance the viability of the household with the economic autonomy of its members remains.

I think we need to work on both sides of this dilemma. On the household side, I'd argue for a shift in cultural consciousness so that the work of provisioning the household is no longer disparaged as mere housewifery compared to 'real' work in the wider world. Instead, the emphasis might be on both women and men competently but modestly furnishing their households through 'husbandry' – an old English word for farming. It derives from the Norse/Germanic *hūsbōndi* – *bō* meaning to dwell, build or cultivate, while *hūs* refers to house. Hence I submit a gender-neutral plea for husbandwomen and husbandmen to build a house, dwell in it and cultivate around it[8] – whether alone, with same-sex or opposite-sex partners, or in groups. Household farming.

But it can't be assumed that equality on the farm will blossom through consciousness-raising alone. It's necessary to work on the other side of the dilemma by building institutional safeguards against coercion within the family. One of the best safeguards is restricting the size and remit of family networks. Where family structures assume wider political and economic functions, people often cease to be individuals as ends-in-themselves pursuing their chosen life projects. Instead they become mere parts of a larger corporate whole, and their individuality easily becomes subordinated to a wider family name. Corporate kinship of this kind often traps women particularly within elaborate codes of conduct concerning honour, shame and control, entrenching their subordination to male kin and to men in general. But it can also entrench seniority, preventing adult men, too, from attaining full autonomy and making them servants in another's household.

Small farm societies haven't often fitted this corporate or 'extended' family pattern historically, and there's a lot to be said for ensuring that remains true in the future.[9] Nowadays, centralised states and monetised market exchange are bulwarks against family extension. They pose their own problems that we'll examine shortly, but they can also prevent family coercion through creating opportunities for individuals – women and youths in particular – to quit an unsatisfactory farm household and form a new one through means such as divorce, off-farm education, land purchase and financial independence.

The possibility of being able to do this depends on the existence of a kind of wider political playing field or public sphere, a space of rational debate available to all where decisions arise out of argument, not social standing. The way this has played out historically is in efforts to extend who can claim both protection *from* the state against non-state actors like violent partners, and who can claim protection *against* state discrimination towards certain groups – women, homosexuals, ethnic minorities – with the implication that those who have rights must somehow be visible to the state.

So there's an upside to the public sphere and visibility to the central state in checking abuses that might otherwise remain hidden, but the glare of the state has its downsides, too. Quite apart from the often erosive effects of centralised states on localised small-scale farming, state social policies in various places and political colours have often involved chauvinisms of their own that put married, heterosexual working men of the ethnic majority centre stage. For this reason, modern identity politics has often been suspicious of allying with governments. Access to decent wages and, crucially, to property, rather than to government social policy, is seen as a safer bulwark against oppression.[10] This brings us back to the need for people of all kinds for a 'recaptured garden', or a field of their own in the rural-agrarian situations to come.

In summary, there's a difficult tension between the ecological benefits of the household as a self-supporting entity without inherent and problematic tendencies to economic growth, and the social disbenefits of households that repress some of their members, especially women. The best way of resolving the tension is to place household farming within a wider public or state space, but not necessarily one like the modern, centralised, welfare nation-state. I return to this issue in Part IV.

A difficulty with my argument is that the forces eroding the existing political economy that make a small farm future more likely will probably also erode the potential to create or maintain public spheres. By that account, a small farm future could be an unattractive one for women and other people at risk of being subordinated in it, a point that should be troubling for those of us who think that such a future may await us whether we like it or not. There are no guarantees that a future turn to agrarianism won't be accompanied by a turn to patriarchy and other forms of domination. But we have resources for fighting collectively against that outcome, such as concepts of the public sphere, formal equality, individualism and individual rights.

CHAPTER THIRTEEN

Complicating the Commons:
Holding and Sharing the Land

A good deal of discussion in the alternative farming and alternative economics movements nowadays promotes the idea of 'the commons', emphasising the need to replace private property with more collective forms of land use. But when we look at historic small farm societies, common property and private property rights usually occur together. Indeed, perhaps the most striking thing for those of us raised on the notion that private property is an invention of modern capitalism is the presence of something akin to private ownership in numerous non-capitalist small farm societies historically. In Robert Netting's words: 'Where land is a scarce good that can be made to yield continuously and reliably over the long term by intensive methods, rights approximating those of private ownership will develop.'[1]

Still, the way private property rights work in the global capitalist economy isn't conducive to economic localism and small farm societies. Arguments for small-scale farming therefore need to accommodate themselves to these apparently contradictory facts. This is the purpose of the present chapter, where I suggest that the most important thing to get right in a small farm future will probably be the *public* allocation of *private* property rights that make widespread household farming possible. This applies whether the household comprises kin or non-kin.

Of Private Property

A while ago, I went to a meeting in my hometown about re-wilding the British countryside. The atmosphere was hostile to farmers, casting them as poor custodians of the country's natural riches. The loudest cheer of the evening went to a panellist who said the government should nationalise the country's farmland and administer it in the public interest. I felt the ghost of Jean-Jacques Rousseau stalking the hall: 'You are lost if you forget that the fruits of the earth belong to all and the earth to no one.' Or maybe the even pithier Pierre-Joseph Proudhon: 'Property is theft.' It seems hard to argue that anybody has any kind of original, natural or inalienable right to own a part of the Earth, especially if their actions have a negative impact on others.

Yet looking around the audience – many of whom I knew – it struck me that few of them owned farmland, whereas many of them owned their own houses, and it seemed to me doubtful that a call to nationalise their homes in the public interest would have gone down as well, despite the national crisis in affordable housing. It would be easy to make accusations of hypocrisy, but probably more productive to investigate whether there are underlying complexities in our concept of property that might explain such different contextual attitudes. And, more to the point, whether these complexities inform how landholding could be organised in a small farm future. The answer to both questions, I think, is yes.

Not long after that first meeting I went to another one, this time comprising mostly young alternative farmers with impressive credentials as radical activists of an anarchist bent. Talk at this latter meeting focused on how to find affordable farmland to buy in order to have the freedom and security to farm as they wished.

So is property theft, or is it freedom? There's much to be gained from viewing it as both, but to understand how, and the implications for a small farm future, we need to probe into the meaning of 'property'. Perhaps I can make the key point up front with a historical example. According to historian Robert Allen, the heyday of peasant farming in England was the 17th century, after the Tudor courts gave security of private, owner occupier tenure to peasants whose rights to property had previously depended on the whim of landed gentry. The demise of peasant farming, Allen says, came in the 18th century when the development of modern mortgages incentivised wealthy landowners to raise money against the security of land, enabling them to consolidate smallholdings into great estates.[12] These bookends of the peasant experience in England dramatise the two faces of private property – security and self-determination on the one hand, speculative concentration of value on the other.

Let's pause to consider the way private property generally functions. Take the toothbrush that I buy from a pharmacy. The money I pay gives me the right to enjoy its benefits, in this case its capacity to keep my teeth clean. But the important relationship is actually between me and other people, not me and the toothbrush. When I hand over the money, the vendor honours the contract by giving me the toothbrush, and the other people around me also honour the contract by not stealing the toothbrush from me and appropriating its benefits to themselves. My property is a relation between me and other people in respect of an owned thing, not fundamentally a relation between me and the thing.[13]

Now suppose instead of a toothbrush I buy some farmland. In many ways, it's a similar transaction. The purchase gives me the right to appropriate the farmland's benefits to myself. In this case, the benefits are more complex and varied, but what secure property rights in farmland have generally meant historically is the opportunity for well-being and a complete life. From my land I can grow food to eat, collect or extract water to drink, grow or extract fuel and building materials to make and heat a house, and generate produce that I can sell to obtain the things I need that aren't so easily provided from my land.

People sometimes oppose the idea of landownership because of the perceived hubris in claiming to own a work of nature that long preceded the claimant's birth and will long outlast their death. But that's not fundamentally what landownership is about. Its real crux is, as with my toothbrush, the agreement it involves between me and other people over the right to its benefits. So it's not surprising that the farmer-activists I mentioned wanted to buy land, nor that the activists of an earlier generation hankered after 'three acres and a cow'.

This is property as freedom – the ability to provide for yourself and control your destiny. Article 25 of the UN's Universal Declaration of Human Rights states that 'everyone has the right to a standard of living adequate for the health and well-being of himself and of his family, including food, clothing, housing and medical care and necessary social services'. Sexist language aside, the best way of delivering on this in the future will probably be by ensuring that everyone has secure access to enough farmland to provide most of these things for themselves.

Currently, few people enjoy such access. In some places, this is because of inadequate legal title that prevents them from securing access to land and its products, something that could arguably be improved by stronger private property rights. But it's also because of the tendency of private property to concentrate in few hands, which isn't likely to improve with stronger private property rights. Here is where the similarities between owning a toothbrush and owning a piece of land break down, essentially for two reasons.

First, because land is a necessary prerequisite for most human activities, because it's a limited and non-expandable resource in space and an almost unlimited one in time, then in situations when it's tradeable for money on open markets its value tends to appreciate over time, rather than depreciate as with most other forms of capital. Or as Mark Twain famously put it: 'Buy land, they ain't making it anymore.' Since land is so precious as a future asset and a store of value, demand for it bids up the price on open markets, especially when there are other major ways of creating value for which land can act as a repository, as is the case in capitalist societies. In this situation, land soon becomes impossible for most people to afford, precisely because (unlike toothbrushes) they ain't making it any more, unless its price is checked by society-wide agreements. My argument is that its price *does* need to be checked by such agreements if private property rights are to be liberating rather than exclusionary.

The second difference is that, unlike the two almost-identical toothbrushes you and I might buy from the pharmacy, every piece of land is different. That doesn't necessarily matter, because the price it commands in an open market should reflect its specific quality, inasmuch as this is possible. But suppose a road is built alongside the cheap and isolated farmland I once bought. Suppose houses, shops, schools and factories come in its wake. My farmland has now become prime urban real estate – not because of anything I've done but because of a broader public creation of economic value from which I, as an individual landowner, stand to benefit privately. Again, the result of this is that the most economically remunerative land quickly prices most individuals out of the market – the problem of Ricardian rent (see Chapter 1, 'Crisis #9: Political Economy', page 53).

Private property, then, is intrinsically a *social* relation between people, not an individual's innate prerogative. And since private property is a collective social arrangement, it doesn't have to be as totalising as it's become in the capitalist societies of the Global North. Even here it's not total. The money that my wife and I handed over in 2003 for the land we now farm bought the exclusive right to generate an income from the land by farming it. It didn't buy the right to live permanently on it; that's something we've had to establish through bureaucratic procedures so laborious that 16 years later I'm writing these words in a new farmhouse that we've occupied for only a matter of months, and that we're unable to sell on the open market. It would be easy to complain about the idiocies of this process, but without something like it Britain's farmland would long since have disappeared under golf courses, condominiums, racetracks, warehouses and any number of other enterprises that offer a better return on investment than growing vegetables.

So private landownership can involve a complex bundle of rights that can potentially be separated out: the right to farm, but not to build a house; the right to earn, but not to bequeath to descendants or exclude passers-by; the right to grow crops, but not to erode the soil. There's no compelling reason to suppose that the only option available to a society that wishes to safeguard wildlife, soil or public access to farmland is to place the countryside entirely in the hands of the state, a method of land allocation that has problems of its own. In fact, both unchecked privatisation and unchecked statism can end up looking quite similar – remote and unaccountable decision making in the hands of the few that alienates most people from self-determination. Is there another way?

The Commons

Yes, according to a growing band of thinkers. The commons. The word, and the idea, originate in the shared spaces and resources that ordinary people have used and still use in traditional agrarian societies across the world in order to make their livelihoods: common pastures where people graze their livestock, common woodlands where they gather wood for multiple purposes, common watercourses where they abstract water for irrigation and so on. A commons isn't the private property of any single person, nor is it controlled by a state or public authority ostensibly in the general public interest. Rather, it's a resource used by a group of people who organise among themselves to determine the nature of their individual and collective use. As commons activist David Bollier puts it: 'A commons is *a resource + a community + a set of social protocols*.'[14]

The drawbacks of both unfettered private property regimes and bureaucratic statist ones have become increasingly clear in a world that's been so blighted by their excesses. For many people the idea of the commons suggests an alternative whose time has come, again. But there are problems with it. Let me broach them by first providing a summary of what I'd call the 'myth of the benign commons' widely recycled in the alternative agriculture and alternative economics movements, which goes something like this.

Before modern capitalism arose, people shared resources in the form of commons. But then the wealthy landowners enclosed the commons for their own private use, turfing the peasants off the land so they became landless labourers – a rural and, later, an urban proletariat, the foot-soldiers of the new capitalist economy. In 1968, ecologist Garret Hardin published an influential article called 'The Tragedy of the Commons' in which he argued that commons were a disastrous – a 'tragic' – way of organising economies, because in a commons it's in nobody's individual interest to limit one's resource use to safeguard long-term sustainability. Hardin's intervention further fuelled the already well-advanced process of converting commons into private property. But he'd fundamentally misunderstood the nature of commons, as demonstrated by political scientist Elinor Ostrom, who showed that people self-organise locally to manage resources successfully and sustainably long term. So what's needed today to combat the environmental degradation and social inequality of private property is a greater emphasis on commons – not just in the original, narrow agricultural sense but in a wider sense of what political theorists Michael Hardt and Antonio Negri call democratic 'rights of the common' that go beyond property and potentially apply to everything in our populous, urban, modern societies.[15]

There's a grain of truth to much of this, for some times and places more than others. But it's also misleading, not least because it mixes up several different things: the practical tasks that commoning arrangements aim to achieve; how such arrangements emerged and changed historically in relation to wider forces; and how people can best organise themselves politically to achieve various practical and ethical ends today. It's worth looking at the way agricultural commons worked historically so we can see the problems they solved in agrarian societies, and the problems they didn't, without concluding that some fuzzy notion of commoning is the answer to all contemporary problems. Table 13.1 tries to unpick this, distinguishing between aspects of traditional commons that may be more (*left-hand column*) or less (*right-hand column*) appropriate to present circumstances.[16]

A commons is a form of non-kin-based household-to-household co-operation . . .

Whereas a typical form of property and economic rights-allocation in non-capitalist and stateless societies has been based around kin groups, commons involve the relatively unusual innovation of collaboration between unrelated local households of similar social standing engaged in similar subsistence

Table 13.1. The characteristics of commons

A COMMONS . . .	
1. Is a form of non-kin-based household-to-household co-operation	2. Is usually geared to the use of extensive and irregularly yielding resources in situations where livelihoods depend on exploiting, but not over-exploiting, a local ecological base
3. Often arises out of agreements between potentially antagonistic kinds of people or social interests . . .	4. Usually involves a small group of intimately known individuals of similar social standing who co-operate long term with no anonymity from penalties for misbehaviour
	5. Usually operates as a corporate group with closed membership
6. Accommodates itself to commercial or capitalist forces outside the commons, usually by trying to mitigate their negative effects rather than challenging them outright	
7. Often limits use to basic needs, promoting community efficiency, not economic efficiency	
8. Involves sanctions against free-riding . . .	9. . . . which sometimes fail
10. Involves input/extraction rules to achieve locally specific ends	

tasks. This potentially fits well with household farming and a wider public sphere (see Chapter 12, 'Households, Families and Beyond', page 171).

A commons is rarely a voluntary and ad hoc form of co-operation, such as mutual help between neighbours undertaken through personal choice. Instead, it often includes everyone in a locality who's engaged in similar subsistence activities, whether they're friendly with each other or not. It therefore requires more formal organisation.

... which is usually geared to the use of extensive and irregularly yielding resources in situations where livelihoods depend on exploiting, but not over-exploiting, a local ecological base ...

These include things like seasonal pastures, wild game or firewood gleanings from surrounding forests, or aquatic resources such as fish or irrigation water. They rarely include intensive cropland (gardens, arable fields) which can be intensified through individual or household labour. This is a key point, implying there are transaction costs to maintaining commons, which are probably worth paying only when doing so is easier than the alternatives. It also implies that commons work best where people are reliant for their daily living on fundamentally local resources that are susceptible to over-exploitation.

The main way this has worked historically in the northerly latitudes with which I'm most familiar is common pastures for livestock, enabling small-scale farmers lacking land for a commercial herd to keep animals for milk, manure and other default services that make the most of livestock's ability to tap the local nutrient base. Many commoning arrangements have involved complex mixtures of private and common property rights enabling small-scale farmers to manage indivisible resources like cows that exceed their private capacities but enable them to make a better livelihood and, collectively, to optimise use of local ecological resources through combining different property regimes.[17] A tight smallholder farmscape in 2050 Britain (see Chapter 11, 'Can Alternative Agriculture Feed Us?', page 150) would be ripe for such mixed private-collective forms of property.

It can be useful to think in terms of what I call the 'elemental commons': fire, water and earth. That is, commons are most typically formed around 'elemental' features of the larger local landscape that elude individual control and optimisation. In some places this will be fire risk, in others flood risk or irrigation water availability, and in others the demands of the farmed earth, such as the need for shared pastures, shared draught teams or shared crop diversity through collective plant breeding and seed saving. Commons are organised around the wider features of the local landscape that limit individual human control, but don't intrinsically supplant it.

Commons often arise out of agreements between potentially antagonistic kinds of people or social interests . . .

For example, the commons and guilds that emerged in medieval Europe involved agreements for mutual benefit between landed gentry and commoners about extending the latter's access to gentry land in the context of population growth and commercialisation. In this respect, commons usually require a weak but not completely absent higher political power.

A commons usually involves a small group of intimately known individuals of similar social standing who co-operate long term with no anonymity from penalties for misbehaviour . . .

. . . because everybody needs a stake in thrashing out the rules and in enforcing them against each other. In a commoning situation where individual members lack a monopoly of coercive power, the most effective method is usually self-control due to reputational risk among people with whom one has important long-term economic relationships. For this reason, commoning doesn't always work well in modern urban-capitalist settings outside of crisis situations. The costs of walking away are too low, which is why initiatives like community gardens often fold when key individuals burn out or move away. Intimate local interaction also lowers the costs of managing and monitoring the commons. But a downside, certainly to the modernist mind, is the intrusiveness of the local reputational management involved – the 'goldfish bowl' of village life, the poison in its gift, its petty rumours and gossip.[18]

It usually operates as a corporate group with closed membership . . .

. . . closed membership being one of the main ways in which functioning commons manage to avoid Hardin's tragedy by restricting who can exploit the resource. A commons is not a free-for-all. Of course, this raises questions about who's in and who's out, on what grounds, whether the ins become a closed clique or caste, and whether the outs can make a livelihood without access to common resources. Although modern proponents often present the commons as more co-operative than other economic institutions, their potential exclusivity needs to be taken seriously if they're advanced as a true model for political co-operation. In Europe, commons share origins with the trading corporations that pioneered capitalist profiteering. In other words, the interests of the commoners aren't necessarily the same as the common interest. And even among commoners, day-to-day operation of the commons has often been in the hands of higher-status people, such as wealthy peasants, village elders or local dignitaries; the management doesn't necessarily operate uniformly in everyone's interest.[19]

It accommodates itself to commercial or capitalist forces outside the commons, usually by trying to mitigate their negative effects rather than challenging them outright . . .

Despite these shared origins, many premodern commons in Europe protected their members from the challenges presented by an increasingly commercialised and monetised society; it was a kind of welfare system prior to true state welfare or private charity. They also tried to protect the integrity of the village economy without challenging the wider economy. For example, private sale of any resource taken from the commons might be forbidden, while commercial production on private land might be allowed.

It often limits use to basic needs . . .

The welfare function of the commons often amounts to allowing people, especially poor people, to meet basic needs, not wants. It may be more economically efficient to turn the commons over to private use (greater output for a given input), but less socially efficient (less community well-being for a given input).

It involves sanctions against free-riding . . .

Despite the strong incentives of local reputation, historical and legal records are full of cases where people were tempted by self-interest and fell short. Selfish individualism isn't limited to capitalist societies or Western societies.[20] Successful commons needed to devise effective sanctions against free-riding . . .

... which sometimes fail

Effective sanctions aren't easy to achieve, particularly in large-scale, differentiated societies like most modern ones, where reputational status is less total. The historical record is also full of cases where commons have failed. While Elinor Ostrom's work is often invoked as a disproof of Hardin's tragedy of the commons, she herself stated that his model isn't wrong; it's simply one possible outcome among several.[21]

A commons involves input/extraction rules to achieve locally specific ends ...

Agricultural commons always have a specific, practical and local aim: What is the best way to nourish enough cows from these fields? What is the best way to ensure that everybody's crops get enough irrigation water from this river? They don't concern themselves with more abstract speculations: What kind of politics best fits the human condition? Does sharing rather than private ownership make for a better society? Although many commoning arrangements are similar, they're always uniquely addressed to locally specific ends.

When a commons is enclosed and turned into private holdings, it is often because powerful local actors have usurped it in their own interests to the detriment of the commoners, but not always. It may be because the commoners themselves have decided there are better ways of organising things. For example, if the price of fencing goes down and a herder's wages go up, enclosure may become preferable for local smallholders. Conversely, if the risk of wildfire or the costs of individual cultivation increase, the conditions may turn away from private ownership and towards the creation of new commons. The ending or the creating of commons isn't always a reflection of broader political dynamics. Sometimes, it's simply the price of a fence.

If we recall my modelling for 2050 Britain (see Chapter 11, 'Can Alternative Agriculture Feed Us?', page 150) – a world of densely populated farmland, churning population movements, high demands on farmland productivity, low availability of energy and other resources, and weakened central states – then there are aspects of commons that may be appropriate to the radically altered situation (those in the left-hand column of Table 13.1) and other aspects that seem less appropriate (those in the right-hand column of

Table 13.1). Sometimes the case is arguable and they could plausibly fit in either column, but what seems clear is that commoning alone is insufficient.

In loose provisioning situations where population pressure on the land is low, commoning agreements may be all that's necessary for people to make a livelihood. The classic case is a foraging society, where hunting or gathering rights need to be thrashed out between people but there's little need for tight private property boundaries. But in tight situations of intensive cropping, like the one I projected for the crisis conditions of 2050 Britain, regimes of small-scale private proprietorship usually emerge.

Property regimes of all kinds are intrinsically social. Ultimately, they can only function through widespread and ongoing consent. In the tight farming situations of the future, the real need will be to replace the extractive, inequitable and speculative private property regime of our existing political economy, which is justified with the increasingly threadbare myth that private self-interest generates public benefit, with collective agreements about a fairer distribution of private property that enables most people to access small parcels of productive farmland. In such a situation, smallholders would develop innumerable local commons over time that optimised responsible use of the local ecological base. I don't mean to understate how intensive that process would be – the joys and frictions of neighbourliness, the endless curation of interactions, tensions and gossip that go into creating local forms of co-operation up to and including a formal commons. But that's not currently the most challenging task. The most challenging task is to develop the *collective* agreements over the *private* property rights enabling widespread access to farmland. This is what I call creating the 'tight commons', and it's key to a small farm future.

Perhaps the enthusiasm for commons in alternative economic thinking arises more from a commitment to human solidarity in the face of con-temporary crises and the cold workings of modern property markets, and less from a detailed interest in how commons practically work. I readily endorse that commitment to human solidarity, but I worry that contemporary interest in the collaborative commons, circular economies, and open source solutions sometimes overplays an enthusiasm for collaborative work simply because it *is* collaborative, at the expense of carefully analys-ing whether it generates successful long-term social relations.

Usufruct and the Small Proprietor

Many of us today live surrounded by our personal possessions in small urban residential units. These units and their contents seem obviously 'ours', while almost everything else – at least to those with progressive politics – seems obviously a collective product. As theorists of the 'non-property commons' Michael Hardt and Antonio Negri put it: '[Our] conception of the common is aimed at social wealth, not individual possessions: there is no need to share your toothbrush or even give others say over most things you make yourself.'[22] I suspect the audience at the re-wilding talk I attended seemed keen on nationalising farmland, but not so much their own private housing, for similar reasons.

But this distinction makes less sense from an agricultural perspective, where the issue isn't toothbrushes or even houses but large forms of working capital like fields, hedges and livestock. For farmers, these are rarely 'social wealth' any more than a toothbrush is. If such items must be fully shared, it's hard to see how people will democratically create livelihoods in socially efficient ways that don't get bogged down in endless disputes over priorities and free riding. Better a small farm future of resource-constrained tight farming where you have the autonomy to make most things yourself, including a livelihood, and where democratic consensus building can focus more narrowly on essentials like finding a just division of land, and on caring for those who can't care for themselves. The advantage of examining actual agricultural commons of the past is that it enables us to see how people tried to achieve this kind of harmony in tough, tight farming situations – sometimes successfully, sometimes not, but rarely in the absence of any private property.

There are likely to be difficult tensions around this point in the move towards a small farm future. In crisis situations, there are often a lot of people on the move with profound unmet needs, and the sedentary 'who's in/who's out' logic of a traditional agricultural commons isn't a humane basis for meeting them. This has prompted various practical and theoretical attempts to rethink commons in a more fluid, open and inclusive way fitted to present circumstances, for example in the concept of 'liminal' urban commons applied to inclusive self-help initiatives arising during Greece's economic crisis.[23] I don't mean to deny that this kind of commons will remain important, but my argument is geared more to avoiding and stabilising crisis situations by building local agrarian autonomies, and as this happens I suspect that liminal commons will probably transition towards more recognisably traditional forms of agricultural commons.

I've made a case for private property as a building block for those local agrarian autonomies. In fact, I'd argue there's a case for largely *inalienable* private property in a small farm future. Why inalienable? Well, consider an alternative like usufruct, which is sometimes advocated in alternative economics circles. The idea is that nobody 'owns' the land, but that individuals can have the right to its 'fruit'. In other words, you can farm the land and make your living from its produce. Usufruct is, in Murray Bookchin's words: 'the freedom of individuals in a community to appropriate resources merely by virtue of the fact they are using them. Such resources belong to the user as long as they are being used. Function, in effect, replaces our hallowed concept of possession.'[24]

The problem lies with the 'as long as they are being used' because it leaves unclear who gets to decide what counts as appropriate use. Consider the allotment-holder ejected from her plot because the allotment association deems she's not using it properly. Perhaps she thinks she's allowing wild plants to grow to encourage beneficial insects, whereas the association considers her untidy plot to be ruined by weeds. Who's right? And who gets to decide? Or consider the dispossession of Native Americans justified by John Locke on the grounds that they weren't 'improving' their land as Europeans did (see Chapter 1, 'Crisis #7: Land', page 48). Again, who's right? And who gets to decide?

The provisional nature of usufruct rights in the face of the opinion of key power brokers or the kind of local dignitaries who've historically been in charge of commons is one reason why inalienable property rights are so appealing, and why people are often willing to do a lot (or pay a lot) to acquire them. Consider again the alternative farmers at the meeting who were anxious to acquire private land.[25] The difference between usufruct and private property is security of tenure, and it's this that renders property as freedom in a 'three acres and a cow' sense. Security of tenure also works as a good bet against enclosure, engrossment and the financialisation of farming. If you're the possessor of inalienable property rights, then nobody can turf you off or increase your rent and squeeze more surplus and productivity gain out of you.

As with anything, there are downsides to inalienable property. A pressing one today is how to ensure that those who have it don't pursue private ends that threaten collective goods like uneroded soil and clean water – the 'it's my land and I'll do what I like with it' problem. This is less of a problem in a society of tight small-scale farming fully engaged with its local ecological base, where the consequences of doing what you like are more apparent and more likely to react back directly on the doer. But more generally the solution depends ultimately on the fact that buying private property rights is not the same as buying the right to do absolutely anything on one's property without any sanctions available to the wider community. Hard libertarian adherents of private property rights might say that such sanctions would revert private property to mere usufruct. But since, as I've stressed above, private property rights are – like all property rights – inherently collective in their very constitution, then every property regime is usufructuary in the final instance. The point of stressing inalienability is that it creates some security around landownership, making arbitrary eviction difficult – and this is important for a prosperous and sustainable small farm society. But it's not a sufficient condition in itself for sustainability. A wider commitment to sustaining the local ecological base is also required.

Since this isn't a technical or policy-focused book, I don't propose to wade into the minutiae of how best to create a private property regime appropriate to a smallholder-householder society, something that's in any case unknowable outside the future play of politics. But a few remarks on the possible avenues are in order.

One way of trying to stop land price speculation from destroying access to farmland is through controlling politically who can buy farmland, for example through limiting farm sales to people who are active farmers or established members of the local community. But if the allocation of farm property is left to nebulous collectivities like 'the local community' then it's a fair bet that its control will be in the firm grip of the strongest local voices and power brokers. If, on the other hand, land is available for sale to anyone willing to pay for it, the possibilities for ownership are widened – land as freedom, the 'three acres and a cow' dynamic once again. The advantage of money is that it's more fluid and less 'sticky' than established status hierarchies. The trick is to make use of this fluidity to create markets for farmland that are socially levelling locally – which may be where the case I've been

making for a 'tight commons' of family farming connects with more col-
lectivist household models like workers' co-operatives and community land
trusts geared to preventing speculative increase in land value.

The problem is to strike a balance between this fluidity and the danger
that it permits an influx of speculative capital raised elsewhere to heat land
prices beyond the capacities of the local farm economy. The best way of
avoiding this danger is to limit the possibilities to accrue liquid capital.
Such limitation is in keeping with the idea of an economy based on tapping
renewable local flows of energy and resources, rather than drawing upon
concentrated stocks.

One way of achieving this balance is heavy gift or estate taxes to prevent
the concentration of wealth by stopping its transfer at death from parents
to children. In this way, farmland can circulate back into the market at
affordable prices. A downside is that this breaks the generational link
between a family and its farmland that can act as a foundation for good
long-term land husbandry. Still, the burdens of taking on and honouring the lifework of one's parents weigh heavily on some people. Estate
taxes offer an escape – and historical evidence suggests that small-scale
proprietors can be unsentimental about inheritance if they're confident of
obtaining land to make a livelihood by other means.[26] The way this could
work in a small farm future is through development banks that accumulate
the rural capital renewably generated from local land and provide loans to
young farmers to buy farms – loans that could realistically be paid off over
the course of a farming career.[27]

There's a 'tragic' problem with the money- and market-based
approaches I've emphasised if they're to deliver a small farm future – a
'tragedy of the privates', not the commons. These approaches require
the existence of a state to underwrite commons, private property and
monetised exchange, which is in keeping with my arguments earlier for
a public sphere to guarantee gender and other rights. But only if everyone trusts the state to secure a fair distribution of social assets will they
support it rather than keeping faith with more personal welfare arrangements, which historically have usually involved family networks that
come with all the problems of corporate kinship I mentioned earlier. So a
small farm society of widespread private ownership and family farming is
only likely when there's a state willing to redistribute land as smallhold-

ings in the common interest. This situation hasn't been commonplace historically, but in Part IV I address how it might become more common in our crisis-wracked future.

For now, I'll simply add that I don't propose my argument for small farm private property in a colonial spirit to suggest that societies organised in other ways must be restructured. Sometimes efforts to create entitlements to private land for disadvantaged groups backfire, or merely open the way to powerful outside players. So I'm not proposing private, inalienable land title as a one-size-fits-all solution. I'm just suggesting that it's a well-understood feature in many societies, especially ones that for better or worse have experienced 'modernisation'. And since it's compatible with the requirements of small farm societies in tight farming situations, there's little point making the job of constructing the latter even harder by abandoning it on principle.

CHAPTER FOURTEEN

Going to Market

In a small farm future of self-reliant but not entirely independent house-hold farming, what might the world of trade look like? To help sketch an answer, I begin with four snapshots from the present.

1

There was an old baker in my hometown, whose excellent bread everyone loved. Having toiled through many a start in the small hours through his working life, he'd reached a point of financial comfort that prompted him to close the shop on Mondays so that he could have a full weekend off. In the summer a neat, handwritten sign on the bakery's locked door would announce his summer holiday and the reopening date. Over the years the holidays got longer. His customers didn't mind. They were always ready to buy his bread when it was available. Eventually the holidays exceeded the shop's opening times. Not long afterwards he retired, sold the shop and holidayed for good.

2

I sometimes raise a couple of pigs in a woodland area on my farm. I feed them a minimum of purchased, grain-based compound feed, and they forage for grass, roots, crab apples and hazelnuts in their enclosure, supplemented with potato out-grades and other waste fodder from the garden. They're a costly product, in a sense, because I spend precious time and labour getting food for them. And I could probably turn their lot over to a more remunerative use. On the other hand, it costs little money to feed them, they turn low-grade food into high-grade meat and fat, I like going to feed the pigs, and they have a healthy, varied life and diet that's manifest in the quality of their meat. It's impossible to buy pork like this in the shops. Sometimes I've sold a little at a premium to reflect this quality. Other times I've been unable to agree on a price with would-be customers. For me, the pork is so steeped in my practices and values on the farm that I struggle to turn it into a quantitative value. For the customer, there's any number of other calls upon their money. The result is that I don't usually sell my pork, but eat it at home.

3

In his book *Coasting*, Jonathan Raban describes the local economy of a marshland community in 1980s Britain.

> *The place was a hive of tiny, tax-free private enterprises. Up every lane there was a brick bungalow with a notice nailed to a tree, advertising the spare-time products of the industrious householder. BIRDTABLES FROM £7.50   LACE BEDSPREADS   KOI CARP   POTTERY LOGS SAWN TO ORDER   POND LINERS   HONEY   GOATS' MILK   PEDLAR DOLLS   ROTTED MUSHROOM COMPOST EGGS LAID WHILE YOU WAIT   TOMS GLADS AND CUES REPLACEMENT WINDSCREENS   DWARF LOP RABBITS MAGGOTS   SWEET CORN   TERRIER MEAL   HORSE PELLETS   KARATE LESSONS   HAIRCUT, SIR?   GOLDEN LABRADOR PUPPIES READY SOON   CLAY PIGEONS CREAM TEAS, WELDING & RESPRAYS   BABY BUNNIES PULLETS' EGGS BY THE TRAY   PORK SAUSAGES AND SHOE REPAIRS   CONCRETE TUBS FOR SALE[28]*

4

An experience I've had in rural parts of poorer countries: shops are few and far between, and sell a poor selection of over-priced branded products from global manufacturers. It's a mystery where people get their food from. But once invited into a resident's home, you find a sly abundance of locally produced wholefoods, sourced through processes invisible to the newcomer's eye.

None of these snapshots bear much relation to the way modern food markets work in wealthy countries today. In theory, these modern markets fit at least one criterion economists use to identify efficient private markets. They involve large numbers of both producers (farmers) and consumers (the general public). But in practice that producer–consumer relationship is mediated by a highly concentrated middleman sector. For example, more than three-quarters of the UK grocery trade is controlled by just five huge retail companies.[29]

The buying power of this sector exerts a downward pressure on farm-gate prices and food-sector wages, while the sector as a whole relies on cheap, polluting fossil fuels and a handful of commodity super-crops. Still, it does a good enough job of getting nourishment into the bodies of people in their multitudes at checkout prices cheap enough that even poorly paid workers – many employed in the food sector itself – can keep paying into the wider economy, especially when their incomes are topped up by government welfare benefits. All this feeds into a tenacious mythology of food-sector efficiency and affordability, implicitly supported by government welfarism, that militates against any radical overhaul of the system.

A good deal of effort in the alternative farming and alternative economics movements dedicates itself to opening out that concentrated middleman sector, for example by supporting direct farmer-to-customer retailing or wholesale co-operatives that don't disproportionately extract value from producers. A second strand of economic thinking focuses on the tech revolution that's creating new and more distributed forms of peer-to-peer 'collaborative consumption' or 'collaborative commons' such as Airbnb and open source industrial design.[30] I happily endorse the first of these trends, and remain sceptical about the second, but the small farm society I envisage represents a more radical break with the status quo than replacing corporate supermarkets with farmers' markets or tech platforms. In the rest of this chapter, I'll look at the market implications of the four snapshots I began with, in which that radical break is assumed.

Market Optionality

Both the baker and the pig farmer described above were interested in going to market, but not in the sense that they *had to* go to market to guarantee their well-being, or that they had to seek the maximum return on their capital there, as is the case in capitalist market society. Going to market and finding a market price was an option, weighed against others.

A vacationing baker and a pig-producer who won't sell his pork are anti-heroes in the capitalist romance. There may be room for a few such renegades, but if everyone behaved like that the capitalist economy would cease to function. Then again, if everyone behaved like that it would imply that everyone was in the same privileged position with respect to the market, and weren't fundamentally dependent upon it. The *capitalist* economy would cease to function, but the economy – whose etymology derives from the Greek word *oikonomia*, meaning household management – would be just fine.

I argue for a small farm economy of this kind, in which economic sovereignty is dispersed. Missing here is the 'consumer sovereignty' of capitalist society, a phrase that over-dramatises consumer power. True sovereignty involves more than being able to walk away from a deal. Instead I suggest a sovereignty of the producer and the household, a self-reliant producerism rather than a market-reliant consumerism. But even then, household farmers can't produce everything for themselves. They'd still want to go to market, selling some of their wares and using the revenues thus generated to buy the things they didn't produce.

Where does money fit into this householder economy – the kind of economy where currency is scarce, and not wasted on things like food, clothes or even dwellings that are easily produced at a zero money price on the holding? The argument of orthodox modern economics is that economising of the household farm is a false economy; its members are better off getting paid work and buying the things they need from specialist providers. Sometimes household farmers make the same judgement, especially when the wider economy forces their hand, although this is often a strategy to retain the farm for long-term security, not abandon it. Still, small-scale farmers do try to retain autonomy by preserving the zero-price household economy as best they can. Such efforts are likely to spread and deepen in the future as a response to interlocking global crises.

Pioneer economist Adam Smith famously wrote in *The Wealth of Nations* (1776): 'It is not from the benevolence of the butcher, the brewer or the baker, that we expect our dinner, but from their regard for their own interest. We address ourselves, not to their humanity but to their self-love, and never talk to them of our own necessities but of their advantages.'[31] This isn't how people behave in societies where capital hasn't fully penetrated, however. In such societies, shopkeepers and merchants offer credit to specific local customers based precisely on their 'own necessities'. And the merchants trust the customers upon their honour, locally known and jealously guarded, to redeem it in the future.

This credit function could be seen as a form of commons, which is enclosed or fully privatised only when the shopkeeper stops offering this provisional, grounded, local trust and instead deals only in money from all comers. Monetisation involves another kind of trust: that the issuing authority will redeem it. The issuing authority is usually the state, classically personified by embossing the head of the emperor or monarch on the coin. In heavily monetised societies, you may not trust your neighbours, but you have to trust the state in the form of your coin. In small farm societies, it's more likely to be the other way around.

Adam Smith thought that monetised market exchange grounded in private interest expressed tendencies hard-wired in human nature, and that centralised states inevitably arose in response. I don't share that view, but I accept it's unlikely (and perhaps not wholly desirable) that small farm societies of the future will exist with complete independence from centralised states – the remnants of our present ones. I envisage that the power and reach of many states will weaken and the attraction of household farming for building economic security and local autonomies from weak states will grow. In this scenario, markets would be partially de-commodified and de-monetised in the manner of my opening snapshots, which would become more typical of economic life. This establishes a tension between state-backed land markets (see Chapter 13, 'Usufruct and the Small Proprietor', page 184) and more autonomous, less monetised local farm economies. This tension is likely to emerge from real political conflicts in the future, which I discuss in Part IV.

Trust

All four snapshots involved trust of some kind between producers and consumers. The consumer trusts, for example, in the qualities of the product or in the producer's farming practices. The more that transactions resemble modern norms of monetised, globalised exchange, the more abstract trust must become. When we pay in a store for pork raised in another country and fed on soy grown in yet another one, trust must instead be based on the architecture of governmental, legal, fiscal and commercial agreements that routinise trust-at-a-distance between strangers. This symbolic economy risks overrunning the biophysical world on which it ultimately depends.

For example, futures markets were invented in Chicago in the 1860s to solve the problem of trading grain efficiently. Within a decade of their invention, speculative trade in the futures exceeded trade in the actual grain by a factor of ten, while today such fictitious capital exceeds trading and investment capital by a hundred to one worldwide.[32] From one perspective, this is the strength of symbolic systems. They abstract from grounded local qualities like a specific farmer's wheat harvest, a bakery keeping idiosyncratic hours or a fodder-conserving keeper of pigs, creating levels of global linkage and value that enable more human action than would otherwise be possible. The problem is that this abstraction incurs debts in the biophysical world that must ultimately be redeemed by people or ecosystems, debts that by the nature of the symbolic overrun are hard to pay. The result is usually violence against people or the natural world – from bust speculators in 19th-century futures markets, to colonised peoples forced to pay someone else's debts, to any number of pervasive global crises today.

In other words, human symbolic systems like money are potentially limitless, whereas humans themselves and the physical world they inhabit aren't. If our limitless symbolic systems are allowed to drive the flow of service from this real physical world, then it's likely that the physical world and some of the people in it will suffer degradation. It seems wiser to establish trust by setting limits around our symbolic systems that are plausibly driven by the capacities of the physical world and its human inhabitants.

Illegibility

All the snapshots also involved the 'illegibility' of the small producer, by which I mean they resist being easily 'read' by governments, or other outsiders, or even by insiders. This is problematic from the perspective of capitalist economics, because it reduces measurable economic output. It could also be problematic for the would-be shopper who finds that the pork's not for sale, the bakery's closed, or there's no bakery at all. It might not be so problematic from the perspective of the farmer or the baker, or from the wider perspective that what's good for raising short-term economic output might not be good for long-term ecological health.

Still, even if there's a good ecological case for favouring producers over consumers, the resulting producerism can, like consumerism, easily become just another form of economic self-interest if it helps the cause of farmers or shopkeepers at the expense of everyone else. The only really satisfactory way of dealing with this is if enough of the population are farmers or shopkeepers themselves (farmers, mostly), so that farmers' special interests approximate to the people's general interests. There are so many ways in which a widespread turn to small-scale farming is likely to advance people's general interests that this is less problematic than it might otherwise be.

Poverty

That leads to another possible problem, however. A nation of small-scale farming is a nation in poverty. I've already discussed this, arguing that equitable small farm societies wouldn't be able to generate the levels of material plenty that we take for granted today, but they could probably generate a materially adequate way of life for most people beyond the capacities of our present unequal world.

To put it another way, maybe a world in which most people live in genteel agrarian poverty is better than our present one where so many live in deep landless poverty, while a few live in luxury. While we lost souls of 21st-century capitalism might bemoan the loss of our laptops and foreign holidays, there's another and perhaps better world of pleasure to be gained by working in the garden and engaging in such activities as raising pigs beyond the compass of the money economy.

But for all that, the suspicion lingers that a genuine small farm economy might be a hard, hand-to-mouth grind. Or conversely that it might not be hard enough.

On the first point, consider Raban's marshlanders. Most of their activities involve reworking material from elsewhere that a small localised economy couldn't itself produce. With its welders, windscreens, concrete and plastic pond liners, this is not an autonomous economy. If it were, life might be very much harder than the cheerful wheeler-dealing that Raban describes. Maybe there's scope for such a secondary economy to persist long into the future after the primary one has died – like the protagonists in Russell Hoban's post-apocalyptic novel *Riddley Walker*, who spend their days excavating things from a pre-apocalyptic waste dump. But this surely isn't an enticing basis for projecting a small farm economy of the future.

But on the second point, note the frenetic industry of the marshlanders. Though they might not be able to make windscreens or concrete from raw materials, they're not shy about generating an economic surplus however they can. If you build that up over time, then something like the present symbolic economy of an accumulative capitalism easily re-emerges. Adam Smith wrote famously in these terms of 'a certain propensity in human nature . . . to truck, barter and exchange one thing for another' which is 'common to all men'.[33] This has nourished a view of history as mere rehearsal for modern capitalism, featuring our forebears as frustrated profit-makers waiting for their opportunity to close in on the main chance.

Such views underestimate the diversity of economic ideologies across times and places. Even so, where strongly monetised market exchange exists, evidence suggests that small-scale farmers and traders are usually motivated to participate in it. Modernisers have often feared that when an independent peasantry dominates the countryside it focuses on self-provisioning, cutting off urban and industrial development, but this hasn't usually been the case. Indeed, invoking the ghost of Adam Smith's trucking and bartering bakers and butchers, left-wing movements have often been suspicious of the petit bourgeois world of small-scale farmers, shopkeepers and tradespeople not because of its poverty or simplicity but because of its acquisitiveness – small-scale farming as small-town capitalism. This misses the point that bakers and farmers aren't intrinsically any one kind of economic agent. Everything depends on how people connect with wider economic, political and cultural circuits.

From another perspective, talk of whether a small farm economy can generate prosperity or not is irrelevant. Historically, a debt-financed commercial capitalism exploded out of Europe in a colonial expansion that reorganised local economies into a global profit-maximising nexus later turbo-charged by the exploitation of fossil fuels. This has led to numerous ecological, political and economic crises, which seem soluble within the present global order only through fanciful promises to spread wealth to all the world's people while simultaneously unpicking the ecological damage that's already occurred in spreading it to a few. What's left when this illusion has passed is the possibility of a less symbolic economy, based on what people can renewably provide from the land, the atmosphere and the waterways. Whether or not we judge that economy to be prosperous by present standards is beside the point.

This viewpoint has an ancestor and champion who some might find surprising – Adam Smith.

The 'Natural' Economy

This interpretation of Smith was developed in a thought-provoking book by the late Giovanni Arrighi.[34] Smith, Arrighi argues, distinguished between the 'natural' path of economic development based on a virtuous circle of expanding domestic agricultural and manufacturing industry, and the 'unnatural' path based on long-distance colonial trade. Smith's model for 'natural' economic development was the Qing-dynasty China of his day. His model for 'unnatural' development? The colonial commercial empires of European powers like England and the Netherlands.

In this view, China represented a 'stationary state' involving a refined and technologically sophisticated but labour-intensive and resource-conserving society of domestic trade and marketing. It had no tendencies towards amplification or self-transcendence, as was the case with the European powers through their labour-saving technical innovation and militarily enforced long-distance colonial trade. The Chinese situation has been called a 'high-level equilibrium trap' (HLET) – 'trap' in the sense that its stable equilibrium didn't prompt the kind of endless accumulation and revolutionary making and remaking of the economic landscape that occurred with European capitalism, ultimately enabling Europe and its offshoots to extend its dominance over the world.

But it now seems clear that this model of endless growth and commodification is itself a trap, fuelling contemporary crises. Viewed from these present crises, the HLET of Qing China doesn't seem like such a bad 'trap' to fall into. The point I'm making is not that 18th-century China represents some acme of global civilisation that we should try to restore today, but that the basic patterning of a stable, labour-intensive, differentiated, resource-conserving market society with securely tenured agrarian labour and other practical trades provides inspiration for developing sustainable forms of economic sovereignty in the present.

The Violence of Things

The things that the baker and the pig farmer produced were immersed in unique qualities, particular values, and local knowledges both for the producers and the potential customers: good bread, well-raised pigs, care of the land, the virtues and vices of labour and so forth. These are qualitative values about provisioning that can't ultimately be reduced to a market price without being somehow violated. The household farm economy generates values and is itself a value beyond market price, which must therefore be defended politically.

These values aren't just given in the nature of the world. They involve shared human ideas, symbolic systems or symbolic economies that transcend what's immediately present physically. So while there's a good case for creating small farm societies deeply grounded in a local ecological base, this amounts to something less than arguing for an entirely 'natural' or local human ecology, the position sometimes taken up by proponents of deep ecology. Our dramatic contemporary crises suggest a need for people to find an economic spirituality that keeps them closer to their local ecological bases, but they won't necessarily find that spirituality by simply mirroring the wild or the natural.

Still, symbolic economies that stray too far from their ecological base easily become dangerous. This is the process I mentioned earlier where, crudely, people with too much money can degrade the physical world and degrade other people by drawing too much service from them. To put it more generally, turning qualitative relationships into quantities is ripe with possibility for violence. Sometimes the violence seems trivial ('it pains me to turn all the values I've invested into raising this pork into a money price'). But this dynamic is at the root of wider and more extreme violence, the violence of the impersonal sanctions that creditors and states enforce against those they consider indebted. This was the fate of Qing China's stationary state, violently subjugated in the 19th century by capitalist states that mobilised a quantitatively larger symbolic economy of money, and of numerous people today wracked by hunger, poverty, war and dispossession in the face of the same violent symbolic economy.

A lot of contemporary thinking about the virtues of the market, economic development and the mythologies we invoke to justify them – the invisible hand of the market – romanticises the benign aspects of money, debt and markets, while hiding this violence. Agrarian advocates like me are often criticised for trying to deny the poorest inhabitants of the Earth their chance of redemption through market capitalism. Meanwhile, the richest capitalist powers build virtual and, increasingly, actual walls to keep these inhabitants from a share of their riches. This violent underbelly needs more exposure.

I'm not so naïve as to think that the more optional relationship to markets afforded in small farm societies automatically banishes all violence from them. I'd simply say the sources of tension are obvious and chronic – property boundaries, inequality, gender difference, political factionalism – and require ongoing effort to defuse them. This acknowledgment strikes me as preferable to the romantic notion in capitalist society that the growth of the economy makes everyone happier. The trick is to make use of the more benign aspects of monetary and non-monetary societies, while trying to safeguard against their less benign ones.

Market Society Versus Capitalist Society

To move towards a small farm future, it's probably necessary to prevent money as the medium of exchange in market society from turning so easily into money as a more abstract form of value (capital or interest) typical of capitalist society. Is such de-abstraction even possible once the genie of the symbolic economy, in this case capitalism, is out of the bottle?

I don't know. If it is, it will require a wholly different global geopolitics than what we presently have (see Part IV). One approach to such de-abstraction is to destroy resources before they over-accrue, so they don't turn into forms of capital with a dangerous liquidity that might threaten the social order. Feasting, gifting, playing and elaborate ritual observances have been the favoured means of doing this. We see this, for example, in the ceremonialism and ritual exchanges characteristic of numerous foraging societies, and the endless saints' days and carnivals of medieval Europe. Some analysts suggest that we shouldn't think of these societies as ones that have failed to develop, but as societies that have looked into the oracle, seen what development involves, and then deliberately created institutions to ensure it doesn't happen.[35]

No doubt, there's a lot to be learned from societies that make social meaning around the idea of *enough* and the pleasures of the here and now. More modernised versions of this idea that have begun to gain ground around the fringes of mainstream politics include such things as limiting the weekly labour input of employees, or imposing finance taxes to tame the overheated speculative financial sectors of modern capitalist societies, the premier symbolic economy of today. Political philosopher Richard Dagger makes the case for a civic economy that retains market relations but prevents them from corroding into abstract capital. Dagger sets out various features of the civic economy that keep the market to its bounds in this way, including these two:

1. *Taking work and the workplace seriously.* Capitalist thinking judges work and the workplace largely by their ability to generate profit. A civic society first defines its goals, which might include an ethical conception of good work, and then judges itself in terms of their realisation. So it may consider cheapness or productive efficiency to be lesser goals than the provision of fulfilling work, limiting the death-by-competition struggle of capitalist market society. One way of doing this in a small farm society would be ensuring widespread, secure tenure of farmland capable of providing a livelihood. Outside farming, sustaining secure employment in low-carbon sectors that serve the civic economy would be another way of taking the workplace seriously. The standard criticism of this approach is that it reduces the profitability of industry and the incentives for labour-shedding innovation. In a stationary, low-carbon economy, these are advantages.

2. *Taking community seriously.* For Dagger, 'economic decisions must sometimes be regarded as public decisions because of their effects on communities'.[36] The interests of the community might sometimes take precedence over the interests of the economy. Of course, 'community' is a troublesome word. Who does it include? Who does it exclude? And what does 'it' want? These are difficult questions, but Dagger is surely right that giving markets precedence over collective decision making doesn't provide

better answers. Market transactions don't reveal our 'true' preferences any more than our actions in voting booths or the civic organisations we join.

Sometimes, introducing *more* market competition might be beneficial. For example, in the UK's highly concentrated grocery sector, there's a case for 'taking community seriously' through effective anti-monopoly measures that level the playing field between small-scale local producers and corporate retail giants. This is not about giving special help to small-scale producers, but of no longer giving special help to large-scale ones. Favouring *market* solutions sometimes amounts to disfavouring *capitalist* solutions, which are not the same thing.

But sometimes it *will* be necessary to limit competition in the public interest. Orthodox economic theory takes a dim view of such protectionism because it risks favouring monopolists who can dictate prices to their advantage in the absence of wider competition. Yet there are plenty of examples of protectionism in the present global economy, including the farm subsidies of wealthy countries that undermine the unsubsidised agricultures of poorer ones, limitations on the global free movement of labour, and intellectual property rights such as patents. If such protectionism is so rife within the global capitalist economy despite its rhetoric of open market competition, the case for protecting markets shouldn't be controversial.

Even so, just forms of market protection usually require anti-monopoly policies and low barriers to entry, which, again, in farming situations points to many small-scale, securely tenured producers. This would move protectionism towards more co-operative and internationalist models, and away from corporate monopoly. The advantage of protectionism is that it allows societies to pursue their chosen economic goals without having them undermined from without. Indeed, there's a growing movement for what Colin Hines calls in a recent book 'progressive protectionism'.[37]

Although I endorse aspects of Hines's argument, I also think there's a have-my-cake-and-eat-it aspect to his view that localised economies can still bring forth the kinds of sophisticated consumer products currently furnished by the global corporate capital economy. I doubt, for example, that a small farm society would have the capacity to produce the computer on which I'm writing these words. For those of us who think the ability of global industrial society to keep churning out such products will be increasingly limited anyway, or who measure human progress by criteria other than the ease of cut-and-paste editing, that's not a major worry. But if I had to furnish my livelihood largely from my local ecological base, I'd be sorry to see my chainsaw go. A serious debate on how to secure a realistic industrial base for a sustainable human ecology and a convivial economy is sorely needed, but it's scarcely happening currently – mostly because of the 'progressive' ideologies that police all hints of economic 'backwardness' (see Chapter 2, 'Wicked Problems', page 81).

I can't pursue that debate here, but it seems likely that in a small farm future there would be more local artisanal production supportive of the agricultural economy and pursued alongside it. It might be the kind of world that we currently recall mainly through our surnames – one of Smiths, Carters, Hedgers, Coopers, Weavers, Tanners, Wrights and Thatchers. Hopefully, we could add some new names to the list. Electrician. Plumber.

This idea of an artisanal economy needs rescuing from its associations with both high-cost contemporary elitism and sepia-tinged nostalgia. I invoke it here only because it seems more renewably compatible with the small farm societies likely to emerge from the present crises. But it's worth recalling that even within advanced modern capitalist societies, the realities of a relatively autonomous local artisanal economy aren't so distant. In the 19th-century United States, agricultural equipment companies like McCormick had to invent almost the whole modern armoury of easy credit, advertising and marketing (including marketing the idea of being 'modern', and notions of efficient modern farming) in order to wrest money from doubtful farmers. As late as the 1950s and 1960s, farm machinery from McCormick and other manufacturers still had a human-scale, almost backyard feel compared to the farm machinery of today.

At much the same time, rural retailers struggled to shift groceries in bulk to people accustomed to growing their own gardens. And countries that have experienced major economic disjunctions in recent times from the global economy – such as Cuba, Argentina and Greece – have furnished numerous examples of self-organising making do.[38] I don't make these points to suggest that it will be easy to recreate a semi-autonomous, artisanal agrarian economy, so much as to raise the possibility that there are economic resources within our existing societies and within recent historical memory that might enable us to imagine how we could – and that this might be useful in a future world that will probably demand such adjustments from us.

Around a century ago, the waning of this artisanal economy in the face of monopoly capital prompted socioeconomic movements like syndicalism, guild socialism, distributism and agrarian populism, together with academic disciplines like home economics, which contended over how to reconcile industrial development with social well-being. These movements faded with the postwar turn to a rampant industrialism underwritten by big government, big corporations and mass society, which was then seen as the optimum route for general human betterment. Despite their eclipse, they lit a path for some of the more unorthodox currents of thought among conservatives, leftists and environmentalists that have endured as a counterpoint to the dream of industrial progress.[39] Now that that dream itself has run its course, the issues they raised seem worth airing again. Some of their concerns need updating, while some are best left forgotten. But many of them speak to contemporary dilemmas and have influenced my analysis here. History hasn't progressed beyond the need for local agrarian and industrial autonomies, but delivered us into a moment when they're relevant again. Maybe it's time to re-examine some of the ideas that attended them the last time they had political currency.

CHAPTER FIFTEEN

The Country and the City

A world of small-scale household farming would involve a significant redistribution of population away from large cities and towards towns, villages and the countryside, so it seems necessary to write about the settlement geography of a small farm society. There's little point trying to specify exactly what some idealised landscape of small-scale farming would look like, since so much depends on local biophysical and human factors, and on the future history of how small farm societies emerge. All I can realistically achieve is a little groundwork, laying an alternative trail to the widespread modern view that humanity's future is inevitably urban.

One plausible reason for this modern view is that urbanisation has been a dominant force in recent global history, and the idea of reversing the flow of humanity that's added more than twice as many people to urban areas than rural ones since 1960 is daunting.[40] But it may be no more daunting than continuing to provide these urban billions with food, water, sewerage, energy, shelter, work and other necessities of urban life into the future. And since prodigious urbanisation has been an unprecedented transformation of the human condition that's occurred only recently, it's hard to dispute the possibility of heading in a different direction. People tend to go where they judge they're most likely to find peace and prosperity. In the future there's a good chance that that will generally be in the countryside.

I begin by questioning some of our modern suppositions about the virtues and vices of both the urban and the rural that implicitly shape our thinking. History has furnished us with economic and political ideologies that have pinned their hopes on either a rural or an urban life of some kind as a favoured ideal, perhaps a utopia. It's also furnished many examples of rural and urban dystopias, sometimes arising as a direct outcome of the

Table 15.1. Rural and urban utopias and dystopias

RURAL		URBAN	
Utopia	*Dystopia*	*Utopia*	*Dystopia*
Close-knit village community	Caste society, serfdom	'City air makes you free'	'City air makes you ill' – the slum
Back-to-the-land, rural communes	Maoism	'City upon a hill' Garden city Eco-city	The long footprint

drive towards utopia. Some examples relevant to the possible course of a small farm future are identified in Table 15.1.

The idea of a stable, close-knit village community is a standard of ruralist thought, a 'moral economy' of mutually supportive face-to-face relationships in contrast to the impersonal and dysfunctional city. This view isn't always fanciful, but creating uncoerced relationships with other people is always difficult, in the countryside as well as in the town, and earlier I emphasised the importance of the modern public sphere as a safeguard against village hierarchy.

Pure ruralism also risks vulnerability to the power of aristocrats and strongmen. The reduction of peasantries in medieval Eastern Europe to the status of bonded serfs has been attributed to the lack of market towns that in Western Europe checked landlord power through a semi-commercialisation of rural society somewhat along the lines of the kind of marketing arrangements for small farm society that I suggested in Chapter 14.[41]

So maybe there's something to be said for the slogan of the medieval burghers that 'city air makes you free'. Urban romanticism nowadays endlessly elaborates this modernist narrative that you can be who you want to be in the city. But despite modern advocacy for the 'vibrant' urban slum, there's little evidence for any hard geographical division between a static/oppressive countryside and a dynamic/liberating city.

In fact, there's a counterpoint to the idea that city air makes you free. City air (and water) makes you ill. High-density urban living creates prodigious public health challenges that are only remedied through costly inputs in energy and infrastructure, inputs that disproportionately benefit the better off. This process has its own geographies and histories. Early 19th-century

London, for example, drew in working people from a landlord-dominated countryside of underemployment, but was so unhealthy that it could only sustain its population through continual in-migration. By century's end, London's population came to enjoy levels of health, prosperity and welfare the envy of working people throughout the world, but largely because as the capital city of a rising global power it had exported much of the misery to its dependencies elsewhere. Even pro-urban analysts who've looked carefully at the evidence concede the depth and intractability of issues like urban poverty, underscoring the point that the violence, squalor, social breakdown and political inertia is hardly an attractive path towards human 'development'.[42] It seems even less likely to be so in the future.

An alternative strand of rural utopianism proceeds from the view that a specifically *modern* rural life could in theory be optimal, without taking a position on the lot of traditional rural dwellers. There've been any number of back-to-the-land experimenters and rural intentional communities that have put this idea to the test in modern times – sometimes quite successfully, sometimes not. Often, they've been middle-class movements in which people have used accumulated fiscal and social capital to swim individually against the current of the mainstream economy. The question is whether such experiments will remain a fringe activity or presage a wider turn towards rural sustainability in a post-capitalist future.

Perhaps endorsing such utopias of voluntary simplicity in the countryside could help prevent a more troubling counterpart – dystopias of involuntary simplicity. The obvious example is Maoism, from Mao Zedong's Cultural Revolution in 1960s China to other Maoist regimes such as Cambodia's genocidal Khmer Rouge, where urban dwellers experienced an enforced rural 're-education'. Maoism is alien to Western political thinking, but its legacy persists in many populous countries of the Global South. In the face of climate change and other crises it's entirely possible that state-centred, anti-capitalist and ruralist 'Climate Mao' regimes may arise.[43] As the consequences of global inequality and ecological crisis bite, a turn to voluntary rural simplicity sooner may prove a price worth paying to avoid involuntary Maoist simplicity later. Calls for a more rural, labour-intensive economy often get damned by association with Maoism, but ironically it may be that only by choosing a small farm future voluntarily in the here and now can we avoid having a worse one imposed by Maos of the future.

Still, for the time being voluntary *urban* middle-class utopias remain more palatable to the modern mindset. The 'city upon a hill' combining a righteous urban community with honest agrarian toil pioneered in New England by the Pilgrim Fathers has invested the thinking of many an urban visionary down to the present. A difficulty with this tradition is that it tends to involve ripping up the existing script and starting over again with a whole new geopolitics, which is problematic when, as in New England and in most other places, there are already people in place with other ideas. More recent urban utopias like the Garden City movement found ingenious ways around this to blend the best of the urban and the rural. But, as with back-to-the-land rural utopianism, they've made limited headway in the face of a capitalist geopolitics unsympathetic to dispersed and self-reliant patterns of settlement. This geopolitics has been a more powerful driver of urbanism than any rural counter-utopia, given the need for a concentrated industrial or post-industrial labour force and the prevalence of rural workers without secure access to their own land.

Other urban advocates press the claim that city life has a lower environmental impact than rural life because of its dense infrastructural linkages, such as mass transit, cycling and cheap-to-heat apartment blocks. Certainly, wherever people live high-impact modern lives it's easier to lessen their consequences a little by living them in cities rather than the countryside. But this hardly proves that mass urbanism is the optimum settlement pattern long term, especially since rural decline caused by urbanist policies underlies a good deal of rural impact. In fact, cities use resources and produce wastes and pollution disproportionate to their population size.[44] This is partly because these impacts are driven by wealthy people, who tend to live in cities, rather than from urban settlement as such. But it also seems likely that the constant destruction and regeneration of the urban built environment does increase their impact relative to the countryside.

There isn't any single optimal settlement pattern for humanity. But in a future where people are probably going to have to spread out across the world's habitable landscapes to skim their renewable bioenergetic flows, I see the various urban and rural utopias and dystopias shown in Table 15.1 as a set of inspirations and cautions to inform that process.

But let's turn from this generalised take on settlement patterns to the more specific question of resource economics or energetics. How do food and the other necessities of life get moved from their place of production to the city? And why?

In 1826, Johann Heinrich von Thünen published *The Isolated State*, one of the first attempts to analyse the spatial and economic connections between city and country. Figure 15.1 represents his analysis pictorially. The upper panel (Figure 15.1.*a*) stays fairly close to von Thünen's original; the lower one (Figure 15.1.*b*) involves some of my own modifications.[45] The figure shows a series of concentric agricultural zones around the city as the centre of a geographic circle, conditioned by the price city folk would pay for different crops, the costs of transporting them to the centre and thus the gradient of land rent.

Von Thünen's model involved a gradation from high-value, intensive, high-transport cost crops like vegetables and dairy products necessarily produced in the urban periphery through to successively lower-value crops with increasing distance from the urban centre, such as timber, cereals, rangeland livestock and – in some circumstances – trapping and hunting products.

At a time when land transport involved horses, von Thünen addressed himself to the issues of moving goods with them, feeding them, and making use of their manure for farming. If the Great Horse Manure Crisis (see 'Introduction', page 5) was ever a real crisis, the alleged fear that the streets of large cities would be buried under the manure of their equine traffic could only have emerged in super-sized cities like London with a colonial relationship to the wider world that broke the link with their local hinterlands. By contrast, for the productive zones edging von Thünen's cities, as for most organic farmers today whose mixed land usages are calibrated to productive possibilities, it was scarcely possible to have too much manure. Whether animal traction ever becomes a mainstream reality again is less important than the fact that a supposed urban manure crisis suggests a dysfunction of ecological scale, to which the invention of cars wasn't a solution but an escalation of the problem.

Von Thünen placed woodland close to his central zone. In situations where transport is costly and cities rely on wood for fuel and construction material this makes sense. In this respect, the modern view that woodland is a low-value land use best restricted to peripheral areas may not endure. In low-energy situations, woodlands and settlements are intimately related.

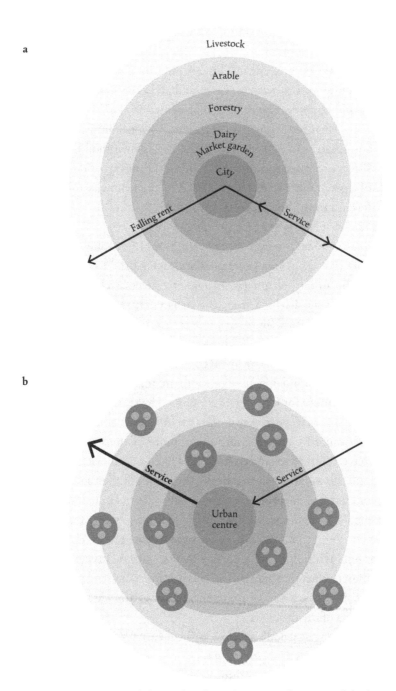

Figure 15.1. Service and the 'Isolated State'. (*a*) von Thünen model, (*b*) rural disruptors

Historian William Cronon draws on von Thünen's analysis when he describes Chicago's rise as the pioneer of global agribusiness, a lakeside intermediary between the northern woodlands and the wood-impoverished but agriculturally productive prairies, especially after railroads lowered the cost of grain transport.[46] Again, this is an indicator of ecological scaling issues in an essentially colonial situation. Chicago wasn't built to ease the burden of living as a dweller in the woodlands or the prairies but to maximise the value it could extract from both zones by linking them together and realising the value elsewhere. Chicago was a forerunner for the colonial relationship with the wider world emblematic of most modern cities, now yet further divorced from their hinterlands.

Von Thünen's model involved some deliberately simplifying assumptions, but the abstraction of his single-city state compared to networked modern cities like London and Chicago isn't a good reason to mock it, as modern commentators sometimes do. Instead it invites us to look at economic relationships and long-distance trade through more critical eyes. In mid-19th-century Germany, the 'doubling distance' – the distance a commodity could be moved before its transport costs equalled the costs of production – for potatoes was 10 miles; for wheat, 66 miles.[47] Part of the impetus for improved transport efficiency, for long-distance trade and for colonialism in modern times has been to break out of such local ecological limitations. But to whose benefit?

Permaculture enthusiasts might spot a resemblance between von Thünen's model and the zoning concept for the permaculture homestead, with the dwelling substituting for the city: the kitchen garden by the house, then orchards, poultry and maincrop vegetables, then field-scale crops and pasture, then rough grazing and woodland, and finally wilderness. Equally, aficionados of world-systems theory might spot a resemblance with the geo-historical structuring of the global economic system. The metropolitan core countries stand in the centre, a zone of high-value farming employing free wage labour around them, a semi-periphery of peasants and share-croppers in colonised countries further out, enslaved or enserfed labour in the periphery. We don't usually think of the homesteader as the colonist of their own property, but its flows of energy and material are organised primarily to the benefit of the homesteader at its centre. The similar patterning of von Thünen's model and of world-systems theory more readily reveals the colonial aspect of the city, the state or the metropolis. In the words of environmental analysts William Rees and Mathis Wackernagel: '[Cities] act as entropic black holes, sweeping up the output of whole regions of the ecosphere vastly larger than themselves'.[48]

The benefits of commercial trade in a household farm society resemble a nested, hierarchical settlement pattern: farms, villages, market towns, regional hubs, perhaps capital cities. There's a line of service and accountability moving outwards (centrifugally) from these nodes or higher-level settlements to the farms scattered across rural space. The higher-level nodes offer benefits to farmers that they can't easily furnish for themselves, such as markets, services, political order. The colonial model, on the other hand, draws service inwards to itself (centripetally) from peripheral zones, ordering rural space not in relation to what that space can renewably provide for its inhabitants, but according to what the higher-level settlement demands. Ultimately this breaks the ecological relation between settlement and hinterland altogether, producing contemporary patterns of 'development' involving a super-urbanism unrelated to local productivity or need, rural depopulation, depeasantisation and precarity. The country serves the city, the city's hinterland becomes the whole world, and therein lie many of our contemporary ecological problems.

Some analysts argue that the densely networked and globally connected aspects of modern cities make them disproportionately productive of human benefits, though others have questioned this result.[49] Indeed, with the COVID-19 pandemic, the global city suddenly lost some of its lustre as a space-erasing, physical-contact-enhancing, economic-efficiency-promoting network that connects people worldwide without firewalls, redundancies or local autonomies of the kind that are built into agrarian localism. As the complex network consequences of the pandemic rippled across the global food supply chain, new customer enquiries at my small farm serving its immediate local market increased by two orders of magnitude.

Pandemics aside, cities have been fantastic accumulators of wealth and resources but in unsustainable ways that now push the human ecological footprint beyond planetary boundaries. And they've done so inequitably, based on a colonial model of centralised resource extraction that conceals its violence through implausible ideologies of trade as mutual benefit enriching all, rather than a centripetal flow that ultimately enriches few.

Pro-urban thinkers correctly insist that no modern nation has prospered without urbanisation.[50] But this neglects not only the ratchet of the capitalist political economy that prevents other kinds of society from flourishing (see Chapter 1, 'Crisis #9: Political Economy', page 53) but also the deep roots of our modern civilisation in urbanism and trade that prevent us from seeing its hidden violence, and from taking seriously any alternatives. Some historians describe commercialism in Europe as a kind of warrior violence, hidden in the guise of trade, that was imposed on a mostly autonomous and peaceful rustic society in the early Middle Ages.[51] Others, more in keeping with mainstream views today, see a greater violence in the landlordism of rustic society, with commercialism offering a route out for ordinary people.[52] I see both commercialism *and* landlordism as rife with the potential for violence, which is why I emphasise small-scale, owner-occupied household farming along with a public sphere and an urbanism that serves farmers, rather than the other way around, as an alternative.

In Figure 15.1.*b*, I've disturbed the smooth centripetal flow of von Thünen's centralising/colonial model by drawing numerous additional centres across rural space. These disruptors could be individual, more-or-less self-reliant household farms like the 'three acres and a cow' smallholdings discussed earlier. Or they could be larger, more-or-less self-reliant rural communities, or mini statelets. The point is, to a large extent they're self-organising, building autonomies that resist the organisation of space towards a powerful centre.

The disruptors may have their own troublesome power dynamics, but these aren't necessarily more troublesome than those caused by the colonial, centre–periphery dynamics of the modern city. The trick is to try to combine features of both entities for optimum results. The advantage of local disruptors is that they minimise trade and enrich people's connections with their local ecological base, whereas trade, in the words of Rees and Wackernagel: 'reduces the most effective incentive for resource conservation in any import region, the regional population's otherwise dependence on local natural capital'.[53] This argument for local ecological feedback helps make the case for a small farm future, but again there's a need for some balance. The point isn't to eliminate all forms of trade in favour of entirely autonomous household economies, but to put some limits around trade in view of its ecological and economic dysfunctions, and to avoid a romanticising language of 'trade-ification' as inherently beneficial.[54]

The settlement pattern of a small farm future best suited to deliver less extractive relationships based on renewable local resources would probably look something like Figure 15.1.*b*, with centrifugal relations of power and service – emphasising what the countryside can draw from urban centres – balancing or exceeding the centripetal ones based on what urban centres can draw from the countryside. It would most likely be a world of farm-steads, hamlets, villages, market towns and regional hub cities, with little need for today's mega-cities. That's why I've made the centrifugal arrow of service from town to country in Figure 15.1.*b* larger than the converse centripetal one.

There are already political developments of this kind: in a new municipal-ism of smaller towns and cities stranded by super-urbanism that are trying to reconnect to their hinterlands in ecological re-localisation movements, in peasant movements and so on. Every situation is different, but it seems clear that current trends towards super-urbanism are unlikely to continue.

CHAPTER SIXTEEN

From Religion to Science (and Back)

S o far I've made the case for a small farm future by addressing the larger structures – ecological, socioeconomic, and so forth – that enmesh human lives. But any vision for the future has to engage individual motivations more personally. It has to work like a story or a song of life: this is who I am, this is what I do, this has meaning. Times of crisis and rapid change often call forth prophets to supply new stories. The best among them can discern and prefigure the shape of the emerging new reality, breathing life into it by naming its spirit or characterising its logic, while somehow relating it authentically to older stories inherited from the past that make it feel familiar and ordained.

I've already mentioned the pioneer of modern economics, Adam Smith (1723–1790), a few times. Smith was a prophet of the modern story that was beginning to fire up during his lifetime, and is probably now reaching its end. He discerned the world of globalised industrial capitalism that largely still lay in the future when he wrote and named its spirit as the logic of competition, by which the self-interest of the individual generated social progress and collective human benefit through the invisible hand of the market. In so doing he told a story that linked the disquieting new society that was emerging to more comfortable old truths, notably religious ideas of divine regulation, order, and progress towards the good that underlay the apparent chaos of human affairs.

Smith was a more complex thinker than conveyed in that thumbnail sketch, or in his undeserved reputation as an apologist for naked capitalism. Even so his story of capitalism has now outlived its usefulness.

Unfortunately, the old stories often get invested with the aura of eternal truths, and so it is with Smith. 'Practical men, who believe themselves to be quite exempt from any intellectual influence, are usually the slaves of some defunct economist',[55] in the words of the defunct economist John Maynard Keynes, and this certainly applies in the case of the defunct economist Smith whenever people claim that the inherent selfishness of human nature confounds the possibility of creating societies steadily adjusted to their ecological circumstances, or that the inventiveness of capitalism is the answer to our ecological predicaments.

So in this chapter I try to tell a new story, though without illusions that my skills as a prophet are the equal of Smith's. In it, I try to explain why people might turn widely to small-scale farming, seeing it as a sensible and life-enhancing response to present times that goes beyond mere necessity and that builds out appropriately from our present culture. In doing so I plan to keep in mind the lessons of Smith's storytelling in its melding of religious, scientific and cultural themes to tell a positive tale of human progress. Among other things, this means I want to tell a story about going 'forwards' to an agrarian future, not going 'back' to an agrarian past, though ironically this involves probing quite deeply into human history in an attempt to reveal some hidden continuities with the past.

I begin with the distinction between the ascetic and the libidinous. Asceticism involves limiting the material needs and pleasures of the body – food and drink, clothes and shelter, human company or sex, solace and comfort, wealth or material things. Its archetype is the religious hermit or renouncer, penniless, naked, fasting, alone. But elements of asceticism are often incorporated in less extreme ways into everyday life in many societies. The libidinous is the mirror of the ascetic, involving the sensory pleasures of the body in the here and now – food, wine, sex, opulence, the satiation of desire.

One story that people build around this distinction in modern life concerns green consumerism. Suppose you choose not to eat meat on environmental grounds. A common anti-environmentalist talking point is that you're virtue signalling, claiming higher social status than lowly meat-eaters through an ascetic display that showcases your focus on more transcendent issues than the pleasures of eating meat. This anti-environmentalist argument is often overplayed, but its libidinous counter-claim to ascetic self-importance is hard to dismiss altogether. Environmentalism needs a better story than the familiar cry of the fun police: 'You shouldn't do that!'

Yet while modernist culture emphasises the virtues of libidinal consumption and indicts environmentalists for their self-important asceticism, it also celebrates a modern asceticism in the form of a commitment to industrious, capital-forming labour. This is a staple of modern politics, with its endless idealisations of the virtues of hard work as a route to personal and national success, typically without acknowledging the structural reasons why some people and some countries remain poor however hard they work. This emphasis on working hard and playing hard is only one version of the good life, and its celebration of ascetic labour and libidinal consumption isn't well fitted to our times.

Perhaps it's worth contemplating its opposite: work easy, play easy. Libidinal labour, in which we take our time to enjoy the passing and immediate pleasures of convivial work, and ascetic consumption, where we're at peace with the fact that our work doesn't produce enough surplus to feast on meat, or computer games, or a round of golf every day. The modern play hard mentality may balk at this, yet psychologist Mihaly Csikszentmihalyi has reported that people are generally happier at work than at leisure despite claiming the opposite, because modern work is better than modern leisure at prompting a state of flow, in which our faculties and skills are fully engaged.[56] The stories of progress that we've inherited from thinkers such as Adam Smith tell us that we wouldn't like a small farm future because of its balance of work and play, but findings like Csikszentmihalyi's suggest this may not be true. And maybe the fact that even today many people dream of retiring to a small property in the country to grow a garden and tend animals after a lifetime of hard wage labour in the city is suggestive of that.

So while it's often assumed that an environmentalist ascetic orientation towards leisure and consumption won't play well with humans because a libidinous orientation is written into our nature, it could be that the issue isn't human nature so much as the stories we customarily tell ourselves about when and where and how we should be invoking the ascetic and libidinous sides of ourselves. Historically, one of the main contexts for ascetic performance has been in the religious and the sacred, particularly to the degree that asceticism often becomes a collective experience rather than an individual status claim. Whereas my abstinence on environmental grounds from a libidinous practice like eating pork might threaten to divide me from my community of revellers, a Jew or Muslim's abstinence from eating pork *connects* them to a community as well as a tradition and a sense of the sacred that makes the sacrifice easier. In fact, it's no sacrifice at all except in an etymological sense (sacrifice = making sacred).

Nevertheless, all aspects of human action are prone to status competition or virtue signalling, including religious forms of the sacred, which may be the ultimate form of status. People in every society create status rankings, but also critique and undermine them. Perhaps a quotation from Richard Powers's novel *The Overstory* is enough to make the point: 'So-called *Homo sapiens* fail[s] at even the simplest logic problems. But they're fast and fantastic at figuring out who's in and who's out, who's up and who's down, who should be heaped with praise and who must be punished without mercy. Ability to execute simple acts of reason? Feeble. Skill at herding each other? Utterly, endlessly brilliant.'[57] The passage suggests not only a ready truth about human pecking orders but also the readiness with which we can name and subvert them to keep status competition in check, a duality that some anthropologists argue is deeply embedded in the evolutionary history of our species.[58]

Perhaps we could define the sacred, at the most general level, as the 'stuff' around which people build their status claims and pecking orders, the thing they claim to have that makes them superior to others. For this to work, sacredness has to be in short supply, something that can be jealously guarded by its gatekeepers. Otherwise everyone can claim their piece of it and there can be no pecking order.

Let's now put this to work in a brief reflection on the history of human religion. In the early religious thought of the world's foraging and nomadic peoples, it seems likely there was typically no clear distinction between the sacred and the profane in everyday life. Humans moved in a world of spirits, of which they formed a part, and it's no accident that foraging societies are usually organised around equity and the rooting out of claims to higher status.[59] The agrarian and world religions that mostly succeeded these earlier ones represented a revolutionary break in which the divine stands *outside* the physical world that humans inhabit. Sacredness is removed from everyday life into a more transcendent realm that humans must imperfectly try to reach by going beyond their ordinary, profane existence and towards the divine.

This transcendent sacredness is easier stuff on which to build pecking orders. When people don't rub shoulders with the sacred in daily life the stage is set for high-status gatekeepers to claim privileged access to it. This was the reality of most premodern agricultural societies, with their low-status peasant farmers and their high-status priests, merchants and warrior aristocracies. Also, the rupture between the sacred divine and the everyday profane creates two main forms of religious practice or knowledge. One is a kind of self-critical humility based on acknowledging that people are flawed and ignorant seekers after a sacredness they can never fully attain. The other is a self-important claim to have got hold of a piece of sacredness beyond lowlier people.

We should also note that the great world religions – Buddhism, Christianity and Islam in particular – were, in their inception, essentially the religions of traders and merchants that took a new turn in allying with ordinary people rather than with religious and political elites. Their universalism removed people from the particularities of family, custom and place in much the same way as market trade did, and their complex theologies of sin, suffering and redemption were modelled after the actual economy of money, debt and its forgiveness. Perhaps this is another way to reprise the benefits of a money economy, despite the downsides: without the fluidity of money to dissolve it, status gets sticky and its local gatekeepers can keep too much of it for themselves. There's something to be said for religions that spread sacredness or love around as if it's as limitless as money.

Bringing the story up to the present day, the rupture between the sacred and profane worked by the agrarian religions created a secular logic that ultimately prompted their own overthrow in the form of modern science. The route to unlocking the mysteries of the transcendent changed from spiritual introspection to practical enquiry into the vastness of space-time or the minuteness of atomic and cellular architectures. I don't mean to minimise the differences between modern science and premodern religion. But it's worth emphasising a continuity. As a mode of enquiry, science in the form of the scientific method has sharpened the self-critical pursuit of transcendent religious knowledge by flawed and ignorant humans into an edifice of progressive knowledge which has been so spectacularly successful that, ironically, we've returned to a way of being not so different from an ancient world of spirits, where everyday objects like mobile phones, virtual assistants and robotic machinery work in mysterious and uncanny ways beyond the comprehension of most of us.

But in the process, science and progress have slipped the moorings of self-critical practice to become transcendent ideals, perhaps the major form of sacredness in our times. Prophets of science and progress like Steven Pinker and Richard Dawkins then present the 18th-century Enlightenment that laid the foundations for modern science as exemplary not of self-critical enquiry but of sacred truths to be defended from infidels and heretics, which is why their denunciations of religion end up sounding so dogmatically religious. The commitment to transcendent truth is basically the same.

Let me be clear that I have no objection to science as a practice of self-critical enquiry in the form of the everyday work that scientists do. The idea of science as transcendent truth, the sacredness of our times manifested in ideas like scientific agriculture or science-based policy is more problematic. I don't think commitment to science as transcendent truth will end well. To chart a different course into the future, I first want to dial back into the premodern religious past and its status orders, with particular attention to the traditions of carnival. These traditions have also been broached by the late David Fleming, theorist of a lean, localist future that in many ways resembles my vision for a small farm future. Fleming argued that, after global capitalism, successful societies will have to be built on local cultures and identities as worthwhile ends in themselves, involving the 'fortitude to affirm the place you live in as special' derived from 'the story of you and the people you know, set in the place you know, which asserts your robust presence'.[60] And he argued that one way of creating these 'stories of you' is through rituals, of which carnivals are an important historical example.

Fleming was aware that local culture and identity aren't inherently benign, as when local gatekeepers of traditions act violently against those they perceive as threatening those traditions. He was inviting us to think about how best to avoid such violence and shape local societies in a future where localism is likely to be the reality whether we like it or not. But he sometimes soft-pedalled the potential for violence in local cultures, for example in his view that carnivals promoted peace.[61] In truth, they sometimes explicitly directed violence against outsiders. In this, and other aspects, carnival openly modelled all the tensions and contradictions of local society. Medieval carnivals were often associated with trading and markets at feasts and fairs which broke open communities and mingled strangers with each other – occasions of feasting and playing, the exchanging of things and the exchanging of sex, and a jocularity that mocked notions of closed boundaries and firm identities. Carnival imagery of the grotesque emphasised bodily functions and pleasures shared among all people and animals – sex, eating and excreting. Carnival also often made an oppositional play around this point, personifying the libidinal pleasures of 'Carnival' as a fat young man with an insatiable appetite for meat and sex, contrasted with 'Lent' as a thin old woman characterised by asceticism and restraint.[62]

For the reformers of the early modern period in Europe, this was all too much. The spirituality was too vulgar and too implicated with the mundane particularities of life, and they sought to remove it to a higher plane of transcendent and respectable godliness. They were largely successful, and their version of ascetic industriousness was one of the forces behind the accumulative urge of early capitalism reacting against the capital-burning rituals of agrarian society. Modern societies have now grown wealthy on the back of that initial ascetic capitalist urge. They have rediscovered the pleasures of the flesh, considering it a triumph of modernity against tradition, while forgetting that agrarian medieval societies got there first.

There's no reason to privilege this modern version of 'work hard–play hard', and good reasons to seek alternatives. In seeking them, the status orders involved in these premodern agrarian rituals and their modern reversals are pregnant with implications for alternatives, and specifically for a small farm future.

Many premodern agrarian societies elaborated the various status orders – priest, merchant, warrior and peasant – into cultural self-conceptions, as with the medieval European distinction between 'those who pray, those who fight, and those who work'. The *varna* categories of ancient India presented a similar scheme. Anthropologist McKim Marriott classified these orders in terms of their idealised strategies for the exchange of things.[63] Table 16.1 presents a simplified and modified rendition of his thinking.

Table **16.1.** Transactional and status strategies

	GIVES	RECEIVES
Saint	√	×
Warrior-lord	√	√
Household farmer	×	×
Servant	×	√
Outlaw		
Monster		

In Table 16.1, the saint achieves status of a sacred, otherworldly kind by giving things away and receiving nothing. This is particularly the strategy of the ascetic religious renouncer. The warrior-lord achieves political honour of a profane, thisworldly kind by both giving and receiving, especially in his archetype of the king. a benefactor of public or religious works, but also an avid and perhaps predatory collector of tribute or taxes. The household farmer achieves thisworldly honour by being beholden to nobody, aiming at a self-sufficiency that neither gives nor takes. We still find an echo of that in stereotypes of the modern farmer: stingy, unimpressed by fashion, given to make do and mend. The servant's low status accrues because they receive but do not give. They're a dependent in another's household. Beyond these four categories of normal society and standing at its edge lies the outlaw. He is the archetypical bandit. He takes, using the predatory violence of the king or warrior, but gives nothing. Beyond even the outlaw lies the monster, a malevolent and almost unintelligible figure of questionable humanity at the boundaries of the known or civilised world.

The scheme in the table isn't supposed to be an unbiased accounting of what actual people in each category contribute to society. A dependent peasant cultivator serving their lord probably gives much more material service to society than the lord. Instead this is an ideological representation of status in the form of that limited sacredness that people try to access and cultivate in order to raise their standing in the human pecking order. In particular, we're looking at a common reckoning of status and sacredness in premodern agrarian societies through which people played status games by seeking to adopt an available persona and its exchange strategy. While we might think that nowadays we're 'practical people' quite exempt from such cultural influences, in truth we're not. Something similar to these personae and their strategies operates in our contemporary capitalist societies, and will probably also operate in small farm societies of the future. In other words, this status order is widely generalisable.

Table 16.2 attempts to weigh these strategies in the context of: (1) premodern agrarian societies, (2) modern capitalist ones and (3) post-capitalist agrarian societies. The ticks or crosses show the weightings I propose for each role in each type of society. For warrior-lord, I've substituted 'big man' to reference a wider sense of status achieved through extensive exchange networks, what anthropologists sometimes call 'big man' societies.[64] A big man could conceivably be a woman, but it represents a characteristically masculine kind of behaviour – the guy in the bar who buys everyone a drink and affects to be everybody's best buddy so long as they keep according him the honour and deference he expects. That, writ large and made routine, is how many states and economies operate.

In Table 16.2, I propose that premodern agrarian societies filled all six status boxes. They were full of ascetic, otherworldly saints or renouncers (Lenten figures) and also full of kings or would-be kings acting as big men (Carnival figures). They weren't short of outlaws or bandits either. Nor were they short of monsters – a category that medieval Europeans filled with Jews, 'Turks' and witches, and which was later applied by Catholics

Table 16.2. Transactional and status strategies in three different societies

	PREMODERN AGRARIAN	MODERN CAPITALIST	SMALL FARM FUTURE?
Saint	✓✓	✓	✓
Big man	✓✓	✓✓	?
Householder	✓	✗	✓✓
Servant	✓✓	✓✓	✗
Outlaw	✓✓	✗	?
Monster	✓✓	✓	?

and Protestants to each other in the wars of religion, providing a semi-racial language of grotesque otherness that became available for any demonised minority of choice. Monsters could become 'enemies within' rather than external threats.

The tricky categories in premodern agrarian societies were the house-holder and servant. A cherished aim was to be an independent householder, the 'three acres and a cow' ideal. Independent households occurred more commonly in some premodern societies than stereotypes of immiserated peasantries under the thumb of feudal domination allow. Nevertheless, people in these societies were often servants or dependents of a wealthier patron or landlord, with a consequently low social status.

In contemporary capitalist societies, the saintly Lenten figure of the ascetic renouncer has largely disappeared. An element of it persists in the honour given sports stars, mountaineers, or artists and writers who put themselves through hell to achieve transcendence. On the other hand, not much honour is accorded the green ascetics who refuse to fly or eat meat. Perhaps the figure of the scientist-scholar carries something of the renouncer spirit, the disciplined and disinterested seeker of transcendent truth who cares little for society's worldly rewards. But, then, nowadays we tend to honour science as a kind of transcendent ideal or form of sacred-ness more than a disciplined practice or a role performed by people who are simply doing a valued professional job.

Outlaws have likewise mostly disappeared from well-established mod-ern capitalist societies. There's no real opportunity for them, given the cen-tralised state's powerful reach, though they're growing at the peripheries of the capitalist world in the guise of monsters spawned by its own disorderly externalities. We see this in 'failed states' and economic basket cases, ter-rorists, drug cartels, Islamist militants and other entrepreneurs of violence. But the big man role has amplified in modern capitalism. In premodern societies, not many people had the power or resources to play it, but the essence of capitalist ideology is that we must all give and take prodigiously in the marketplace. 'The consumer is king' supposedly foments a win-win scenario in which consumers augment their status while spreading social benefit to others.

But in modern capitalism, we again confront a tension of the house-holder and servant roles. Though the rich consumer householders of today's world can easily believe their exchange relationships make them the equal (or better) of any medieval king, their dependence on interconnected global markets to deliver service reveals them to be the mere servants of these markets, precariously situated in relation to the market's global dynamics. This is all the more evident for most of the world's people, who can't pretend to be either kings or king-like consumers.

We often see the proliferation of manufactured things in the modern world as an unremarkable result of our desire for them as ends in themselves. Who wouldn't want all this cool stuff? In this, we fail to see acquisitiveness as a search for modern sacredness and social status, something the advertising industry sees all too well. Yet the accumulation of consumer goods never really works as a status strategy, because ultimately you can't buy your way past what Richard Powers called the 'fast and fantastic' human ability to create pecking orders and limit access to sacred status. The logic of capitalism as an economic strategy demands endless material growth that's ultimately impossible energetically and ecologically. Its logic as a status strategy demands endless material growth that's also ultimately futile culturally, because you can never fully buy your way to sacredness, however much you spend.

What of a small farm future? In Table 16.2, I propose a strong role for smallholding householders who, unlike their contemporary capitalist counterparts, are more truly independent. In practice, such smallholders would probably combine the figures of Lent and Carnival, the ascetic and the libertine, but in a different way to modern life. As in premodern agrarian societies, a good deal of daily life would involve belt tightening and making do. The wise householder doesn't indebt themselves or waste resources trying to build status through consuming like a king. But usually it's possible to create an adequate abundance for the small farm household. Meat on Sundays, Carnival in February, going to market, paying your way and agreeable, self-directed work rather than 'alienated, subservient and degraded work'.[65] Still, in societies with less easy abundance than the fossil-fuelled cornucopia of rich countries today it seems likely that the renouncer will return. Those who give up worldly things to pursue a path of transcendence may start to seem less holier-than-thou and more straightforwardly holy.

Put like that, the household farmer could be just another status persona, with smallholders cherishing a fierce, ascetic self-reliance and independence that allows them to look down upon flashy but ultimately servile consumers and other folks with uncallused hands. But if we succeed in creating small farm societies with widespread access to land there's a chance of avoiding a good deal of this chasing after scarce sacredness in the search for higher status. We could hope instead to establish farming simply as a disciplined and enriching vocation of practical knowledge and competence, its own kind of science, and its own kind of religion.[66] This would be the focus point for developing education and welfare policies in a small farm future.

I'm under no illusions that people won't continue to jockey for position in small farm societies of the future, just as they've always done in every other kind of society. But a society of widespread small farm householding offers us the best chance for a less alienated relationship with ourselves, with other people, with other organisms and with the Earth. Perhaps it offers an opportunity to move more easily in a world of spirits, with less concern for status competition.

On the other hand, it's also possible that the crises we face will ultimately revert us to a medieval world of warrior-lords, big men and servile peasants. Such portents of collapse and dystopia loom large in our cultural imagery, but they possibly undersell the complexity of medieval status orders, and oversell our modern escape from them. Still, it's a genuine fear. Despite their complexity, premodern agrarian societies were often casually inegalitarian because control by the few of the labour of the many comes easily in low-energy situations lacking other models to draw upon.

Some analysts argue that inegalitarian labour control was the best way for low-energy societies of the past to organise themselves and create effective social benefit and political institutions, suggesting that a return to low energy necessarily implies a return to inegalitarianism.[67] I'm not sure that's true, except perhaps from an elite viewpoint, but I doubt such inegalitarianism would serve us well in a small farm future built on the remnants of our present populous, mobile, capitalist world with its strong ideals about individual rights. The most promising future for us now is one where we try to retain some of these benefits: the formal equality of individual rights, money as a solvent of status hierarchies, the big man accorded space as an economic connector but kept on a tight political leash. The challenge is to deliver a stable, sustainable and relatively egalitarian society of smallholder householders, built on the openness of the public sphere and the exchange of things, but not destroyed by them.

But I fear that the present trajectory of capitalist societies may indeed terminate in a kind of bad medievalism. Its prophets of scientific progress like Steven Pinker share similarities with its prophets of economic progress like Friedrich Hayek (see Chapter 1, 'Crisis #9: Political Economy', page 65), allotting to ordinary people the role of servants awaiting crumbs from the table of a constantly world-transforming progress orchestrated by and largely serving a narrow big man class. Even if, improbably, this kind of progress succeeds in solving the various biophysical crises we face, it can never deliver the status and honour that people crave. This risks the blowback of populist, anti-technical 'know-nothing', possibly millenarian, revolts – the kind of dystopia depicted in novels like Kurt Vonnegut's *Player Piano* or Nigel Kneale's *Quatermass*, and which in some respects already seems under way.

A better medievalism would more even-handedly juggle the priest-renouncer, big man and householder status roles. This is the story of a small farm future. It would be absurd to try to recreate a medieval sense of status, sacredness or carnival as a model for a small farm future. But we can look to it for inspiration in its open sense of sacredness and its contesting status strategies. Perhaps as important, we can seek to cultivate the rational-technical or scientific skills in the everyday labour of the householder on the farm or in the workshop, instead of confining these skills mostly to a relatively closed caste of scientist-priests, from a handful of countries with the capital to invest in expensive technical training. Of course, I can't predict what either science or religion would be like in a small farm future, but I like to think that both would be based on a thoughtful practice of autonomy, and a resistance to high-flown people claiming that only they can mediate with the gods through churches, nuclear power stations or other elite controls over status.

This nearly brings me to the end of my story, an alternative narrative to that which Adam Smith presented, but geared to the small farm future that's upon us by exploring the dynamics of status and autonomy. If it seems no more than an over-complicated way of saying that in the future we'll have to consume less, I apologise. However, I've tried to show that reduced consumption might not be a simple matter of necessity, but a complex matter of cultural fulfilment. Therefore, the idea of a lower-energy and lower-consumption future might be more than just a futile environmentalist exhortation destined to crash into the real-world rocks of Adam Smith's 'propensity in human nature to truck, barter and exchange'. Smith tried to make the emerging trends of his times intelligible by relating them to a story about human nature, underlying order and community benefit. I've tried to do the same by emphasising the propensity in human nature to seek status, sacredness and autonomy. These aren't a weaker basis for a story than Smith's. If anything, they go deeper into humanity's soul. Perhaps if we balance their inherent tensions well, we'll be able to create a small farm future where, in attending mostly to their own practical competence in providing lovingly and adequately for their households with minimal external dependencies, people will be led as if by an invisible hand to promote the wider public interest of a socially egalitarian, economically sustainable and spiritually fulfilled society.

But the notion that we can change the world through telling stories can be overplayed, because the world is also conditioned by institutions and structures that resist change. This is another story, which I take up in Part IV.

PART IV

Towards a
Small Farm Future

Man cannot control the current of events. He can only float with them and steer.

Otto von Bismarck

CHAPTER SEVENTEEN

The Supersedure State

E ven the most sympathetic reader might by now be wondering how
the small farm future I've been trying to construct throughout the
book could possibly arise from the unpromising political present. For it's
surely unlikely that the governments of the world will collectively engineer
a wrenching change of course to the capitalist juggernaut and nurture a
distributed economy of rural horticulture.

I have to concede that's true, though perhaps it's not quite as unlikely as
at first it seems. It's possible that a combination of emerging crises, along
with the realisation among electorates that mainstream political promises
are irredeemable within the present global political economy, will impel
a new generation of politicians to implement a green new deal involving
rapid decarbonisation, land reform and reinvigorated, distributed rural
economies. Already, radical political parties of various colours are making
electoral gains against more traditionally centrist parties supportive of the
neoliberal status quo. Political change is in the air.

But it still seems unlikely that existing states will be able to deliver a
small farm future, or else rescue the present global order from the crises
enveloping it. This is partly because the depth and speed of these crises
isn't prompting the degree of radical rethinking that's needed to overcome
them. It's also because the very structure of the modern state itself is part of
the problem (see Wolfgang Streeck's consolidation state argument, Chapter
1, 'Crisis #9: Political Economy', page 66). We seem to be living in an age
of zombie liberalism. Neither right-wing versions – that price-responsive
markets will progressively solve current problems – nor left-wing versions
– that justice-responsive governments will progressively solve current
problems and fairly distribute the economic surplus – show any vital signs,

yet they still dominate the political scene. The desire to turn the clock back on the undead politics that generated the presidency of Donald Trump in the United States and similar figures elsewhere is understandable, but it's more productive to acknowledge that the zombie can never be revived and to search for other sources of renewal.

The alternative farming movement generally responds to political shortcomings with bottom-up local transformation. There are countless such projects globally, but probably not enough to bring about the degree of change necessary, not least because of the hostile policy environment they face top-down. While I'm sympathetic to bottom-up change – and like to think I'm involved in it myself – it's therefore necessary to seek larger political contexts within which it can propagate.

So here I turn my attention to those larger political contexts. I'm not looking for false optimism, neat resolutions or unrealistically upbeat endings. Nor am I looking for ways to convince electorates or consumers to vote for small-scale agrarianism. That's unlikely to happen. Still, small-scale agrarianism of some kind *does* seem likely in the future. In what follows, I try to unpick that apparent contradiction, laying out a political path towards better forms of small-scale agrarianism in the hope that it might help efforts in the here and now to avoid worse ones.

How, then, can small farm societies arise out of present circumstances? The exact answers will depend from place to place, but in general they'll be based on building local autonomies from centralised state and market power, the kinds of disruptors shown in Figure 15.1.

Maybe that's not much of an answer. Few local autonomies remain anywhere in the world today, perhaps least of all in the wealthy countries. And of those wealthy countries, my home country of Britain is among the sorriest of the lot, lacking the historical continuity of small-scale agrarianism that clings on in pockets in the Americas, and lacking the local food cultures and peasant traditions that cling on in parts of Europe. Both victor and victim of early modernisation, with few signs of post-industrial or post-imperial renewal that enable it to do more than clutch grimly to its accumulated historical privilege, Britain is a microcosm for the difficulties that lie ahead.

It would be easy to contest that view by listing some of the many inspiring people, projects and organisations working towards more sustainable local economies and food futures in Britain and elsewhere, but I think it would be ultimately unconvincing because their tenacity only underlines how paltry the autonomies are. A more likely path towards building local autonomies is through necessity in the face of emerging biophysical and social crises, many of which are likely to prompt political crisis, including the declining legitimacy and reach of the centralised state.

The outcomes of such political crises will be uncertain and possibly ugly, demanding much of our collective energies and ingenuity to turn them into something positive. But they'll be different from present politics, and that's what I want to work with. The different futures that tug most insistently at our emotions, the ones that are endlessly rehearsed in our fictions and dramas, are collapse, anarchy on the streets or civilisational breakdown. This invites the ridicule of techno-progressives and their views of an upward-trending future. More interesting than this unholy dualism of collapse or techno-utopia, and probably more likely, are medium-term scenarios of decline and retrenchment – a decline in capital and energy availability more than a decline of civilisation or culture. A couple of possible scenarios are what I call 'fortress north' and the 'supersedure state'.

Fortress North

Probably the more likely of the two, 'fortress north' involves the wealthy countries of the Global North defending what they've got. This is essentially what's happening currently, with increasingly regulatory and militarised borders in key interfaces between the rich world and the poor world – USA–Mexico, North–South Mediterranean, Saudi Arabia–Yemen – and a global neoliberal framework that disadvantages poor countries vis-à-vis rich countries and, within countries, poor people vis-à-vis rich ones.

But it's hard to see fortress north benefiting many people, except the very wealthiest, and perhaps not many of them. As political analyst Leon Fuerth put it in relation to the climate crisis:

> Governments with resources will be forced to engage in long, nightmarish episodes of triage: deciding what and who can be salvaged from engulfment by a disordered environment. The choices will need to be made primarily among the poorest, not just abroad but at home. We have already previewed

the images, in the course of the organisational and spiritual unravelling that was Hurricane Katrina. At progressively more extreme levels, the decisions will be increasingly harsh: morally agonising to those who must make and execute them – but in the end, morally deadening.[1]

Indeed, as Katrina and earlier the Dustbowl showed, citizenship in a rich country isn't enough to protect people, especially poor people, from neglect or immiseration at the hands of their own government in circumstances of environmental crisis.

A larger problem with fortress north is that it's likely to sustain existing patterns of energy and resource use – the scramble for tight oil and other mineral reserves among them – merely delaying and exacerbating a time of reckoning. Another is that it's fundamentally unjust. Some might argue that justice is a dispensable luxury when there aren't enough seats in the lifeboat, but it's debatable if even pure self-interest is best served by battening down the hatches. When power blocs pursue blatantly 'me first' policies, the result is often war – and in war situations the ultimate victor is rarely certain.

Even without all-out war, the near future is likely to see local and global migrations, mostly climate-induced, on an unprecedented scale. Militarised attempts to control them will likely prompt increased authoritarianism, surveillance and economic contraction that are worse for their supposed beneficiaries in the wealthy countries than the problem, even if successful in their own terms. And the chances are high that they won't be successful, with consequences that could be worse still.

A world in which millions of people feel impelled to seek a tolerable life by moving from their natal lands doesn't seem intrinsically desirable to me. But rather than unjust, futile and politically dangerous border mobilisations to stop it, I'd argue that we should take seriously the 'human right not to have to migrate' by trying to mitigate the environmental drivers, economic inequalities and social injustices behind mass migration. It's probably too late to do this adequately to prevent large-scale migration from happening anyway. In a world of rising temperatures, melting ice caps and melting global capital reserves, it seems likely that a lot of people will be moving away from the mostly coastal mega-cities where jobs serving the nodes of global capital will be increasingly thin on the ground, and indeed where ground itself will be increasingly thin on the ground. For rural areas, that means there'll be a lot of incomers from near and far looking for agricultural land on which to make a living. It's not hard to imagine the problems this could cause. But, following the permaculture dictum that 'the problem is the solution', it's worth trying to imagine the problems it could solve.

The Supersedure State

The situation I've just described might conform to what I call the supersedure state. 'Supersedure' is a term I've borrowed from beekeeping, where it can refer to an unusual situation of queen succession. Normally, when worker bees decide that an old queen is no longer fit for purpose they create special queen cells and carefully raise up a batch of new queens. When the new queens are almost ready to hatch the old queen heads off into exile with a few loyal servants. The first new queen to emerge kills her sisters, and the new regime is installed. This, give or take a few details, is also roughly how political succession occurs in many human societies. But in a supersedure situation, the queen dies or otherwise goes off duty unexpectedly, before the workers have a chance to bring new queens through. They do the best they can, improvising new queens out of the worker cells. The queens thus produced are usually weaker than the genuine article, but they're better than nothing under the circumstances.[2] This situation of the supersedure state – making do under the bad circumstances bequeathed us by zombie liberalism – is, by analogy, what I suggest human societies now need to attempt as best we can.

Globally, there are a few centres of political and economic power whose influence seems unlikely to disappear any time soon – the United States, China, Western Europe, Russia – together with other regional powers like Australia, India, South Africa and Brazil. Fractally within each centre, there's a centre–periphery structuring of territorial-political space similar to the one shown in Figure 15.1. This is usually organised around the capital or major city or cities. In the United States, for example, the focus is the northeast – Washington, DC, and New York City in particular – and, to a lesser extent, the West Coast cities. In the United Kingdom, the focus is England, and in England the focus is the southeast, especially London.

It seems likely that under the force of the various crises outlined in Part I, the power of these centres – manifested materially in control of energy and capital, and culturally in political legitimacy – will decline. They'll be less able (though not completely unable) to control and co-opt the territorial space nominally within their jurisdiction, and less able to draw or give service, such as taxes and state welfare services, from or to their peripheries. This will open the way for people in the peripheries to develop local political organisation with some autonomy from the weakening state centre. Already, municipalities like Preston in northwest England have gained attention by trying to regenerate their economies and reconnect with their hinterlands, with less reliance on central government or world market solutions. But this falls a long way short of complete autonomy, and since there isn't any other fully worked out political alternative to the waning liberal state it's doubtful that Preston or larger regional blocs will break completely from London. We're witnessing supersedure, not secession. I use the term 'state centre' to refer to these weakening but still powerful remnants of the old political order we're likely to see in the future, usually based around the old capital cities and the wealthy regions surrounding them that remain loyal to them, and where the familiar trappings of economic and political power remain concentrated.

The conservative journalist and politician Boris Johnson has framed this bluntly in economic terms: 'I am sure they are an estimable bunch, but Preston Council are not the locomotive of the UK economy.' For Johnson, this accolade goes to London, which, in his words, 'is to billionaires what the jungles of Sumatra are to the orangutan. It is their natural habitat.'[3]

Interestingly, Johnson became British prime minister after an election that tilted in his favour largely thanks to voters in northern cities defecting from their traditional support for leftist parties because of his promise to deliver Britain's exit from the European Union – another supersedure, perhaps, and one that ironically seems certain to further hasten the economic decline of England's north, at least in terms of conventional economic development. This result involves Johnson's government in a difficult balancing act between its natural affinity for the billionaires of London and its refractory new constituency in the north. If it and its successors can pull this balance off long term, then my analysis of the supersedure state will be disproven, at least for Britain. But I doubt they can, and I'm not ready to withdraw my analysis yet. As this book is going to press, tensions between municipal, regional and national politicians in the United Kingdom and elsewhere in the world concerning not only the COVID-19 pandemic but also worldwide protests arising from the Black Lives Matter movement in the United States suggest on the contrary that the balancing act is already getting harder, even before the political, economic and ecological blowback of present crises is fully apparent.

So in supersedure situations, state centres can still direct resources outwards to serve their interests, but they're limited in their ability to fully organise their peripheral zones. In the future, it seems likely that their capacities to project resources will further diminish, prompting graduated retreats by the state into its core geographic territory. Already, state centre politics in some places – including the United States and England – is assuming more of a symbolic and self-referential character than the characteristics of a rational, modern, managerial state that reaches out into the economic fabric of local life. Its concerns are with 'making America great again', 'taking back control', combating 'fake news', ending 'vassalage' to the European Union, controlling immigration and gesturally reinvesting in fossil fuel industries in the face of climate change. In the United States, while state and national politics still sometimes entertains the possibility that climate change is a hoax worked by scientists, environmentalists or the Chinese government, city politicians in places like Miami are left to figure out how to deal with the rising sea levels threatening to engulf their jurisdictions.[4]

The already daunting in-tray of such local politicians is likely to get worse with diminishing fiscal flows from the centre, diminishing local abilities to raise or pay taxes in the face of economic crisis and, in some areas, increasing migrant flows. In this situation, it becomes necessary for local people and politicians to improvise new kinds of political economy. This has already been happening around the world in disparate situations: Greece's 'liminal' commoning in response to its deep financial crisis discussed earlier (see Chapter 13, 'Usufruct and the Small Proprietor', page 185); the mobilisation of neighbourhood councils of slum dwellers in El Alto, Bolivia, during the gas conflict with the government; mobilisation around local nutrition and food security in Belo Horizonte, Brazil; Cuba's 'special period' in 1990s; the aforementioned case of Preston, England.[5]

These are but a few examples. In the worst cases of state failure, often prompted by climate change-induced 'natural' disasters, the state often enters the fray in the form of militarised authoritarianism and disaster capitalism, both of which are opposed by the 'disaster communism' of local self-help – what Rebecca Solnit calls a 'paradise built in hell'.[6] This is a key battleground of the supersedure state.

Local self-organisation is inspiring, but it's mostly not yet oriented to any thorough reconfiguration of local food production and farming economies, probably because food itself remains relatively easily available through global market routes and because of the persisting disjunction between urban and rural hinterland. Still, looming ecological and economic crises suggest that feeding people in places like Preston may soon no longer be the foregone conclusion it currently is, pushing them towards the need for true local autonomies.

If that happens, we'll be eyeing a supersedure situation, and a confluence of political, economic and food crises. In Britain, it would be another iteration in the cycle of alternative agriculture described by Joan Thirsk[7] (see Chapter 6, 'A Note on Alternative Agriculture', page 116), where the pre-crisis emphasis on producing capital-intensive and labour-extensive grain and meat for non-local use will come under intense local pressure. The alternative is diverse, labour-intensive, energy-light production for local use. A garden future, a small farm future.

Something like a supersedure situation occurred in China in the 1960s, and, for better or worse, underlies the rise to its current global influence. The disastrous economic policy of Mao Zedong's Great Leap Forward in the 1950s led to widespread famine and distress, destroying the credibility of the local state in the form of communist party cadres, which were further weakened by the subsequent Cultural Revolution. This leadership vacuum created circumstances of considerable local economic autonomy, particularly in rural areas, and out of this emerged a local industrialism and peasant entrepreneurialism that predated and shaped the policies of Mao's successor, Deng Xiaoping. Deng's economic reforms are widely credited as the top-down cause of China's economic miracle, but bottom-up dynamism in the semi-chaotic circumstances of Mao's rule was more to the point.[8]

This raises the spectre of the bottom-up reinvention of capitalism by local peasant entrepreneurialism. But everything depends on context.

China's centralised state co-opted and amplified its local dynamisms, and was able to place it on the global economic stage through circumstances that seem unlikely to repeat themselves elsewhere in a world entering economic and ecological crisis. Perhaps a better lesson comes from an earlier point in China's history: a chronic or long-term 'high-level equilibrium trap' with expensive resources and capital, abundant labour, and effective local markets (see Chapter 14, 'Going to Market', page 198). As I argued earlier, this situation is less of a 'trap' than most of its alternatives.

But exactly how a supersedure situation plays out in any given place depends greatly on the shaping of local politics. Here's a possible scenario:

1. The demand for both luxuries and necessities, including food, is only partially met by resources flowing from state centres. This calls forth local supply.
2. Rising energy, resource and capital prices and high or rising local populations create economic distress and a large local supply of labour.
3. These circumstances combine to create a high demand for agricultural land with an inflationary effect on price. This is offset by wider demonetisation and the crisis of capitalism's symbolic economy that currently holds agricultural land prices at artificially high levels relative to returns from farming.
4. In populous supersedure states there would be a low land-to-labour ratio. Efficient production would tend towards tight farming and commons, with private owner-occupation or secure tenancy on small, substantially self-reliant farms.

The critical social question revolves around points 3 and 4. At present, landownership in many wealthy countries is concentrated, but landowners generally lack decisive political or economic power *as* landowners. Landownership is a result rather than a basis of power, or a historical hangover from a landed past. The important thing in a supersedure situation is to unlock land concentration as a matter of citizenship rights. Urban–rural or international migration arising out of the crisis conditions prompting the rising populations (see point 2) could create the necessary pressure for that unlocking, so long as citizenship rights aren't restricted to privileged 'here first' minorities. The temptation to restrict citizenship in this way – the fortress north approach – is always strong. But in situations of pervasive global crisis it might be easier to resist, especially if it's true that modern civilisation is transcending violence, as some people claim. One way or another, this view soon seems set to undergo rigorous testing.

Turning broadscale land holdings into smallholdings may not be so hard to do in light of changing economic demands on land, since large-scale farmers tend to see land as a commercial factor of production which they wouldn't retain for the sake of it with these changing demands. There are well-established procedures for compensatory land reform that could bring such farmers onside.[9] The complicating factor is that land can be a high-value capital asset, which could make landowners want to hang onto it. It's possible that a landowner class might form in alliance with the local or centralised state, imposing quasi-feudal domination and Ricardian rent on relatively powerless, underemployed and landless citizens and newcomers.

But there are various factors pushing against this outcome. The grip of central political power would be weakening in a supersedure situation. In wealthy countries, where capitalism and modernity are entrenched, that power or its memory will probably remain strong enough for it to project itself territorially as rational-bureaucratic governance rather than the private power of local landlords or big men. Also, there would still be a strong if diminishing urban framing to social life that would make it harder to hold people in rural subjection. The dangers to the urban state centre of hosting multitudes of disaffected poor and landless people may be enough to stymie alliances between local state actors and aspiring rural aristocrats. Most importantly, there would still be the legacy of the painstakingly assembled public sphere (see Chapter 12, 'Households, Families and Beyond', page 171) in which individual human rights hold their own against mere power or status.

So in this kind of supersedure situation, large-scale landholding by wealthy absentee owners would probably come to seem unattractive in the face of the weakness of state centres to underwrite it. In a country like Britain where there's considerable landownership by a remnant aristocracy with semi-local loyalties, matters may be more complicated. But such landowners might find that serving their local society and selling land or renting it on favourable terms to small-scale tenants is the most attractive possibility. This, after all, is what many of their medieval and early modern forebears did.

Even so, there's a danger that a supersedure state might replicate economically sapping forms of landlordism and rent extraction. The best way to prevent this is probably by buttressing a public sphere geared around a human right to land. That may be more easily achieved in supersedure situations because the idea that the capitalist growth economy can deliver prosperity for all will no longer be credible. The onus will be on individuals and communities within the supersedure state to deliver it for themselves.

Betting the Farm:
Defending the Supersedure State

How would a supersedure state defend itself from its enemies? The answer first requires an analysis of who its enemies are.

The most persistent point of tension for any supersedure state would be the relationship with its declining state centre. It would doubtless have to take a firm stand on many issues vis-à-vis the centre, but not to the point of open military conflict, because it would lose. This needs stating plainly. Radical theorists of eco-anarchist secession sometimes extol the virtues of citizen militias for defending the realm, but this is surely illusory. True, dedicated guerrilla cadres with intimate local knowledge and the enormous motivation of defending their farms and homes can be a long-term thorn in the side of would-be invading states, as has been repeatedly demonstrated through history. But if state centres with standing armies want to assert control badly enough, history also demonstrates that it's ultimately hard to stop them.

In worst-case scenarios, the state centre will deploy its full battery of warplanes, artillery and (these days) drones, and surveillance apparatus against its own rebellious peripheries. This happened when General Franco called in Luftwaffe airstrikes against Gernika during the Spanish Civil War, and more recently with the Assad regime and its allies' onslaughts against civilian resistance in Syria. In earlier ages, states employed foreign mercenaries without local loyalties to put down regional revolts. Time and again, the hierarchical and concentrated political, economic and military power of state centres has found successful ways to prevail against the more distributed and networked power of citizenries. We remember the occasional exceptions to this precisely because they're so unusual. Even then their success often results from revolutionaries adopting the methods of the state centre, with unhappy later results.

The more likely way for supersedure states to thrive in the face of state centre hostility is to practise what theorist of peasant anarchism James Scott calls the 'weapons of the weak', the 'arts of resistance' and the 'illegibility' of local rural economics to central state penetration. This involves finding at the level of the political community equivalents to the individual peasant skills of 'foot dragging, dissimulation, desertion, false compliance, pilfering, feigned ignorance, slander, arson, sabotage and so on'.[10] It may be necessary for supersedure states to form citizen militias and engage in a certain amount of symbolic sabre-rattling as a part of those arts of resistance to dissuade state centres from going to the trouble of hostile engagement. Given their waning power, that may not be so hard to do.

More important than militias is, once again, the universalist public sphere. Franco could call in his airstrikes because his foes were beyond the pale for his administration, with no seat at the table; this is more or less the definition of war. By contrast, the English Peterloo Massacre of 1819, in which government troops killed fifteen peaceful protestors, prompted a crisis of political legitimacy for the British government. And yet there was far greater carnage going on in its slave colonies and elsewhere in its burgeoning empire at around the same time. Amid hierarchies of state power, some lives matter more than others. In restraining state centre violence, nothing is more powerful than an insistence on shared human rights.

Another possible threat comes not from the 'home' state centre, but from rival ones. This seems less likely, except for people in the unfortunate position of occupying border spaces between centres, places like present-day Crimea, Kashmir and Kurdistan. Whereas state centres have a strong record of quashing dissent in their backyards, the history of foreign adventurism is more spotty. The United States, which probably has the strongest claim in world history for truly global dominion, achieved many victories through hard and soft power during the 20th and early 21st centuries. But the failures of its hard power in Vietnam, Afghanistan and Iraq, and of soft power in relation to other blocs like Russia and China, signal its limits, and perhaps its future decline. I see plenty to fear for the future in the machinations of United States, European, Russian and Chinese power, but outright military invasion actually comes low on the list.

A greater threat than invasion by soldiers is probably invasion by capital. Historian Steven Stoll describes, for example, how Appalachian agrarians fended off an army raised by Alexander Hamilton in the 1790s to impose a tax on their whiskey production, but failed to fend off the coal-mining entrepreneurs who ultimately destroyed a possibility of a smallholding livelihood in those same mountains: 'An army could invade but never dominate the mountains. Capital moved differently. It acted through individuals and institutions. It employed impersonal laws and the language of progress. Mountain people knew how to soldier and hunt, to track an animal or an enemy through the woods. But few of them could organize against an act of the legislature or to stop a clear-cut.'[11]

So it's worth thinking about how capital might move into and challenge a future supersedure state. Probably the least threatening way is through rural gentrification, when wealthy people buy smallholdings or even largeholdings and set themselves up in farming. By doing so, they make themselves part of the supersedure state's political community and subject to its jurisdiction, thereby giving it the opportunity to keep their landlordism in check. I don't discount the dangers of such landed economic power parlaying itself into political power, a reinvented aristocracy, but in a supersedure situation of substantial abandonment by state centres and a strong emphasis on shared local self-reliance, the chances of overcoming such moves are good.

The same applies with yet greater force to absentee large-scale landlordism. Presently land prices are high in countries like the United Kingdom partly because they're a juridically and economically safe bet for the global wealthy to park money. That would be much less true in a supersedure situation. Wealth would want to stay closer to the centre. So billionaires would prefer the natural habitat of London, just as orangutans prefer the jungles of Sumatra. It is an especially apt comparison from Prime Minister Johnson, as in both cases their habitats are diminishing, threatening the extinction of the species.[12]

The penetration of footloose capital – as happened in Appalachia – is more problematic. Places with substantial, recoverable mineral deposits are probably going to be out of luck – and as capital seeks increasingly tight and fragmentary mineral and fossil fuel reserves, there's a danger that its disruption to local human ecologies will become even more widespread.

Already, there's a kind of militarised envelope for global energy, mineral and logistics flows that destroys civil society and the possibilities for even the most basic form of decent life for the civilians who are unfortunate enough to be caught up in it – in Iraq, the Democratic Republic of Congo, Brazil, Honduras and many other countries besides. It is what philosopher Étienne Balibar describes as the division of the world into 'life zones' and 'death zones'.[13] Ironically, this fuels part of the global migrant flows that are perceived as a threat to wealthy countries; in a sense, it spreads the dysfunction back to its origin. The main sources of hope here are a declining viability of resource extraction, or a faltering of global capital that outruns its ability to fund militarised resource extraction, or the rise of post-capitalist economies and public spheres strong enough to challenge it.

Another possibility is that once the destructive energies of present crises have worked themselves through, the world will repeat something like the cycle of capital formation that forged the modern world system from the 15th century to the present. With the unravelling of the present global economy into more disparate state centres, and with many people living lives of relative agrarian self-sufficiency in their peripheries, there's a chance that the history of land grabbing, enclosure, labour coercion, industrialisation, trade wars and trade treaties that's occurred over the last half-millennium will repeat itself – not in its exact details, of course, but in its general shape.

This is possible in the longer term. It's made less likely by the greater balance of economic forces across the globe: there are no more Americas to 'discover', no more continents of mineral and agricultural riches to be colonised, monopolised and cashed out on by European seaborne empires in a quest for global power. Doubtless it's for this reason that the capitalist urge today has become extra-planetary, with its dreams of asteroid mining and space colonisation.[14] Cultivating a historical memory of how violent and ultimately dysfunctional the first historical episode of capital formation proved may help to prevent the misery of a second instalment.

There's little that agrarians in supersedure situations will be able to do about most of these capital-penetration threats. I can offer only two possibilities beyond what I've already suggested. The first is to keep the lid on capital locally by tying it firmly to more-or-less sustainable cycles of production, to localism and dwelling in the land. Historian Ellen Meiksins

Wood has argued that the glories of democratic Athens emerged after the statesman Solon outlawed debt-peonage and created an alliance between peasant-citizen small-scale farmers and reformist elements within the aristocracy.[15] An enduring supersedure state might need a latter-day Solon to outlaw or at least to limit debt-collateral, preventing people from raising liquid capital against the security of a farm estate and then putting it to work in any number of ways that undermine local agrarianism. A supersedure state can't allow people to bet the farm.

For that to work – and this is the second possibility – agrarians would have to convince themselves and others that their way of life was basically agreeable. They would have to overcome the 'language of progress' with a different narrative. Steven Stoll describes how important the battle for narrative control is: whereas Appalachian agrarians were once admired for their hardiness and vigour as pioneering frontier folk, their public representation changed over the course of the 19th century to a racialised image of degeneracy, the hillbilly. Too many representations of the joys and sorrows of agrarian life today traverse similar ground.

When I first presented some of these ideas on my blog, one commenter suggested that if I wanted to create an enduring peasant republic I'd better figure out how to build a wall around it. Of course, that would be impossible. But it would also be unnecessary. The polities that really invest in walls – from ancient China to the contemporary United States – are always large in scale and centralised. That's not to say there'd be no external threats to a supersedure state. It's that the walls such states would need to build would be subtler than physical ones. They would mostly be economic, sociological, cultural and psychological – and they would probably be at least semi-permeable to most kinds of people, but impermeable to most kinds of money.

CHAPTER EIGHTEEN

From Nations to Republics

In order to put the case for small farm supersedure states on a firmer political footing, it's important to briefly examine the political traditions we can build on to deliver such a future, and ones we probably need to lay aside.

A good deal of politics in the modern era has focused around the conflicts and concords between classes standing in different economic relations with each other – peasants, landless workers, entrepreneurs, capitalists, manufacturers, salaried professionals and landowners. I can't possibly summarise the vast historical complexities of this process, but I think it's fair to say that the main political traditions emerging out of it – the ones that have dominated politics in the modern era – have stressed that the conflicts and concords between economic classes drive social progress, and that this progress has prompted the decline and increasing irrelevance of peasants and small-scale farmers to modern life.

This applies both to pro-capitalist and anti-capitalist political thought. Among the latter, the disdainful view of peasantries and small-scale farmers associated with most currents of Marxism has been particularly influential. In 1899, the Austrian Marxist Karl Kautsky formulated what he called 'the agrarian question', which asked: 'In what ways is capital taking hold of agriculture, revolutionizing it, smashing the old forms of production and of poverty and establishing the new forms that must succeed?'[16] Most analysts – pro- or anti-capitalist – still frame their thinking about small-scale agrarianism in similar terms, assuming its demise at the hands of global capital is inevitable and, usually, desirable.

But I'd argue the time is upon us to pose a new agrarian question that asks in what ways local, low-impact, labour-intensive, non-capitalist agrarianism might take hold after capital has smashed itself. Even Marxist critics of peasant agrarianism like Henry Bernstein have started to feel their way towards this new agrarian question:

> *Advocates of the peasant way argue that it does not represent nostalgia – worlds we have lost – but that contemporary peasant movements incorporate and express specific, novel and strategic conceptions of, and aspirations to, modernity, and visions of modernity alternative to that inscribed in the neoliberal common sense of the current epoch. This is a plausible thesis, always worth investigating in particular circumstances, but [its] principal weakness . . . is its lack of an adequate political economy.*[17]

I've done my best in this book to sketch that adequate political economy, but I'd argue that the shoe is now on the other foot. The thesis that further de-peasantisation, urbanisation and industrialisation are the best ways to deliver long-term human well-being is worth investigating in particular circumstances, but it no longer seems plausible as a general prescription for human development.

Instead, I'd emphasise the need for the 'recaptured garden' (see Chapter 3, 'The Return of the Peasant', page 93), where access to small plots of land buys relief for workers subject to the pitiless dynamics of global capital. As the economic and environmental dysfunctions of these dynamics spread, it seems likely that an increasingly large proportion of the world's people will want to buy out of the global capitalist economy as best they can. Globally, we're going to be reinventing peasantries – in fact we already are.[18] And I think it *will* be peasantries, in the plural – people responding to their local situations in many different ways, albeit with a similar focus on creating local livelihoods from the land – rather than a globally unifying process of further modernisation and class consolidation.

Of course, there's always class conflict and jockeying around economic resources in every society. The same will be true in a small farm future. But if we continue to see economic class conflict as the major 'progressive' force driving humanity 'forwards' out of farming and into urban-industrial prosperity, we badly misunderstand the forces shaping the world to come. It's time for other stories.

In fact, there's long been another story – and perhaps a more power-ful story than class – claiming people's loyalties in the modern world: the nation. Many historians regard the Peace of Westphalia that concluded Europe's brutal Thirty Years' War in 1648 as the start of a modern interna-tional system of state sovereignty, in which each state has exclusive jurisdic-tion over a bounded territory – a world of nations ruled by nation-states. Prior to Westphalia, and for a long time afterwards, the political field in Europe was peopled with a wider range of entities claiming sovereignties of one kind or another: city-states and city leagues, small principalities, reli-gious authorities, various remnants or reconfigurations of larger empires, and sovereign monarchies like France and England. It's possible that more fractured forms of political sovereignty like this will return, and in many ways the supersedure state would fit that situation.

But the nation has a larger emotional pull that may also persist long into the future. Its key idea is of cultural unities that create 'a people' rather than a random collection of individuals. The curious thing is that historically this was rarely the reality on the ground. After Westphalia, it took centralised states centuries of military, police, cartographical and intellectual labour to breathe organic life into the idea of the nation-state. It was a process of 'inventing' national traditions and histories, 'imagining' a national community through creating national memories, literatures, languages, memorials and media, and creating the idea of humans as a mass force, a population, transcending their individual animal natures.[19] The victory of the nation lies in how self-evident all this now seems, rather than something that was painstakingly constructed.

Even so, the victory is partial. In most places, there are counter-narratives involving different stories about how the nation should be constituted, different historical memories, and different cultural accents. In the 1950s, Leopold Kohr advocated for political disunion: Scotland, Wales and England instead of Great Britain; Croatia, Serbia, Slovenia, etc. instead of Yugoslavia, and so on. His argument influenced a great deal of political-environmentalist writing of the 'small is beautiful' variety. Some of the disunification Kohr advocated has since come to pass, at the cost of considerable and complex bloodshed in some places. Kohr claimed that his disaggregated Europe represented the continent's 'natural and original landscape',[20] but I find this unconvincing, another modern piece of nationalist myth making with its own silenced counter-narratives. It neglects the fact that, in Europe and elsewhere, people have often lived with some conviviality in large, multinational empires that claimed their allegiance despite differences of language, religion and culture-history.[21] Perhaps this can inspire us to make the most of future supersedure states.

Still, these modern stories of the nation have an impressive power, engaging the emotions and drawing connections between specific local places and people, and unknown places and people elsewhere in the territory that get sprinkled with the same emotional fairy dust. When the English writer Edward Thomas was asked why he'd volunteered to fight in World War I, he famously scooped up a handful of soil and said: 'Literally, for this.'[22] The fact that it's easy to understand his meaning – a tiny bit of unremarkable physical stuff standing powerfully for a symbolic and emotional entity, England, that he's willing to die for – speaks once again to the success of the idea of the nation in knitting together politics and emotions, the local and the non-local. Nobody is prepared to die for the World Trade Organization.

A contemporary current of environmentalist thought follows this path. Ultimately, the argument runs, environmentalism is about getting emotionally connected with the local. Paul Kingsnorth writes,

> *the old left-right political divide, which had been looking iffy for years, [is] being supplanted by a new binary: globalism versus nationalism. Nationalism, in the broadest sense of the term, [is] the default worldview of most people at most times, especially in more traditional places. It was a community-focused attitude, in which a nation, tribe or ethnic group was seen as a thing of value to be loved and protected. . . . As ever, those who can harness people's deep, old attachment to tribe, place and identity – to a belonging and a meaning beyond money or argument – will win the day.*[23]

Kingsnorth sketches this 'broadest sense of nationalism' rather *too* broadly, however. Certainly, people have long sought satisfying emotional identities beyond money or argument. They've also long sought concord and alliances born *out of* argument; in other words, they've sought satisfying politics. Neither is a deeper or older human urge than the other, but the modern nation has only become a repository of emotional identity *because* of money and argument, *because* of politics – a politics that often silences its counter-narratives. More sceptical views emphasise that the modern nation isn't some pre-political touchstone of authentic identity but a result of politics, specifically modernist politics that tries to erase class conflict in favour of the nation-state.

The danger is that in our modern plural world, people who fall outside the realm of the nation's supposedly singular boundaries can easily be turned into monsters, and subjected to extreme, possibly genocidal, violence. This has happened often enough in the modern history of nationalism. So while there's much to be said on environmentalist and other grounds for engaging the emotions locally, invoking an ill-founded idea of the tribe or nation as simple, authentic, pre-political belonging is a bad basis for a new politics of localism and attachment in the modern world.

A better approach might be to recognise that almost everyone in the world today is a child of a failing modernity. So when it comes to building small farm societies of the future, instead of seeking some kernel of 'real' local culture or peasant ness as a marker of authentic membership in the political community, it would be better to start over with the people who are actually there. And probably easier, too. Debating with your neighbours when it's best to mow the meadow around here is a better way to start building community than debating how best to worship God or vote in the national election. It's said that in the United States today, more than half of politically engaged citizens who support one of the two main parties live in fear of the other party.[24] This isn't a good basis for a healthy public sphere. Perhaps if we placed more emphasis on a politics of practical local livelihood rather than a politics of emotional identity at the level of the nation-state, we'd improve it.

Localisms worth their salt must find ways to respect existing local mores, especially ones grounded in successful long-term land husbandry. But I'd argue against excessive deference to local tradition and 'the way we do things around here'. Most 'local' agricultures nowadays ultimately serve global commodity markets. In a supersedure situation, the 'way we did things' and served those markets clearly won't have worked out. People will be facing wholly new situations – situations that can be informed by prior cultural practices, but not by clinging to realities that no longer exist. In this sense, the cultural cross-fertilisation brought by in-migration could prove more advantageous than a deep attachment to place filtered through modern nationalism, which has never been about the particularity of place. Perhaps it helps to cultivate a sense of culture not as a fixed thing that people have, but as an improvised, shared and performative thing that readily assumes new forms. That is, more a process than a structure.

The challenge in a supersedure situation is to build something new politically on the existing foundations of a farmed and settled landscape. What might make it easier in this situation is that the key task is simplified: creating local livelihoods from local land. So the colour of your God or how you say 'good day' will matter less than whether you can put food on the table, and whether you can work with others to resolve disagreements. For sure, the way that people interact would be conditioned, and potentially conflicted, by prior cultural practices. The challenge would be figuring out how to transcend them.

There's a political tradition older than nationalism which addresses that challenge. Civic republicanism was first articulated in ancient Greece and has been repeatedly reinvented ever since. Key elements of civic republi-canism, most of which distance it from political parties or countries apt to bear the republican name, are:[25]

- The republic is a political community that's deliberately constructed so that people can agree how to live alongside each other. It's not based on any prior 'natural' community or on shared identity. It therefore requires a foundational moment, entity or person to establish its institutions.
- The politics of the republic are geared to defining the *values* that guide its citizens' behaviour. Society is not therefore regarded as just the sum of individuals' preferences or utilities, as in capitalist market societies. The guiding values are more important than other possible desired ends, like efficiency, return on investment, or consumer choice . . .
- . . . but in relation to that last point, the politics of the republic are also geared to *non-domination* of citizens by any particular interests, includ-ing paternalistic or clientelistic claims that the state, the economy or other agents beyond the citizens' control know their interests best and are best equipped to deliver them.
- The republic is not committed to a single view of the good life, recognis-ing that there can be differences of opinion that must be reconciled for convivial political life, but not necessarily be definitively resolved.

- In this respect, the republic takes seriously differences between citizens, emphasising *dialogue and recognition*.
- In this respect also, the republic emphasises *realpolitik*, the practical solution of specific political problems, rather than romantic conceptions of a perfectible humanity or polity.
- Republicanism therefore sees citizens as neither intrinsically good nor bad, but potentially prey to *corruption*, where private interest dominates public interest.
- Republicanism favours rough equality of wealth and status – though not an insistence on absolutely equal outcomes – in order to prevent corruption and clientelism.
- Republican politics emphasises participation by all citizens, irrespective of rank or wealth.
- Republicanism also emphasises collective institutions to build civic consciousness, such as schools, militias, civic service, civic religion.
- Unlike empires, republicanism tends to draw fairly tight territorial bounds around a political community of citizens who interact with one another in the conduct of practical daily life. Historically, the classic manifestation of a republic is the city-state. A global or a limitlessly expanding republic is a contradiction.
- Republicanism often emphasises the independent self-reliance of the private householder, set within a civic commitment to the values of the republic.
- Republics are mindful of political failure and disarray. In John Barry's words: '[They] attempt to build an enduring and safe home for human lives in a world ruled by contingency and filled with potentially hostile agents.'[26] Historically, republics have often been militarist and masculinist.

The influence of this civic republican thought on my attempts to grapple with the shape of sustainable small farm societies of the future is probably clear, encompassing problems that the tradition helps to solve, like control of markets and forming the political disruptors I discussed in Part III, and problems that it raises, such as gender issues.

Historically, republican thought often comes to the fore in times of trouble and the breakdown of an old order. It was invoked in the

Enlightenment thought that created modern political ideals of freedom and democracy, notably in the founding of the French and US republics. Thomas Jefferson famously imagined an agrarian republic where 'those who labor in the earth are the chosen people of God'.[27] But arguably he did little as a politician to help bring such a republic about, and republican politics lost out globally in that era to commercial-capitalist interests that invoked the politics of liberalism. Yet with liberalism now in zombie mode – increasingly mired in political corruption, economic crisis and ecological blowback – thinkers since the 1980s have begun to reappraise the republican tradition as a worthy one for our modern times of trouble.

In a supersedure situation, the republican emphasis on defining common values – civic virtue – through open deliberation helps guard against the potential factionalism, prejudice and narrowness of localism, the poison in the gift of local community (see Chapter 13, 'Complicating the Commons', page 181). In this sense, republican politics provides a better grounding for localism and the commons than vaguer appeals to the virtues of local community.

Some critics of republicanism fear that its concept of civic virtue too easily devolves to a tyranny of the majority. In this view, it's better to embrace a pluralism of endless political horse trading without any sense of ultimate virtue, rather like the structure of the capitalist marketplace. One line of defence against that charge proceeds from emphasising the importance of autonomy and dialogue in republicanism. But I'd also like to defend it in the practical context of a small farm society of the future.

In such a society, where small-scale farmers enjoy a significant degree of self-reliance, the collective political agreements that it's necessary to make are more limited and therefore probably less oppressive than those to which we're accustomed in modern bureaucratic societies. And people would be keenly aware of the necessity for those agreements because they'd know what happens without a tight, place-based sense of civic virtue – market penetration, ecological overshoot, loss of self-reliance, surrender to generally hostile wider political control.

But when I say that self-reliance makes for a less oppressive collective politics, this returns us to the discussion of households and families (see Chapter 12, 'Households, Families and Beyond', page 165). Family self-reliance isn't necessarily less oppressive if you're oppressed by your family, as has often particularly been the case historically for women. The republican answer to this proceeds from its sense that the political community is an artificial construct that's always open to further deliberation, so arguments that it's 'natural' for men to rule over women, or for any category of person to rule over another, should be unacceptable to republican thought. This was the line that Mary Wollstonecraft took in her *Vindication of the Rights of Woman* (1792), one of the first feminist tracts, and one couched in explicitly republican terms. It's why I've consistently emphasised deliberation and the public sphere while rejecting the idea of given 'natural' communities.

Invoking Thomas Jefferson as a republican ancestor raises comparable issues in view of his simultaneous enthusiasm for small-scale agrarian freedom and his ownership of an enormous slave plantation. I have little interest in working through Jefferson's personal contradictions, but they're a warning against front-parlour republicanism that ignores the underlying oppressions enabling it. There's genuine political inspiration to be drawn from small-scale agrarianism in the United States, but the slave-based cotton and tobacco capitalism of the US South can't be written out of the picture as an enabling force upon it. The wider lesson for agrarian republicanism in our probable patchwork future of distressed capitalism, growing state failure and border/resource militarisation is not to build the congenial abundance of a small farm republicanism unwittingly on other people's misery.

CHAPTER NINETEEN

Reconstituted Peasantries

I've argued that the most realistic and promising future for humanity given the present historical moment is one in which large numbers of us turn to small-scale farming for self-provisioning and mostly local marketing. I've suggested some ways that this might happen politically. But I'll readily admit they amount to something vaguer than a confident and fully specified political programme.

Maybe this is a failing of my analysis. Or maybe not. Confident programmes are a tic of modernist politics in its taste for single keys that explain the forward march of history, whether it's the profit motive, democratic freedom, the inevitable march of science and Enlightenment ideals, or class struggle. Since I don't subscribe to single keys, forward marches or inevitability, the politics I've outlined is vaguer and less certain of success. Still, focusing on how people will have to make a living from the local ecological base, create local autonomies and build local commons to make that possible without succumbing to the inequities that have bedevilled both premodern agrarian societies and modern capitalist ones has led me to highlight forms of republican and agrarian politics that may be equal to the task. To me, these seem less vague than touchstones of political faith like 'progress', 'technology' and 'community'.

The scoping exercise that I've done in these pages falls short of describing exactly how the present global political economy will fail and what will replace it – an impossible task, of course. But the failure is virtually certain nonetheless. So the question is how best to prepare for what's to come. Predicting a 'climacteric' before 2040, when a confluence of crises of the kind examined in Part I will force systemic change, David Fleming wrote: 'The task . . . is not about wrestling with the controls of economics to force it in the direction of degrowth, but about getting ready for the moment when the coming climacteric does the heavy work of degrowth for us.'[28]

I'm more sympathetic to Fleming's argument than I once was. After all, if even so expert a helmsman as the 'Iron Chancellor' Otto von Bismarck thought that humans could only float with the current of events, then I'm happy not to try wrestling overly with economic controls. Instead, like Fleming, I think it makes sense to prepare for a time when the current of events delivers degrowth by default. The sobering thing is that there are so many ways in which the heavy work of degrowth could be destructive of human well-being, and only a few in which it's otherwise.

This impending reconfiguration of the global political economy has no exact historical parallels, but it's not unprecedented. There have been numerous instances of de-centralisation and re-peasantisation in world history, with complex consequences that are by no means always reducible to a single story of decline, collapse and immiseration. We tend to settle on that narrative because elites with the strongest interest in the prior status quo are the ones who get to leave their stories for posterity. But historically the unravelling of economic linkage has been less widely mourned by ordinary people than we often suppose when we swallow elite stories that romanticise economic growth.[29] Still, I'm under no illusions that building future peasant societies in places like Western Europe and the United States is anything other than an enormously tall order. Part of what makes it so difficult is the impossibility in our culture of imagining that it might be a step worth taking.

But at least there are sources of historical inspiration for taking that step. Here, I'd like to highlight just one, and perhaps not the most obvious: the reconfiguration of Caribbean societies after slavery. Plantation slaves in the Caribbean count high among the most exploited and brutalised workers in the capitalist world system, ever. Yet in the aftermath of and around the margins of the slave plantation system they built successful peasant lifeways on the foundation of their 'captured garden' provision grounds, not necessarily because they wanted to, but because they had no alternative.

These reconstituted peasantries were instrumental in creating Creole societies built from prior African, Amerindian, Asian and European foundations but representing new cultural assemblages in new situations.[30] It's not necessary to romanticise what these societies were like to make my point. Before and after slavery, they involved racism, privation and brutal disparities of power. But the fact that their peoples still created recognisably local cultural syntheses in those circumstances is testament to the power of culture to make new worlds. The reconstituted peasantries and creole societies of the future are unlikely to look much like the ones of the 19th-century Caribbean, but we could do worse than learning from their example. In particular, we can learn from them that creating peasant societies isn't about trying to restore a lost past. It's about trying to create a workable future.

The Nyéléni Consensus

Another window into that future was produced in the Malian village of Nyéléni in 2007, when the Forum for Food Sovereignty convened by the international peasant organisation La Vía Campesina produced its eponymous declaration, including this passage: 'Food sovereignty is the right of peoples to healthy and culturally appropriate food produced through ecologically sound and sustainable methods, and their right to define their own food and agriculture systems. It puts the aspirations and needs of those who produce, distribute and consume food at the heart of food systems and policies rather than the demands of markets and corporations.'[31]

Food sovereignty emphasises 'growers and eaters' allying politically at the local level rather than 'producers and consumers' relating to each other only by seeking the best price in the market.[32] It can be hard birthing such grower/eater alliances out of familiar market relationships, as I know all too well from personal experience as both grower/producer and eater/consumer. As a grower, I notice that the checkout price of food bears little relation to its true long-term social and environmental costs of production. My business is fortunate in that many of our 'eaters' recognise this and are prepared to pay a little more than they would for world-market produce.

But occasionally we've encountered eaters as consumers with a strong sense of the priority of their demands over us – the consumer as king. In these circumstances, we've sometimes walked away from a customer, much to their astonishment, since the dominant model has it that it's always the customer who walks.

Of course, we're in a privileged position to do so (and most of our customers are in a privileged position to pay more than they strictly must). I'm sympathetic to would-be customers who can't afford our produce, albeit sometimes a little sceptical of how people define the affordability of food in view of other things they spend their money on. I'm less sympathetic to the notion that food sovereignty is therefore a boutique movement catering only for the middle class, especially since the cheapness of world-market food arises in considerable measure through the poverty it inflicts on many of its workers and wider publics. The unaffordability of good food must be set against the greater unaffordability of housing and land conditioned by capitalist land markets.

As an eater/consumer, there are various ways in which I try to support growers and other pioneers of local economic autonomy by spending my money on products I believe in, and various ways in which I fail, falling back on world-market routes. Rather than engaging in tiresome debates about the virtues and vices of our individual consumption choices that assume those choices are a deeper reflection of our true preferences than our citizen concerns, it seems better to invest our energies as best we can in building local economic autonomies whose products become the easiest ones to prefer. A focus on shopping habits is only one aspect of that work. Another that I'd like to emphasise more strongly is 'de-commodification' – reducing the focus on commodity exchange in the capitalist marketplace as a way of delivering a just and sustainable society. Withholding produce from a pernickety customer and eating it myself is one small step towards de-commodification.

Bigger steps are necessary, of course, but there are worse ways of beginning than further building consensus and alliances around the Nyéléni declaration. Inevitably, a programmatic statement like Nyéléni is lacking in detail, and involves possible contradictions, as its critics have charged. For example, Bina Agarwal writes,

Can consensus really be reached or would we merely get majoritarianism? What space would dissenting voices have? How would perspectives stemming from gender, caste, ethnicity, and so on be incorporated, if they diverge from one another or from the majority? Although these are general questions of presence and representation that can apply to many contexts, they are particularly complex when applied to issues of livelihood and survival under substantial inequality and diversity between peoples and nations.[33]

These are good questions, which I've done my best to answer in this book. In the crisis situations we now face, consensus is best approached as a (republican) politics of recognition based on autonomous economic agents (peasants, small-scale farmers, growers). Building local consensus around producing livelihoods out of the immediate ecological base, though complex and rife with potential for domination, is probably *less* complex and more potentially egalitarian than the drive to build a global capitalist political economy. In that respect, this book is intended essentially as a defence of food sovereignty principles and a working through of some of their difficulties. The difficulties, I'd argue, are less severe than those bedevilling other kinds of political economy. Suppose we tried to build a global 'Nyéléni consensus' to outflank the present 'Washington consensus' of global free-market integration? I think such a reboot would improve fairness, human well-being and global stability, both political and ecological. But, as Agarwal reminds us, it's not a panacea.

The Auto-System

In many places, it would be better to work on building such consensus by fostering local autonomies rather than agitating against state power. The latter approach, encompassing class and nationalist politics, anti-globalisation protests and identity politics, are sometimes called 'anti-systemic movements' and it's not my intention to criticise them or minimise their importance. But I'd like to speak up for what might be termed 'self-systemic' or 'auto-systemic' movements. The word 'self' in English, with its connotations of 'selfishness' and 'self-sufficiency', doesn't capture the collective spirit within which this enterprise is conceived. Self-reliant farming on a small, self-owned plot needn't be intrinsically selfish, and could be a key building block of a self-systemic society as part of a wider movement. Other languages have words with a more plural sense of 'ourselves' – like the Spanish *autoorganización* (organising for ourselves) – that better capture what I'm driving at. An auto-systemic movement isn't aiming primarily to critique or topple the existing wider political economy, but to build superior alternatives to it.

The autonomies I've emphasised bear on politics, on money and markets, on communities and on land. How they work in any particular place and time will vary. In our populous, mobile, globalised, capitalist world, I've stressed the importance of a strong public (or republican) sphere. As communities develop new commons through self-provisioning from the local ecological base, everybody's voice counts, not just that of local elites or the shadowy collectivities that politicians often invoke – 'the real people', 'the silent majority', 'local communities', 'local people' and so forth.

As we build these autonomies, for a long time to come there'll be enormous spillovers from the wider global economy that perturb the impetus to localism, arising especially through the search for cheap energy. Perhaps they'll resemble the secondary economy of Jonathan Raban's marshlanders (see Chapter 14, 'Going to Market', page 191). The challenge is to be aware of the contradictions of our localism, honest about its shortcomings, well-humoured about its hypocrisies and welcoming to whoever is willing to help improve them. Just as world-system attributes will continue to perturb the local, localisms must try to perturb the local manifestations of world-system attributes and scramble the centripetal pull of state centres.

In many places, one of the hardest but most important dimensions of that scrambling is drawing rural land into a more localised economy, whether as private holdings or commons. Small areas of urban greenspace are easily, if often transiently, commoned into community gardens and allotments, but it's also necessary to repurpose huge swathes of agricultural cereals and grasslands as small mixed farms, smallholdings, cottages and commons. Aided and abetted by zoning restrictions, this land tends to be locked in a world-system spiral of Ricardian rent and entry barriers to farming that puts it beyond the reach of any but a lucky few. This is a key battle to be won.

An important dimension of local action is the question of 'ecologically sound and sustainable methods', as articulated in the Nyéléni declaration. In Part II, I examined various candidates for what might constitute such methods – organic farming, no-till farming, regenerative agriculture, permaculture, perennial cropping and forest gardening, as well as more conventional options like the arable corner. All of these have valuable things to teach, but the lesson of localism is that no one label fits every circumstance. As people build new local agricultures, new property relations and new commons, a dose of scepticism about off-the-peg systems and third-party audit schemes like organic certification is in order.

Better than scepticism, is a knowing indifference to 'off-the-peg' systems, including most of the ones touted in the alternative agriculture movement. By 'knowing indifference', I don't mean not caring. I mean absorbing the underlying philosophies and applying or not applying them judiciously in ways that are sensitive to local contexts and constraints.

In other words, the small farm future I propose is more de-commodified and supple than organic certification, or any other defined agricultural system. In such a future, 'knowing indifference' would help people figure out workable low-input, low-money farming styles for themselves that are fitted to their circumstances, protecting them from get-rich-quick gurus and false prophets who lie in wait in the alternative farming world just as much as in the mainstream one. Pure 'indifference', on the other hand, would mainly penalise the farmer, not the customer, with self-correcting consequences. But indifference to ready-made solutions must turn into attentiveness to local specifics. Indeed, part of the idea of the auto-system is the complexity of how people would have to consciously define themselves in their localities as producers and consumers of food and fibre. Sometimes this might be as producers of home fare, sometimes as buyers or supporters of produce from known local farmers, sometimes as citizens helping to define the tight property commons through which local access to land is allotted, sometimes as commoners themselves and only sometimes as consumers buying more distanced market commodities. An auto-system draws farms into their localities through a richly connected set of local producers, consumers and citizens, who are often the same people at different moments in their daily lives.

CHAPTER TWENTY

Dispossessions

My argument, then, is that to address and adapt to our pervasive contemporary crises it will be necessary for many people across the world to go 'back' to the land, creating livelihoods out of their local ecological base in ways that rely less on the symbolic economy of money, global finance and capital accumulation. That process will be conditioned by legacies of the past dispossession of ordinary people from access to productive land in ways that cast long shadows into the present. Part of that legacy is a tendency to read historical dispossession through simplistic moral scripts – either a 'progressive' enthusiasm for the coming of urban-industrial society or a 'romantic' lament for the rural worlds we've lost.

Neither of these scripts serve us well in the present historical moment. But the best way of moving beyond them is probably to embrace our historical relationships with the farmed landscape rather than ignoring them. Needless to say, I can't do that here in any depth even for a single place or country, let alone for the whole world. But it's worth reflecting briefly on a few historical experiences in order to sketch some of the issues involved.

One window into this is populism, a form of politics that mobilises an idea of 'the people' against other adversarial forces, which has risen to prominence in many countries recently, including the United States, Britain and other Western European countries. Before this present global populist moment there was another one, stretching roughly from the middle of the 19th century to the middle of the 20th, which likewise claimed to speak for ordinary people at a time when many of them were small-scale farmers. In parts of Africa, Asia and Latin America many people still are, and numerous forms of agrarian populist politics have arisen in them – sometimes contesting colonial or capitalist forms of control, sometimes organising around land and labour rights, and sometimes conforming to existing local structures of power.

Closer to the centre of capitalist power, the first era of populism saw the emergence in the United States of the Farmers' Alliance and the People's Party, which were active from the 1870s to the 1900s. The history of this movement has been painted in starkly different colours by succeeding generations of US historians – as a popular democratic frontier response to commercial control from the east, a backward-looking movement of rural reactionaries, and a movement of radical and presciently anti-capitalist resistance to economic 'progress'. Probably, it was all those things and more. But historian Charles Postel's proposition that fundamentally it represented the last throw of the dice for a 'progressive' rural capitalism largely on-message with prevailing trends in US politics seems convincing.[34] The populists wanted industry, science, progress, political influence, but they wanted it in a plural world of thriving rural farm communities. For better or worse, those things came to pass, but in a state-directed, urban-commercial world utterly different from, and hostile to, the ruralism of their imagining.

The US farmers' movement was among the last major political mobilisations of working-class people around a progressive, rural and agrarian vision in a Western country. Such visions have largely since been pressed by minority middle-class movements of back-to-the-landers, something that seems destined to change soon. The farmers' movement hands forwards a conflicted legacy of how that future may unfold. Against a background of economic distress among small-scale farmers around the world at the end of the 19th century, it was suspicious of commercial credit, bankers and merchant middlemen, favouring farmer co-operatives and rural self-help for reasons I find entirely plausible. But at its worst, this shaded into anti-Semitism, racism, anti-immigration and anti-elite conspiracy theories, all with troubling contemporary resonances.

With hindsight, it's easy to see that the first populist moment involved a clash between more grounded national rural capital of the kind that I've argued must be supported in a small farm future, and more virtualised global commercial capital. It was a prescient battle to reclaim Main Street from Wall Street that the populists lost. Barely a century later, as global commercial capital exhausts both itself and planetary capacities, we've arrived at a second populist moment with similar economic stakes, and much higher ecological ones.

Part of the battle in the United States is to reclaim populism from its bogeyman status in 'progressive' liberal politics, which is exacerbated when figures such as Donald Trump clothe themselves in the mantle of pro-working class, reformist populism with little genuine commitment to that cause. Like all political labels, 'populism' has acquired so much baggage that it's hard to form a clear politics around it, but I'd argue against seeing it merely as a demagogic appeal to the base instincts of 'the people'. What's worth rescuing from the traditions of US populism, and from their theft by cynical contemporary politicians, is a scepticism towards, but not outright hostility to, the centralised state as the fundamental force of politics, an emphasis on a politics supporting producerism and personal livelihood, and a commitment to social improvement rather than the endless revolutionary, world-transforming 'progress' associated with political traditions like neoliberalism and communism.

Turning to another part of the world's capitalist heartlands – my own country, England – a different rural history presents itself. Earlier, I argued that a peasant class of small-scale farmers was defeated in lowland England in the 18th century by large landowners, not because the latter were more efficient farmers but because they were better able to organise property regimes in their favour. The result was a large-scale rural landlordism of little relevance to England's emerging capitalist economy, but one that's created a rather deadened and static imaginative hold on English visions of the countryside ever since. With its rise as an industrial power, England's countryside began emptying of its labouring class, and the theatre of their political activism became urban. They strove for better pay and conditions, winning them from the state against capital through their power as industrial workers, and they strove for a 'recaptured garden' in the form of urban allotments for growing fruit and vegetables. This happened so long ago that barely a trace of rural radicalism persists in the country's historical memory, and conservative thought has made over the countryside in its own image as a bastion of stability and bluff good sense against the corrosive forces of urban change and rights claims.

For example, in the late Roger Scruton's book *News from Somewhere* the rural commons that he celebrates is a conservative, fox-hunting commons aimed primarily at confirming rural status hierarchies, rather than agrarian production or smallholder autonomy. The only class distinction Scruton admits into his rural vision is between the employed and the self-employed – farmers being in the latter group, and gaining his approval for cheerfully tolerating the industrial injuries they sustain as under-labourers in the capitalist economy, while their urban counterparts wallow in a sickly modern 'culture of compensation'.[35] It's likely that in the future the jobs and associated employment rights these urban workers painstakingly won from reluctant employers will disappear, and people will be thrown back into relying upon rural autonomy, neighbourliness and commons. The commons in this new and populous rural world would probably best be articulated in the form of tight property commons oriented to smallhold-ing, and therefore necessarily articulated *against* rural big men, large land-holders and the cap-doffing world that Scruton celebrates. The traditions of progressive US agrarian populism, though unfamiliar in England, could be informative in this respect.

Celebrated British nature writer Robert Macfarlane displays a less partisan agenda than Scruton in his interesting essay on the 'eeriness of the English countryside'.[36] In contrast to Scruton, the ghost of class conflicts past makes it into his vision. But only peripherally. Macfarlane mentions an English landscape constituted by 'uncanny forces, part-buried sufferings and contested ownerships' and currents of thought 'sceptical of comfort-able notions of "dwelling" and "belonging"' (Scruton's book, by contrast, is subtitled 'On Settling'). These are exactly the kind of counter-narratives to a nationalist sense of belonging that I mentioned earlier. But Macfarlane never brings centre stage the idea that the English countryside might be eerie because it's full of defeated ghosts.

I feel these ghosts around me as I work my holding – family ghosts of ancestors who left the land as labourers or petty owners in Ireland and Scotland in the 19th century, making their way from Celtic periphery to Anglo centre, some of them working the coalfields we now know helped build the fossil-fuelled economy that may ultimately impel us back to the land in a damaged world. But I also feel the different ghosts of an occasion-ally hostile localism directed at a stranger like me born and raised into another emptied farmscape fully a hundred miles from where I now live and where, even there, other people still had a better claim to be a 'real' local than me. These are the same ghosts invoked by a writer like Scruton in his pastiche of yeoman stability. I think we need to bury them.

There's an eeriness, too, in the green deserts of cereal and ryegrass monocultures, the countryside emptied of people, the invisibility of farming to so many people for whom the countryside is at best a place for wildlife and rural recreation. Current zoning regulations, allied to the symbolic economy of capitalism, make a reinvigorated countryside of smallholdings a virtual impossibility in England at present, and the idea of a countryside 'ruined' by people living and working in it is widely shared. People *living* in the countryside in lowland England earn on average about £90 per week more than those living in urban areas, whereas people *working* in the countryside earn on average about £90 per week less than urban workers, the discrepancy arising because the countryside acts as a dormitory for wealthy urban workers. As the 'Equality in the Countryside' manifesto from which those figures were taken puts it: 'The countryside does not currently generate wealth, it imports it, and it imports the people who earn it.'[37]

If the arguments put forward in this book are borne out, that will have to change. But change is slow in coming, especially when impeded by cultural mythologies of rural timelessness of the kind put forward by Scruton. Encouragingly, new activist organisations are emerging like the Land Workers' Alliance, The Land Is Ours, the Ecological Land Co-op, Reclaim the Fields and XR Farmers, along with the first glimmerings of a movement for land reform.[38] Much of it is being pioneered by well-educated young people who are losing interest in increasingly precarious mainstream routes to economic 'success' and developing a new kind of radical politics. But it remains an uphill struggle. Let us summon the 'uncanny forces' lying dormant from near-forgotten conflicts of the rural past to help them in their work towards the future. And let's summon, too, the experience of peasant movements in Asia, Africa and Latin America who are well ahead of the Global North in developing radical agrarian populisms fit for present times.

There's much to be gained from connecting a land-based peasant politics with progressive populism in the Global North. Progressive populism shares some aspects of its thinking with the traditional left but also with conservative Main Street populism in honouring the lives and struggles of ordinary people. It differs from most other political doctrines in lacking a utopia or a vision of an ultimately perfected political society. Unlike conservatism, it doesn't hanker after a settled, hierarchical social order. Unlike market liberalism, it doesn't believe that private markets maximise value or happiness. Unlike anarchism, it doesn't believe that people are inherently better off without any form of state. Unlike communism, it doesn't believe in the improvement of humankind towards some historically perfected new order underwritten by the state. It's progressive in the sense that it believes people should be able to achieve self-realisation unlimited by gender, economic class or other political identities that might otherwise constrain them, but it doesn't necessarily believe in progress as an intrinsic value. The ideal citizen of its imagining spends a good part of their day striving for flourishing and livelihood. The next day, they do the same again, probably in the same way. There's no higher political purpose.

Such a desire for non-hierarchical decency can seem limited and aimless in capitalist societies relentlessly oriented to the growth of financial capital, and to remaking the world in service of it. But decency, non-hierarchical autonomy and engagement with rather than overcoming of the natural world seems the better bet for creating viable human societies long term. This is where the progressive populisms of today can meet with a small-farm, agrarian populism inherited from the first populist moment in ways fit for present times that enable people to provision themselves locally and take care of themselves collectively in the challenging circumstances that are now upon us. This, ultimately, will be how to deliver a congenial and renewable small farm future.

Does Goldman Sachs Care
If You Raise Chickens?

I was well over thirty before I first raised food for my household. Already a parent, I'd only belatedly started thinking about the future of food and farming. A local farmer had sold me a few point-of-lay hens, and I tended them lovingly in the henhouse that I'd proudly made myself. Not long after I'd started, one of the hens laid the first egg – a perfect brown ellipse, about half the size of anything you'd be likely to see in the shops. I cooked it and divided it up between my family. Each of us got barely a morsel, and I joked that we shouldn't stake a homestead claim just yet. But I couldn't help feeling a wild kind of glee that I think most people feel in some way when they raise food for themselves. It's the same when they fix a car, plumb a bathroom, make a basket or knit a sweater. There are many ways to find fulfilment, but even in our modern commodified society, a lot of people are drawn to practical self-realisation.

There was nothing especially 'ecological' about my first faltering efforts as a chicken-keeper. The hens were a commercial variety, bred for a short life of industrially maxed-out egg production, and I fed them mostly on purchased concentrate feed. Since then I've gone through various episodes of raising chickens, not raising chickens and raising other plants and animals, searching for methods that better approximate to something that will honour the land and my community long term, though never yet quite finding them. Later in my farming career, when I rose before dawn on wet mornings to spend hours picking vegetables for our customers, the glee I'd felt when I cracked that first egg was sometimes diminished. But it has never gone out entirely.

So when I hear the witticism attributed to Jodi Dean, a professor of political science in New York, that 'Goldman Sachs doesn't care if you raise chickens',[1] I have some skin in the game. What does this mean? I think it means that the world is structured by vast collective systems of value-extraction that are not significantly challenged by someone like me just because I produce a few eggs in my backyard rather than buying them in the shops.

That's true, of course. But another truth that's long been known by labour organisers is that existing political structures are challenged only when people act collectively. The same is true of chicken-keepers. And, now that labour can barely challenge a fluid global capital any more through local strikes, perhaps it's time to imagine a different strategy. There's a long history of peasant activism geared to recapturing the garden to draw from. In this book, I've tried to reconfigure it in terms that make sense for the present world-historical moment. That moment involves impending food and political-economic crises, sharpening the relevance of bygone peasant assertions. What will you do when you can no longer rely on the centralised state that you're familiar with to keep supplying you with eggs and other forms of welfare?

Perhaps another dimension of the quotation's dismissiveness towards chicken-keepers is a sense that the modern world is huge, fast, interconnected and highly technological, so any politics able to overturn its dysfunctions must likewise be huge, fast, interconnected and invested in high-tech. This is the critique of 'folk politics' that I considered in Chapter 1 (see Chapter 1, 'Crisis #10: Culture', page 78). As I said there, I think it's mistaken. Increasingly, it seems clear that attempts to co-opt the restless developmental logic of capital and turn it towards more genuine human betterment themselves become co-opted into mere variants of the same logic – the same melodramatic tune of human overcoming, played in a different key. And all these variants of the huge, fast, interconnected, high-tech world ultimately rest on an improbable calculus of energy increase, climate mitigation and economic growth.

So against that, I'd assert the virtues of keeping chickens – something that people were doing long before Goldman Sachs got started, and something I suspect they'll be doing long after it's gone. We have no real idea what a genuine small farm future might look like, because long ago and willingly or not most of us gave up such visions for a fairytale of wealth increase promoted by the likes of Goldman Sachs. We need to find those visions again, regardless of what Goldman Sachs thinks. So I agree with permaculturist David Holmgren's tortoise-over-hare emphasis on 'small and slow' solutions, and in this book I've tried to take those lessons from the henhouse and apply them to world politics.[2]

It's true of course that we're facing some vast and pressing global problems, but one of the main reasons they're so vast and pressing is that we've been unable to think outside the frameworks that continue to generate them, so we keep amplifying them. Humanity is now sailing in dangerous waters. In this book, I've tried to chart what now seems to me our safest course, though without illusions about the difficulties of following it and the chances of success. I think it involves rejecting grand solutionism and creating local autonomies as best we can that may just see us through into a new phase of history, with its own contradictions and difficulties. We need to prefigure it by thinking, and farming, for the long haul. It begins when you start raising chickens.

ACKNOWLEDGEMENTS

Writing this book has been a lonely calling at times, but not an entirely solitary one, so I'd like to record my thanks to those who've helped along the way.

The deepest ones are to Cordelia Rowlatt for supporting this project so unswervingly, for embodying it so ebulliently, and for journeying with me into its heart. Also to my children and wider family, especially Alexandra Rowlatt, for living it with humour, and Dan Smaje for assistance with data analysis.

My thanks to Bernadette Alves, Shaun Chamberlin, Dave Darby, Simon Fairlie, Anthony Galluzzo, Paul Hillman, Andy McGuire, Cordelia Rowlatt, Joan Sheldon, Ted Trainer and Elise Wach for reading and commenting on portions of the manuscript – comments that I sometimes ignored but always thought about, and that greatly improved my analysis.

Thanks also to Michael Albert, Sam Bliss, Ellis Bowdler, Erik Buitenhuis, Steve Caballero, Kris Fowler, Alex Hart, Samson Hart, Miles King, Jake, Oliver and Dan Smaje, Aaron Vansintjan and Professors Ford Denison, Phil Grime and Rattan Lal for discussions in person or by email that helped inform my thinking, and to Giorgos Kallis, George Monbiot and Colin Tudge for small acts of encouragement for my writing. Special thanks to Paul Hillman for the many years of productive conversation and agreeable disagreement that whisper through these pages.

I presented some of the ideas that became Part IV at the Rachel Carson Center for Environment and Society, LMU Munich. My thanks to Robert Baumgartner, Claudio de Majo and Ursula Münster in particular for the invitation and for stimulating discussions.

I first formulated many of the ideas here on my Small Farm Future blog (www.smallfarmfuture.org.uk), where they were honed by the fine insights of numerous commenters. I couldn't wish for a more informed and collegiate online community.

I owe an ironic apology to my neglected garden as I've busied myself instead making a case on paper to tend the soil. At least I had the envy-tinged honour of watching the Vallis Veg team bring forth the fruits of the earth from my study window as I wrote. To them my thanks and appreciation, particularly to Kiki Cendoya for helping to safeguard this book's soul as well as its words.

And a dedication to three of my teachers, two who've sadly passed: Sidney Mintz, Paul Richards and Patrick Whitefield. I was too young and green when you taught me to appreciate what you were passing on. In this book I've done my best to render its due – not through repetition but, I hope, through making it my own.

Finally, my thanks to Shaun Chamberlin, Brianne Goodspeed and the rest of the team at Chelsea Green for helping me bring this book to fruition, and steering me away from the numerous rabbit holes I found it all too easy to fall in.

No responsibility attaches to anyone named above, of course, for any deficiencies in the book or for errors of commission or omission.

NOTES

INTRODUCTION

1. Wild, Tony (2014) 'Can World's Most Expensive Brew Be Made Sustainably?' *The Guardian*, 19 September. My thanks to Paul Hillman for drawing this example to my attention.
2. Sowell 2006.
3. Frase 2016, 101.
4. Bastani 2019; Phillips and Rozworski 2019.
5. See, for example, Bastani 2019; Browne, John (2019) 'Should We Pursue Boundless Economic Growth?' *Prospect*, 30.
6. Francis 1990; Gosho et al. 1984; Wild, Rose (2018) 'We Were Buried in Fake News as Long Ago as 1894,' *The Times*, 13 January.
7. FAO n.d.; Hickel 2017; Holt-Giménez 2019; Milanovic 2016; UNICEF (2018) 'The State of Food Security and Nutrition in the World 2018,' https://data.unicef.org /resources/sofi-2018/.
8. See Morrison, Oliver (2020) '"Cultured Meat Is Fool's Gold": Environmentalists Lock Horns over Controversial Documentary,' *Foodnavigator.com*, 10 January.
9. FAO n.d.; Smil 2017.
10. ILO n.d.; Rosset and Altieri 2017.

PART I: A SMALL FARM FUTURE?

1. Smil 2019, 513.
2. Bradshaw and Brook 2015; Meadows et al. 2004.
3. WDI n.d.
4. Chancel and Piketty 2015.
5. Drawing on Bradshaw and Brook 2015.
6. Schmidt et al. 2017.
7. The figures in this paragraph are calculated from WDI n.d.
8. Todaro and Smith 2015; United Nations, Department of Economic and Social Affairs, Population Division. 2019.
9. Meadows et al. 2004, 177.
10. Malthus 1798.
11. Boserup 1965.
12. A more elaborate analysis is in Vandermeer 2011, 25–61.
13. See Kallis 2019 for a detailed critique not only of Malthus but also of modern concepts of 'Malthusianism' that goes beyond my scope here.

14. A more persuasive (non-Malthusian) argument suggests high fertility among the poor is one among several poverty *traps* that exacerbate poverty, but don't cause it – see Smith 2005.
15. There are numerous versions of this argument, for example, Pinker 2018.
16. Brand 2009, 26, 36, 43, 73.
17. Banerjee and Duflo 2011; Krishna 2013; Levien 2018; Zhan 2020.
18. Figures in this paragraph are calculated from WDI n.d.; and https://www.un.org /en/development/desa/population/migration/data/estimates2/estimates19.asp. The seven countries are the United States, Japan, Germany, the United Kingdom, France, Italy and Canada.
19. Netting 1993.
20. UN (2018) '68% of the World Population Projected to Live in Urban Areas by 2050, says UN,' https://www.un.org/development/desa/en/news/population/2018 -revision-of-world-urbanization-prospects.html.
21. Wesselbaum and Aburn 2019.
22. Bradford 2019.
23. See FAO 2016; IPCC 2018.
24. IPCC 2016; IPCC 2018.
25. FAO 2016; IPCC 2019. The figure may be higher if industrial and food chain emissions are included – or lower with different methane accounting (see Part II).
26. Smil 2017, 228.
27. Nordhaus, Ted (2019) 'The Empty Radicalism of the Climate Apocalypse,' *Issues* 35(4): 69–78, https://issues.org/the-empty-radicalism-of-the-climate-apocalypse/.
28. Hardin 1968. I discuss the question of commons in more detail in Part III.
29. Tainter 1988, 50.
30. WDI n.d.
31. Tainter 1988, 56.
32. IPCC 2018.
33. See, for example, IPCC 2016; IPCC 2018; IPCC 2019; Loftus et al. 2015.
34. Marris, Emma (2017) 'Can We Love Nature and Let It Go? The Case for Interwoven Decoupling,' *Breakthrough Journal*, 7, https://thebreakthrough.org/journal/issue-7 /can-we-love-nature-and-let-it-go.
35. IPCC 2018, 15.
36. Campbell et al. 2007, 85.
37. WDI n.d. (2014 figures).
38. Smil 2017, 458.
39. My distinction between flows and stocks draws from Malm 2016, among others – a different usage from economic convention.
40. Smil 2017, 12.
41. Fizaine and Court 2016.
42. Court 2018, 7. See also Grime and Pierce 2012.
43. *BP Statistical Review of World Energy 2019*, www.bp.com/en/global/corporate/ energy-economics/statistical-review-of-world-energy.html; WDI n.d.

44. Tong et al. 2019.

45. Berners-Lee and Clark 2013; Smil 2010; Smil 2017; Smil 2019.

46. See, for example, Moriarty and Honnery 2019.

47. Berners-Lee and Clark 2013, 81.

48. Meadows et al. 2004; Turner 2008.

49. For example, Kallis 2018.

50. I calculated the figures in this paragraph from the following sources: DBEIS (2019) *Energy Consumption in the UK 1970 to 2018*, London; DEFRA (2018) *Agriculture in the United Kingdom 2017*, London; Pelletier et al. 2011.

51. Fleming 2016, 219.

52. Smil 2017, 358.

53. WDI n.d.

54. Smil 2017, 362.

55. IPCC 2019; Montgomery 2007.

56. On ancient states contrast, for example, Hillel 1991 with Pournelle 2019. On the Dustbowl, contrast Cunfer 2005 with Worster 1979. On British soils contrast Case, Philip (2014) 'Only 100 Harvests Left in UK Farm Soils, Scientists Warn,' *Farmers Weekly*, 21 October, with Committee on Climate Change (2016) *Environmental Audit Committee – Inquiry into Soil Health*, 14 January, https://www.theccc.org .uk/wp-content/uploads/2016/01/CCC-Written-Submission-to-Environmental -Audit-Committee-Inquiry-into-Soil-Health.pdf.

57. IPCC 2019; Rickson et al. 2015; UN (2014) 'UN Agency Calls for Urgent Action to Protect Global Soil from Depletion, Degradation,' *UN News*, 24 July.

58. Soil Association 2010.

59. Smil 2017, 383.

60. Kiel et al. 2010; UNEP 2014.

61. Polimeni et al. 2008.

62. Sverdrup et al. 2012.

63. UNEP 2016.

64. UNEP 2014, 11.

65. WWAP 2012.

66. Foley et al. 2011; IPCC 2019.

67. Nabhan 2002.

68. Parenti 2011.

69. UN Water 2018, v.

70. Lipton 2009, 83.

71. Lambin and Meyfroidt 2011, 3466; Gibbs et al. 2010, 16732.

72. Holt-Giménez, Eric (2014) 'Feeding Nine Billion: Five Steps to the Wrong Solution,' *Huffington Post*, 25 June.

73. Data from WDI n.d.; FAO n.d.; UN DESA (2017) 'World Population Projected to Reach 9.8 Billion in 2050, and 11.2 Billion in 2100,' 21 June, https://www.un .org/development/desa/en/news/population/world population-prospects -2017.html. Country figures exclude small city-states like Singapore. Further

information in this paragraph is drawn from Byerlee et al. 2014 and Gibbs et al. 2010.

74. I use the word 'Creation' to mean the world and its living inhabitants without specific religious commitment on my part – but I like the connotation of a world that's been created beyond human forces.

75. Wilson 2001.

76. IBPES (2019) 'Summary for Policymakers of the *Global Assessment Report on Biodiversity and Ecosystem Services* of the Intergovernmental Science-Policy Platform on Biodiversity and Ecosystem Services,' https://www.ipbes.net/global-assessment -report-biodiversity-ecosystem-services.

77. Byerlee et al. 2014; Kremen 2015; Lambin and Meyfroidt 2011.

78. On these various points, see Letourneau et al. 2011; Perfecto et al. 2009; Phelps et al. 2013; Smith et al. 2012.

79. Kremen 2015.

80. Monbiot 2014.

81. Lambin and Meyfroidt 2011.

82. Morris, Dafydd (2019) 'The Case Against Rewilding – a Welsh Farmer Speaks Out,' *Countryfile*, 19 February, https://www.countryfile.com/news/the-case-against -rewilding-a-welsh-farmer-speaks-out/.

83. Marris 2011, 170.

84. See Callicott 1999, 187–219.

85. Locke 1689, II, 37.

86. Asafu-Adjaye et al. 2015.

87. Figures for 1991 and 2019, WDI n.d.

88. See Part II, Table 5.1 (page 108).

89. FAO n.d.

90. Cronon 1991; Scott 2017.

91. de Ruiter et al. 2018; Pournelle 2019.

92. Carrington, Damian (2017) 'Arctic Stronghold of World's Seeds Flooded After Permafrost Melts,' *The Guardian*, 19 May.

93. WDI n.d.

94. Byass 2015, 2122.

95. Wallace 2016; Wallace and Wallace 2016.

96. Wallace 2016, Loc 577.

97. WDI n.d.; Joyce and Xiaowei 2019; UNICEF (2018) 'The State of Food Security and Nutrition in the World 2018,' https://data.unicef.org/resources/sofi-2018/.

98. Woolf et al. 2018.

99. Armstrong 2017; UN (2018) 'Statement on Visit to the United Kingdom, by Professor Philip Alston, United Nations,' https://www.ohchr.org/Documents /Issues/Poverty/EOM_GB_16Nov2018.pdf.

100. Kennedy et al. 2003.

101. de Ruiter et al. 2018.

102. Tudge 2003.

103. My analysis draws from the thought of Karl Marx 1867 and later writers influenced by it – especially Graeber 2011 and Harvey 2010, who provide more sophisticated analyses than mine here. I'm not an enthusiast for Marxist alternatives to capitalism, but few match Marx's perceptiveness as an analyst of its structure.
104. Overton 1996.
105. Durand 2017.
106. Harvey 2010.
107. WDI n.d.
108. See, for example, Lawton, Graham (2017) 'Effortless Thinking: Why Life Is More Than a Zero-Sum Game,' *New Scientist*, 3156:28.
109. Ricardo 1817, 83.
110. See, for example, Hickel 2017; Milanovic 2016.
111. Heilbroner 1999, 99.
112. For example, Allen 1992; Dyer 2012.
113. The pioneering work is Wallerstein 1974.
114. Hobsbawm 1976; Rodney 1972.
115. Bagchi 2009.
116. Cronon 1991; Wallerstein 1974.
117. Smith 1776.
118. Loewenstein 2015.
119. See Arrighi 2007; Harvey 2010; Hickel 2017; Streeck 2016.
120. Parenti 2011.
121. Donnan, Shawn (2016) 'IMF Economists Put "Neoliberalism" Under the Spotlight,' *Financial Times*, 26 May; Slobodian 2018, 78.
122. For example, Iversen and Soskice 2019.
123. ILO 2019.
124. Benanav 2019; Sayer 2016, 5; Streeck 2016.
125. Klein 2001, 87; Streeck 2016.
126. For example, Ploeg 2008.
127. Pinker 2018, 364.
128. WDI n.d.
129. Suwandi 2019.
130. A plot of GDP per capita for each country without aggregation suggests an inflection point around the top fifty countries or so. My comments here directly contradict Hans Rosling's assertion that there is no longer a gap between the rich, old Western world and the larger part of the rest: Rosling 2018, 28.
131. WDI n.d.
132. Parenti 2011, 241–2.
133. Vinten-Johanson et al. 2003, 256.
134. WDI n.d.
135. Hickel 2017; Milanovic 2016.
136. UN DESA (2017) 'Development Issues #10: International Financial Flows and External Debt,' 24 March, https://www.un.org/development/desa/dpad

/publication/development-issues-no-10-international-financial-flows-and-external-debt/.

137. See, for example, Benanav 2019; Durand 2017; Suwandi 2019.
138. Streeck 2016, 2, 12–14, 58–9.
139. For example, Campbell 2018.
140. Horowitz 1985, xii.
141. Graeber 2018; Crawford 2009.
142. Therborn 2017, 24.
143. Asafu-Adjaye et al. 2015; Bregman 2017, 1; Pinker 2018; Rosling 2018; Warner 2018, 279.
144. Srnicek and Williams 2015, 10, 82, 70, 1–2.
145. Levin et al. 2012.
146. BBC News (2019) 'Extinction Rebellion: What Do They Want and Is It Realistic?' 16 April, https://www.bbc.co.uk/news/science-environment-47947775.
147. Pinker 2018, 109.
148. Honohan 2002, 3.
149. Smith (1776) 1993, 292 (Book IV, Chapter 2).
150. On some of these points, see Benanav 2019.
151. This opposition is formulated by Biehl among many others 1998, 135.
152. Nozick 1974, 311–2.
153. I should add that I'm not persuaded by other aspects of his strongly libertarian arguments.
154. ILO n.d.
155. Stoll 2017, 67.
156. This argument is pursued by Ploeg 2013. See also Netting 1993 and Strange 1988.
157. (2010) 'Quarter of Farming Households Below Poverty Line,' *The Independent*, 30 November.
158. For analysis of this political economy of food past and present see Bello 2009; Cronon 1991; Holt-Giménez 2019; Mazoyer and Roudart 2006; Robbins 2003.
159. ILO 2019; WDI n.d. The exit from farming over the last quarter-century is larger than the figures I've cited superficially suggest in view of increasing population.
160. A selection of such reports: FAO 2016; HLPE 2019; IFAD 2013; IPCC 2019.
161. See Lipton 2009; Stoll 2017; Zhan and Scully 2018.
162. For example, Bernstein 2016; Soper 2020.
163. Netting 1993, 3.
164. Linklater 2014; Lipton 2009.
165. Ploeg 2013.

PART II: SMALL FARM ECOLOGY

1. 'Songs,' Three Acres and a Cow, https://threeacresandacow.co.uk/2014/07/three-acres-and-a-cow-unattributed-broadside-from-late-1800s.
2. Foley et al. 2011, 337.
3. Grime 2001; Grime and Pierce 2012.

4. Grime and Pierce 2012, 163.
5. The ten crops in descending order of land-take are wheat, maize, rice, soybeans, barley, sorghum, dry beans, rapeseed, cotton and millet (Source: FAOSTAT – 2017 data).
6. Van Vliet et al. 2012.
7. For example, Scoones 1995.
8. FAOSTAT n.d. (2013 data).
9. Scott 2017.
10. The figures are potentially misleading looking down the columns because of differences between crops, especially in moisture content (a kilo of potatoes contains a lot more water and less nutrient than a kilo of wheat, which is why far-flung empires with trading commitments have relied on cereals, not root crops).
11. Different perspectives on the Green Revolution are offered by Conway 2012; Patel 2013; Perkins 1997; Stevenson et al. 2013.
12. Smaje 2015.
13. Lynas, Mark (2013) 'Golden Promise,' http://www.marklynas.org/2013/02/golden-promise-how-biofortification-could-soon-be-saving-hundreds-of-thousands-of-lives/.
14. Pournelle 2019, 879.
15. DeHaan et al. 2005, 6.
16. See overviews in Smaje 2015; Crowley and Wingler 2020.
17. Jackson and Piper 1989, 1591; Jackson 2002.
18. Van Tassel et al. 2010.
19. DeHaan et al. 2007, 65–6.
20. The recantation is in Crews and DeHaan 2015, 508. For another demonisation of annual crops, see Shepard 2013. Pournelle 2019 offers a counterweight, as do Foley 2019, King 1911, and Mazoyer and Roudart 2006.
21. Tudge 1998.
22. For some attempts, see FAO 2014; GRAIN 2014; IFAD 2013.
23. Thirsk 1997.
24. Bray 1986.
25. Denison 2012, 7.
26. McGuire, Andrew (2017) 'Don't Mimic Nature on the Farm, Improve It,' Food and Farm Discussion Lab, 1 February, http://fafdl.org/blog/2017/02/01/dont-mimic-nature-on-the-farm-improve-it-1/; Denison 2012, 106.
27. Wood and Lenné 2001.
28. For example, Buchmann et al. 2018; Bybee-Finlay and Ryan 2018; Liebman 1995.
29. Pittelkow et al. 2014.
30. King 1911.
31. Badgley et al. 2007; Ponisio et al. 2014.
32. For example, Brown 2018.
33. See Montgomery 2017 for a detailed overview.
34. I must apologise to a certain soil scientist for once obtusely contesting this point.
35. Lal 2008. For an accessible general discussion of carbon farming see Popkin, Gabriel (2020) 'Can "Carbon Smart" Farming Play a Key Role in the Climate

Fight?' *YaleEnvironment360*, 31 March, https://e360.yale.edu/features/can-carbon
-smart-farming-play-a-key-role-in-the-climate-fight.

36. Mollison and Holmgren 1978.

37. For some critiques and defences of the movement see, for example, commentaries
in *The Land* (2013) 14:14–19; *The Land* (2013–14) 15:32–5. See also Whitefield,
Patrick (2014) 'One of Permaculture's Holy Cows: The Death of the Swale,'
Whitefield Permaculture Courses and Consultancy, 19 April, http://patrick
whitefield.co.uk/one-permacultures-holy-cows-death-swale/.

38. The smallholder-householder adaptation is thoroughly documented in Netting 1993.

39. De Ruiter et al. 2018; Frumkin et al. 2017; Lipton 2009.

40. Netting 1993, 323.

41. Lipton 2009.

42. Lipton 2009, 71.

43. Netting 1993, 27.

44. FAO n.d.

45. Poore and Nemecek 2018.

46. Fairlie 2010.

47. Netting 1993, 139.

48. FAO 2016.

49. Further analysis of draught animal agriculture is provided in Fairlie 2010; Mazoyer
and Roudart 2006.

50. FAO n.d.; IPCC 2019.

51. For accessible overviews of the methane–CO_2 equivalence issue, see Cain,
Michelle (2018) 'A New Way to Assess Global Warming Potential of Short-Lived
Pollutants,' *Carbon Brief*, 7 June; Frame, Dave et al. (2018) 'Why Methane
Should Be Treated Differently Compared to Long-Lived Greenhouse Gases,' *The
Conversation*, 12 June.

52. FAO (2012) 'Livestock and Landscapes,' http://www.fao.org/3/ar591e/ar591e.pdf.

53. For an overview and links, see Rogers, Adam (2019) 'Trying to Plant a Trillion Trees
Won't Solve Anything,' *Wired*, 25 October. See also Fairlie, Simon (2020) 'Quality
Not Quantity,' *The Land* 26:5–6.

54. Stoll 2017.

55. FAO n.d.

56. Raskin and Osborn 2019. See also Hayden and Hayden 2019; Shepard 2013.

57. Stoll 2017.

58. Tawney 1932, 77.

59. de Waal 2018; Pinker 2018.

60. de Waal 2018; Ó Gráda 2009; Stoll 2017.

61. Overton 1996, 141.

62. See, for example, Bello 2009; Davis 2001; Ghosh 2009.

63. de Waal 2018, 76–7.

64. de Waal 2018, 199.

65. de Waal 2018, 165. See also Sen 1981.

66. Ó Gráda 2009.
67. See FAO 2016; IPCC 2019.
68. See the Introduction, page 6.
69. Cotula 2013, 67; de Waal 2018, 174.
70. Overton 1996, 21, provides one historical analysis of these relative disadvantages of small scale, but with little attention to the political forces underlying it. For a more detailed evaluation, see Smaje, Chris (2020) 'Of Scarcity and Scale,' Small Farm Future, 12 April, https://smallfarmfuture.org.uk/2020/04 /of-scarcity-and-scale/.
71. O'Connell, Mark (2018) 'Why Silicon Valley Billionaires Are Prepping for the Apocalypse in New Zealand,' *The Guardian*, 15 February.
72. For example, FAO 2016; UNDRR 2019; Wiebe et al. 2015.
73. For example, Badgley et al. 2007.
74. FAO 2016.
75. WDI n.d.
76. These data derive mostly from Lampkin, Nicholas et al. (2017) *2017 Organic Farm Management Handbook*, Newbury: Organic Research Centre.
77. See Fairlie 2010, 257–76, on wood and 91–105 for another analysis of sustainable and self-reliant UK food production.
78. Trainer 2019 provides an analysis along these lines for Australia.
79. In interpreting the figures, it may help to know that 2,000 calories (roughly the recommended daily food energy intake per person) is equivalent to about 8 MJ. I should also caution the reader not to place too much weight on the precise energetic productivity per hectare figures of the different types of farming shown in the seventh column of Table 11.3, which depend heavily on modelling assumptions. The fact that, together, they meet total energetic requirements (column six) is more important.
80. EAT Lancet Commission (2019) *Summary Report: Food Planet Health: Healthy Diets from Sustainable Food Systems*, https://eatforum.org/content /uploads/2019/07/EAT-Lancet_Commission_Summary_Report.pdf.
81. Zuckerman 1998, 30.
82. Cobbett 1822, 52, 70.
83. Salaman 1949, 542.
84. WDI n.d.

PART III: SMALL FARM SOCIETY

1. Netting 1993, 329.
2. See, for example, Bagchi 2009; Tainter 1988; Wickham 2005.
3. Linklater 2014, 40.
4. Netting 1993, 75. See also Lipton 2009.
5. See, for example, ONS 2017.
6. World Bank, FAO and IFAD 2009, 341.
7. Agarwal 1996, 2014.

8. Some people argue this was more common prior to the widespread monetisation and market linkage of modern economies, for example, Federici 2014.

9. See Laslett 1972; Netting 1993.

10. Fraser 2013; Linklater 2014.

11. Netting 1993, 158. See also Lipton 2009, 177.

12. Allen 1992, 14, 102.

13. This relation between persons, things and property has a murky origin in Roman law, where it bore on the definition of slavery. But in modern societies characterised by individual human rights, I suggest it's a useful way of grasping the concept of property. The latest twist is in attempts to accord legal personhood to non-human entities such as trees and rivers to protect them from people who treat them as mere disposable things.

14. Bollier 2014, 15.

15. The references in this paragraph are to Hardin 1968; Ostrom 1990; and Hardt and Negri 2017.

16. The table draws especially on De Moor 2015; Lipton 2009; Netting 1993; and Ostrom 1990.

17. For examples, see Fairlie 2009; Neeson 1993; Netting 1993.

18. Bailey 1971.

19. See, for example, Dyer 2012, 201–21.

20. See De Moor 2015; Dyer 2012; and, generally, Flannery and Marcus 2012.

21. Ostrom 1990.

22. Hardt and Negri 2017, 98.

23. Varvarousis and Kallis 2017.

24. Bookchin 1982, 50.

25. At a more granular level, usufruct can be either favoured or disfavoured by poor smallholders according to local specifics. Bookchin's discussion of usufruct was more plausibly centred on a low-density foraging society.

26. Dyer 2012.

27. Arguments along these lines, building on the earlier agrarian politics of the sub-treasury, are provided by Strange 1984, among others. See also Postel 2007.

28. Raban 1986, 295.

29. STATISTA (2020) 'Market Share of Grocery Stores in Great Britain from January 2015 to January 2020,' https://www.statista.com/statistics/280208/grocery -market-share-in-the-united-kingdom-uk/.

30. For example, Raworth 2017.

31. Smith 1776, 22.

32. Cronon 1991, 126; Durand 2017.

33. Smith 1776, 21.

34. Arrighi 2007.

35. For example, Clastres 1987; Fleming 2016.

36. Dagger 2006, 163.

37. Hines 2017.

38. This paragraph draws from, among others, Cronon 1991; Cunfer 2005; Mak 2010; Varvarousis and Kallis 2017.
39. Lasch 1991 provides an overview.
40. WDI n.d.
41. Anderson 1974, 205.
42. Satterthwaite et al. 2010, 2815; Smil 2017, 437.
43. Wainwright and Mann 2018.
44. Hoornweg et al. 2011; Rees and Wackernagel 1996.
45. von Thünen 1826.
46. Cronon 1991.
47. Landers 2003, 87.
48. Rees and Wackernagel 1996, 245.
49. See discussions in Orrell 2010; Shalizi 2011.
50. Satterthwaite et al. 2010, 2810.
51. Duby 1974, 147–8.
52. Hart 2004.
53. Rees and Wackernagel 1996, 238–9.
54. Clapp 2017.
55. John Maynard Keynes, *The General Theory of Employment, Interest and Money*, https://www.marxists.org/reference/subject/economics/keynes/general-theory/ch24.htm.
56. Csikszentmihalyi 2002.
57. Powers 2018, 60–1.
58. For example, Boehm 1999.
59. Clastres 1987; Boehm 1999.
60. Fleming 2016, 199.
61. Fleming 2016, 31.
62. Bakhtin 1984; Burke 1994.
63. Marriott 1976.
64. Flannery and Marcus 2012.
65. Netting 1993, 329.
66. Wendell Berry's writings elaborate this point – for example, Berry 2002.
67. Morris 2015.

PART IV: TOWARDS A SMALL FARM FUTURE

1. Quoted in Dyer 2010, 22.
2. Some beekeepers refer to the situation I've described as 'emergency queen replacement', rather than supersedure proper. But I plan to stick with 'supersedure' for various reasons, one of which is that it's a lot catchier.
3. (2018) 'Preston "Not the Locomotive of the UK Economy" Says Johnson,' *Lancashire Post*, 2 October; Nelson, Fraser (2014) 'Boris Is Right – Britain Does Need Rich People. And Plenty of Them,' *The Spectator*, 28 November.
4. Dawson 2017.

5. See Chappell 2018; Varvarousis and Kallis 2017; Zibechi 2010. See also Chakraborty, Aditya (2019) 'In an Era of Brutal Cuts, One Ordinary Place Has the Imagination to Fight Back,' *The Guardian*, 6 March.
6. Solnit 2010.
7. Thirsk 1997.
8. Arrighi 2007; White 2018.
9. Lipton 2009.
10. Scott 1985, xvi; Scott 2009.
11. Stoll 2017, 130–1.
12. Fraser (2014) 'Boris Is Right.'
13. Balibar 2004, 126.
14. For example, Bastani 2019.
15. Wood 1988.
16. Kautsky 1899.
17. Bernstein 2009, 254.
18. Ploeg 2008.
19. Anderson 1983; Hobsbawm and Ranger 1983; Agamben 1998.
20. Kohr 1957, 75.
21. For example, Judson 2016.
22. Discover War Poets (n.d.), 'Edgar Thomas,' https://warpoets.org.uk/worldwar1/poets-and-poetry/edward-thomas/.
23. Kingsnorth, Paul (2017) 'The Lie of the Land: Does Environmentalism Have a Future in the Age of Trump?' *The Guardian*, 18 March.
24. Kidd, Colin (2018) 'In a Frozen Crouch,' *London Review of Books*, 13 September.
25. My account draws particularly upon Barry 2012 and Honohan 2002.
26. Barry 2012, 223.
27. Jefferson 1784, 259.
28. Fleming 2016, 189.
29. See Graeber 2011; Tainter 1988.
30. See Brathwaite 2005; Mintz 1974.
31. Declaration of Nyéléni, 2007: https://nyeleni.org/spip.php?article290.
32. McMichael 2009, 308.
33. Agarwal 2014, 1248.
34. Postel 2007.
35. Scruton 2004, 49–50.
36. Macfarlane, Robert (2015) 'The Eeriness of the English Countryside,' *The Guardian*, 10 April.
37. (2016) 'Equality in the Countryside: A Rural Manifesto,' *The Land*, 19:10.
38. For example, Shrubsole 2019.

EPILOGUE

1. Quoted in Srnicek and Williams 2015, 25.
2. Holmgren 2002.

BIBLIOGRAPHY

Agamben, Giorgio. 1998. *Homo Sacer: Sovereign Power and Bare Life*. Stanford: Stanford University Press.

Agarwal, Bina. 1996. *A Field of One's Own: Gender and Land Rights in South Asia*. New Delhi: Cambridge University Press.

———. 2014. 'Food Sovereignty, Food Security and Democratic Choice: Critical Contradictions, Difficult Conciliations,' *Journal of Peasant Studies* 41(6): 1247–68.

Allen, Robert. 1992. *Enclosure and the Yeoman: The Agricultural Development of the South Midlands 1450–1850*. Oxford: Clarendon Press.

Anderson, Benedict. 1983. *Imagined Communities: Reflections on the Origin and Spread of Nationalism*. London: Verso.

Anderson, Perry. 1974. *Passages from Antiquity to Feudalism*. London: Verso.

Armstrong, Stephen. 2017. *The New Poverty*. London: Verso.

Arrighi, Giovanni. 2007. *Adam Smith in Beijing: Lineages of the Twenty-First Century*. London: Verso.

Asafu-Adjaye, John, et al. 2015. *An Ecomodernist Manifesto*. http://www.ecomodernism .org.

Badgley, Catherine, et al. 2007. 'Organic Agriculture and the Global Food Supply,' *Renewable Agriculture and Food Systems* 22: 86–108.

Bagchi, Amiya Kumar. 2009. 'Nineteenth Century Imperialism and Structural Transformation in Colonized Countries,' in *Peasants and Globalization*, edited by A. Haroon Akram-Lodi and Cristóbal Kay. London: Routledge, 83–110.

Bailey, F.G. 1971. *Gifts and Poison: The Politics of Reputation*. Oxford: Blackwell.

Bakhtin, Mikhail. 1984. *Rabelais and His World*. Bloomington: Indiana University Press.

Balibar, Étienne. 2004. *We, the People of Europe?: Reflections on Transnational Citizenship*. Princeton: Princeton University Press.

Banerjee, Abhijit, and Esther Duflo. 2011. *Poor Economics: Barefoot Hedge-fund Managers, DIY Doctors and the Surprising Truth About Life on Less Than $1 a Day*. London: Penguin.

Barry, John. 2012. *The Politics of Actually Existing Unsustainability: Human Flourishing in a Climate-Changed, Carbon-Constrained World*. Oxford: Oxford University Press.

Bastani, Aaron. 2019. *Fully Automated Luxury Communism: A Manifesto*. London: Verso.

Bello, Walden. 2009. *The Food Wars*. London: Verso.

Benanav, Aaron. 2019. 'Automation and the Future of Work – 2,' *New Left Review* 120:117–46.

Berners-Lee, Mike, and Duncan Clark. 2013. *The Burning Question*. London: Profile.

Bernstein, Henry. 2009. 'Agrarian Questions from Transition to Globalization,' in *Peasants and Globalization*, edited by Haroon Akram-Lodhi and Cristóbal Kay. London: Routledge, 239–61.

———. 2016. 'Agrarian Political Economy and Modern World Capitalism: The Contributions of Food Regime Analysis,' *Journal of Peasant Studies* 43(3): 611–47.

Berry, Wendell. 2002. 'The Whole Horse: The Preservation of the Agrarian Mind,' in *The Fatal Harvest Reader*, edited by Andrew Kimbrell, 39–48. Washington: Island Press.

Biehl, Janet. 1998. *The Politics of Social Ecology: Libertarian Municipalism*. Montreal: Black Rose.

Boehm, Christopher. 1999. *Hierarchy in the Forest: The Evolution of Egalitarian Behavior*. Cambridge, MA: Harvard University Press.

Bollier, David. 2014. *Think Like a Commoner: A Short Introduction to the Life of the Commons*. Gabriola Island: New Society.

Bookchin, Murray. 1982. *The Ecology of Freedom: The Emergence and Dissolution of Hierarchy*. Palo Alto: Cheshire.

Boserup, Ester. 1965. *The Conditions of Agricultural Growth: The Economics of Agrarian Change Under Population Pressure*. London: George Allen & Unwin.

Bradford, Jason. 2019. *The Future Is Rural: Food System Adaptations to the Great Simplification*. Corvallis: Post-Carbon Institute.

Bradshaw, Corey, and Barry Brook. 2015. 'Reply to O'Neill et al. and O'Sullivan: Fertility Reduction Will Help, but Only in the Long Term,' *PNAS* 112(6): E508–9.

Brand, Stewart. 2009. *Whole Earth Discipline: Why Dense Cities, Nuclear Power, Genetically Modified Crops, Restored Wildlands, Radical Science and Geoengineering Are Essential*. London: Atlantic Books.

Brathwaite, Kamau. 2005. *The Development of Creole Society in Jamaica 1770–1820*. Kingston: Ian Randle.

Bray, Francesca. 1986. *The Rice Economies: Technology and Development in Asian Societies*. Berkeley: University of California Press.

Bregman, Rutger. 2017. *Utopia for Realists: And How We Can Get There*. London: Bloomsbury.

Brown, Gabe. 2018. *Dirt to Soil: One Family's Journey into Regenerative Agriculture*. White River Junction, VT: Chelsea Green.

Buchmann, Tina, et al. 2018. 'Connecting Experimental Biodiversity Research to Real-World Grasslands,' *Perspectives in Plant Ecology, Evolution and Systematics* 33:78–88.

Burke, Peter. 1994. *Popular Culture in Early Modern Europe*. Aldershot: Ashgate.

Byass, Peter. 2015. 'A Transition Toward a Healthier Global Population?' *The Lancet* 386:2121–2.

Bybee-Finley, K. Ann, and Matthew Ryan. 2018. 'Advancing Intercropping Research and Practices in Industrialized Agricultural Landscapes,' *Agriculture* 8(6): 1–24.

Byerlee, Derek, et al. 2014. 'Does Intensification Slow Crop Land Expansion or Encourage Deforestation?' *Global Food Security* 3(2): 92–8.

Callicott, J. Baird. 1999. *Beyond the Land Ethic: More Essays in Environmental Philosophy*. Albany: SUNY Press.

Campbell, Colin. 2018. *The Romantic Ethic and the Spirit of Modern Consumerism*. Cham: Palgrave Macmillan.

Campbell, Kurt, et al. 2007. *The Age of Consequences: The Foreign Policy and National Security Implications of Global Climate Change*. Washington, DC: Center for Strategic and International Studies.

Chancel, Lucas, and Thomas Piketty. 2015. *Carbon and Inequality: From Kyoto to Paris*. Paris: Paris School of Economics.

Chappell, Jahi. 2018. *Beginning to End Hunger: Food and the Environment in Belo Horizonte, Brazil, and Beyond*. Oakland: University of California Press.

Clapp, Jennifer. 2017. 'The Trade-ification of the Food Sustainability Agenda,' *Journal of Peasant Studies* 44(2): 335–53.

Clastres, Pierre. 1987. *Society Against the State*. New York: Zone.

Cobbett, William. (1822) 2008. *Cottage Economy*. Bath: eco-logic.

Conway, Gordon. 2012. *One Billion Hungry: Can We Feed the World?* Ithaca: Cornell University Press.

Cotula, Lorenzo. 2013. *The Great African Land Grab? Agricultural Investments and the Global Food System*. London: Zed.

Court, Victor. 2018. 'Energy Capture, Technological Change and Economic Growth: An Evolutionary Perspective,' *BioPhysical Economics and Resource Quality* 3(12).

Crawford, Matthew. 2009. *The Case for Working with Your Hands*. London: Penguin.

Crews, Timothy, and Lee DeHaan. 2015. 'The Strong Perennial Vision: A Response,' *Agroecology and Sustainable Food Systems* 39(5): 500–515.

Crowley, Sharon, and Astrid Wingler. 2020. 'Functional Strategies and Life Histories of Grasses Underlying Yield and Resilience,' *Annual Plant Reviews Online* 3(1): 1–27.

Cronon, William. 1991. *Nature's Metropolis: Chicago and the Great West*. New York: W.W. Norton.

Csikszentmihalyi, Mihaly. 2002. *Flow: The Psychology of Happiness*. London: Rider.

Cunfer, Geoff. 2005. *On the Great Plains: Agriculture and Environment*. College Station: Texas A&M Press.

Dagger, Richard. 2006. 'Neo-republicanism and the Civic Economy,' *Politics, Philosophy and Economics* 5(2): 151–73.

Davis, Mike. 2001. *Late Victorian Holocausts: El Niño Famines and the Making of the Third World*. London: Verso.

Dawson, Ashley. 2017. *Extreme Cities: The Peril and Promise of Urban Life in the Age of Climate Change*. London: Verso.

DeHaan, Lee, et al. 2005. 'Perennial Grain Crops: A Synthesis of Ecology and Plant Breeding,' *Renewable Agriculture and Food Systems* 20(1): 5–14.

DeHaan, Lee, et al. 2007. 'Perennial Grains,' in *Farming with Nature: The Science and Practice of Ecoagriculture*, edited by Sara Scherr and Jeffrey McNeely, Washington: Island Press, 61–82.

De Moor, Tine. 2015. *The Dilemma of the Commoners: Understanding the Use of Common-Pool Resources in Long-Term Perspective*. Cambridge: Cambridge University Press.

Denison, R. Ford. 2012. *Darwinian Agriculture: How Understanding Evolution Can Improve Agriculture*. Princeton: Princeton University Press.

de Ruiter, Henri, et al. 2018. 'Moving Beyond Calories and Protein: Micronutrient Assessment of UK Diets and Land Use,' *Global Environmental Change* 52:108–16.

de Waal, Alex. 2018. *Mass Starvation: The History and Future of Famine*. Cambridge: Polity.

Duby, Georges. 1974. *The Early Growth of the European Economy: Warriors and Peasants from the Seventh to the Twelfth Century*. Ithaca: Cornell University Press.

Durand, Cédric. 2017. *Fictitious Capital*. London: Verso.

Dyer, Christopher. 2012. *A Country Merchant, 1495–1520: Trading and Farming at the End of the Middle Ages*. Oxford: Oxford University Press.

Dyer, Gwynne. 2010. *Climate Wars: The Fight for Survival as the World Overheats*. London: Oneworld.

Fairlie, Simon. 2009. 'A Short History of Enclosure in Britain,' *The Land* 7:16–31.

———. 2010. *Meat: A Benign Extravagance*. White River Junction, VT: Chelsea Green.

FAO. 2014. *The State of Food and Agriculture: Innovation in Family Farming*. Rome: FAO.

———. 2016. *The State of Food and Agriculture: Climate Change, Agriculture and Food Security*. Rome: FAO.

———. n.d. FAOSTAT. http://www.fao.org/faostat/en/#data/.

Federici, Silvia. 2014. *Caliban and the Witch: Women, the Body and Primitive Accumulation*. Brooklyn: Autonomedia.

Fizaine, Florian, and Victor Court. 2016. 'Energy Expenditure, Economic Growth, and the Minimum EROI of Society,' *Energy Policy* 95:172–86.

Flannery, Kent, and Joyce Marcus. 2012. *The Creation of Inequality: How Our Prehistoric Ancestors Set the Stage for Monarchy, Slavery and Empire*. Cambridge, MA: Harvard University Press.

Fleming, David. 2016. *Lean Logic: A Dictionary for the Future and How to Survive It*. White River Junction, VT: Chelsea Green.

Foley, Jonathan, et al. 2011. 'Solutions for a Cultivated Planet,' *Nature* 478:337–42.

Foley, Michael. 2019. *Farming for the Long Haul: Resilience and the Lost Art of Agricultural Inventiveness*. White River Junction, VT: Chelsea Green.

Francis, Daniel. 1990. *A History of World Whaling*. Markham: Viking.

Frase, Peter. 2016. *Four Futures: Life After Capitalism*. London: Verso.

Fraser, Nancy. 2013. 'A Triple Movement?' *New Left Review* 81:119–32.

Frumkin, Howard, et al. 2017. 'Nature Contact and Human Health: A Research Agenda,' *Environmental Health Perspectives* 125(7). https://doi.org/10.1289/EHP1663.

Ghosh, Jayati. 2009. 'The Unnatural Coupling: Food and Global Finance,' *Journal of Agrarian Change* 10(1): 72–86.

Gibbs, H., et al. 2010. 'Tropical Forests Were the Primary Sources of New Agricultural Land in the 1980s and 1990s,' *PNAS* 107(38): 16732–37.

Gosho, Merrill, et al. 1984. 'The Sperm Whale,' *Marine Fisheries Review* 46:54–64.

Graeber, David. 2011. *Debt: The First 5,000 Years*. New York: Melville House.

———. 2018. *Bullshit Jobs: A Theory*. London: Allen Lane.

GRAIN. 2014. *Hungry for Land: Small Farmers Feed the World with Less Than a Quarter of All Farmland*. Barcelona: Grain.

Grime, J. Philip. 2001. *Plant Strategies, Vegetation Processes, and Ecosystem Properties*. Chichester: John Wiley.

Grime, J. Philp, and Simon Pierce. 2012. *The Evolutionary Strategies That Shape Ecosystems*. Chichester: John Wiley.

Hardin, Garrett. 1968. 'The Tragedy of the Commons,' *Science* 162:1243–8.

Hardt, Michael, and Antonio Negri. 2017. *Assembly*. Oxford: Oxford University Press.

Hart, Keith. 2004. 'The Political Economy of Food in an Unequal World,' in *The Politics of Food*, edited by Marianne Lien and Brigitte Nerlich. Oxford: Berg, 199–220.

Harvey, David. 2010. *The Enigma of Capital and the Crises of Capitalism*. London: Profile.

Hayden, Nancy, and John Hayden. 2019. *Farming on the Wild Side*. White River Junction, VT: Chelsea Green.

Heilbroner, Robert. 1999. *The Worldly Philosophers: The Lives, Times and Ideas of the Great Economic Thinkers*. London: Penguin.

Hickel, Jason. 2017. *The Divide: A Brief Guide to Global Inequality and Its Solutions*. London: Windmill.

Hillel, Daniel. 1991. *Out of the Earth: Civilization and the Life of the Soil*. London: Aurum.

Hines, Colin. 2017. *Progressive Protectionism: Taking Back Control*. London: Park House Press.

HLPE. 2019. *Agroecological and Other Innovative Approaches for Sustainable Agriculture and Food Systems That Enhance Food Security and Nutrition*. Rome: HLPE.

Hobsbawm, Eric. 1976. 'From Feudalism to Capitalism,' in *The Transition from Feudalism to Capitalism*, edited by Rodney Hilton. London: New Left Books, 159–64.

Hobsbawm, Eric, and Terence Ranger. 1983. *The Invention of Tradition*. Cambridge: Cambridge University Press.

Holmgren, David. 2002. *Permaculture: Principles and Pathways Beyond Sustainability*. Hepburn: Holmgren Design Services.

Holt-Giménez, Eric. 2019. *Can We Feed the World Without Destroying It?* Cambridge: Polity.

Honohan, Iseult. 2002. *Civic Republicanism*. London: Routledge.

Hoornweg, Daniel, et al. 2011. 'Cities and Greenhouse Gas Emissions: Moving Forward,' *Environment and Urbanization* 23(1): 207–27.

Horowitz, Daniel. 1985. *The Morality of Spending: Attitudes Toward the Consumer Society in America, 1875–1940*. Chicago: Elephant.

IFAD. 2013. *Smallholders, Food Security and the Environment*. Rome: IFAD.

ILO. 2019. *The Global Labour Income Share and Distribution*. Geneva: ILO.

———. n.d. ILOSTAT. http://www.Ilo.org/ilostat/.

IPCC. 2016. *Climate Change 2014 Synthesis Report Summary for Policymakers*. Geneva: IPCC.

———. 2018. *Global Warming of 1.5°C*. Geneva: IPCC.

———. 2019. *Climate Change and Land*. Geneva: IPCC.

Iversen, Torben, and David Soskice. 2019. *Democracy and Prosperity: Reinventing Capitalism Through a Turbulent Century*. Princeton: Princeton University Press.

Jackson, Wes. 2002. 'Natural Systems Agriculture: A Truly Radical Alternative,' *Agriculture, Ecosystems and Environment* 88(2): 111–17.

Jackson, Wes, and Jon Piper. 1989. 'The Necessary Marriage Between Ecology and Agriculture,' *Ecology* 70(6): 1591–3.

Jefferson, Thomas. (1784) 1944. 'Notes on Virginia,' in *The Life and Selected Writings of Thomas Jefferson*, edited by Adrienne Koch and William Peden. New York: Modern Library, 173–267.

Joyce, Robert, and Xiaowei Xu. 2019. *Inequalities in the Twenty-First Century*. London: Institute for Fiscal Studies.

Judson, Pieter. 2016. *The Habsburg Empire: A New History*. Cambridge, MA: Harvard University Press.

Kallis, Giorgos. 2018. *Degrowth*. Newcastle: Agenda.

———. 2019. *Limits: Why Malthus Was Wrong and Why Environmentalists Should Care*. Stanford: Stanford University Press.

Kautsky, Karl. (1899) 1988. *The Agrarian Question*. London: Zwan.

Kennedy, Gina, et al. 2003. 'The Scourge of "Hidden Hunger": Global Dimensions of Micronutrient Deficiencies,' *Journal of Food, Nutrition and Agriculture* 32:8–16.

Kiel, Katherine, et al. 2010. 'Luck or Skill? An Examination of the Ehrlich-Simon Bet,' *Ecological Economics* 69:1365–7.

King, Franklin. 1911. *Farmers of Forty Centuries*. Emmaus: Rodale.

Klein, Naomi. 2001. 'Reclaiming the Commons,' *New Left Review* 9:81–9.

Kohr, Leopold. (1957) 2001. *The Breakdown of Nations*. Totnes: Green Books.

Kremen, Claire. 2015. 'Reframing the Land-Sparing/Land-Sharing Debate for Biodiversity Conservation,' *Annals of the New York Academy of Sciences* 1355(1): 52–76.

Krishna, Anirudh. 2013. 'Stuck in Place: Investigating Social Mobility in 14 Bangalore Slums,' *Journal of Development Studies* 49(7): 1010–28.

Lal, Rattan. 2008. 'Carbon Sequestration,' *Philosophical Transactions of the Royal Society B* 363:815–30.

Lambin, Eric, and Patrick Meyfroidt. 2011. 'Global Land Use Change, Economic Globalization and the Looming Land Scarcity,' *PNAS* 108(9): 3465–72.

Landers, John. 2003. *The Field and the Forge: Population, Production and Power in the Pre-Industrial West*. Oxford: Oxford University Press.

Lasch, Christopher. 1991. *The True and Only Heaven: Progress and Its Critics*. New York: Norton.

Laslett, Peter. 1972. *Household and Family in Past Time*. London: University of Cambridge.

Letourneau, Deborah, et al. 2011. 'Does Plant Diversity Benefit Agroecosystems? A Synthetic Review,' *Ecological Applications* 21(1): 9–21.

Levien, Michael. 2018. *Dispossession Without Development: Land Grabs in Neoliberal India*. Oxford: Oxford University Press.

Levin, Kelly, et al. 2012. 'Overcoming the Tragedy of Super Wicked Problems: Con-straining Our Future Selves to Ameliorate Global Climate Change,' *Policy Sciences* 45(2): 123–52.

Liebman, Matt. 1995. 'Polyculture Cropping Systems,' in *Agroecology: The Science of Sustainable Agriculture,* edited by Miguel Altieri. Boulder: Westview Press, 205-18.

Linklater, Andro. 2014. *Owning the Earth: The Transforming History of Landownership.* London: Bloomsbury.

Lipton, Michael. 2009. *Land Reform in Developing Countries: Property Rights and Property Wrongs.* Abingdon: Routledge.

Locke, John. (1689) 1993. *Two Treatises of Government.* London: Everyman.

Loewenstein, Antony. 2015. *Disaster Capitalism: Making a Killing Out of a Catastrophe.* London: Verso.

Loftus, Peter, et al. 2015. 'A Critical Review of Global Decarbonization Scenarios: What Do They Tell Us About Feasibility?' *WIRES Climate Change* 6:93–112.

Mak, Geert. 2010. *An Island in Time: The Biography of a Village.* London: Vintage.

Malm, Andreas. 2016. *Fossil Capital: The Rise of Steam Power and the Roots of Global Warming.* London: Verso.

Malthus, Thomas. (1798) 1976. *An Essay on the Principle of Population.* New York: Norton.

Marriott, McKim. 1976. 'Hindu Transactions: Diversity Without Dualism,' in *Transac-tion and Meaning,* edited by Bruce Kapferer. Philadelphia: Institute for the Study of Human Issues, 109–142.

Marris, Emma. 2011. *Rambunctious Garden: Saving Nature in a Post-Wild World.* New York: Bloomsbury.

Marx, Karl. (1867) 1990. *Capital.* London: Penguin.

Mazoyer, Marcel, and Laurence Roudart. 2006. *A History of World Agriculture: From the Neolithic Age to the Current Crisis.* London: Earthscan.

McMichael, Philip. 2009. 'Food Sovereignty, Social Reproduction and the Agrarian Question,' in *Peasants and Globalization*, edited by A. Haroon Akram-Lodi and Cristóbal Kay. London: Routledge, 288–312.

Meadows, Donella, et al. 2004. *Limits to Growth: The 30-Year Update.* White River Junc-tion, VT: Chelsea Green.

Milanovic, Branko. 2016. *Global Inequality: A New Approach for the Age of Globalization.* Cambridge, MA: Harvard University Press.

Mintz, Sidney. 1974. *Caribbean Transformations.* Baltimore: Johns Hopkins University Press.

Mollison, Bill, and David Holmgren. 1978. *Permaculture One: A Perennial Agricultural System for Human Settlements.* Sisters Creek: Tagari.

Monbiot, George. 2014. *Feral: Rewilding the Land, Sea and Human Life.* London: Penguin.

Montgomery, David. 2007. 'Soil Erosion and Agricultural Sustainability,' *PNAS* 104:13268–72.

———. 2017. *Growing a Revolution: Bringing Our Soil Back to Life.* New York: W.W. Norton.

Moriarty, Patrick, and Damon Honnery. 2019. 'Ecosystem Maintenance Energy and the Need for a Green EROI,' *Energy Policy* 131:229–34.

Morris, Ian. 2015. *Foragers, Farmers and Fossil Fuels: How Human Values Evolve*. Princeton: Princeton University Press.

Nabhan, Gary Paul. 2002. *Coming Home to Eat: The Pleasures and Politics of Local Foods*. New York: Norton.

Neeson, J.M. 1993. *Commoners: Common Right, Enclosure and Social Change in England, 1700–1820*. Cambridge: Cambridge University Press.

Netting, Robert. 1993. *Smallholders, Householders: Farm Families and the Ecology of Intensive, Sustainable Agriculture*. Stanford: Stanford University Press.

Nozick, Robert. 1974. *Anarchy, State and Utopia*. Oxford: Blackwell.

Ó Gráda, Cormac. 2009. *Famine: A Global History*. Princeton: Princeton University Press.

ONS (Office for National Statistics). 2017. *Families and Households in the UK: 2017*. London: ONS.

Orrell, David. 2010. *Economyths: How the Science of Complex Systems Is Transforming Economic Thought*. London: Icon.

Ostrom, Elinor. 1990. *Governing the Commons: The Evolution of Institutions for Collective Action*. Cambridge: Cambridge University Press.

Overton, Mark. 1996. *Agricultural Revolution in England: The Transformation of the Agrarian Economy 1500–1850*. Cambridge: Cambridge University Press.

Parenti, Christian. 2011. *Tropic of Chaos: Climate Change and the New Geography of Violence*. New York: Nation Books.

Patel, Raj. 2013. 'The Long Green Revolution,' *Journal of Peasant Studies* 40(1): 1–63.

Pelletier, Nathan, et al. 2011. 'Energy Intensity of Agriculture and Food Systems,' *Annual Review of Environmental Resources* 36:223–46.

Perfecto, Ivette, et al. 2009. *Nature's Matrix: Linking Agriculture, Conservation and Food Sovereignty*. London: Routledge.

Perkins, John. 1997. *Geopolitics and the Green Revolution: Wheat, Genes and the Cold War*. Oxford: Oxford University Press.

Phelps, Jacob, et al. 2013. 'Agricultural Intensification Escalates Future Conservation Costs,' *PNAS* 110(19): 7601–6.

Phillips, Leigh, and Michal Rozworski. 2019. *People's Republic of Walmart: How the World's Biggest Corporations Are Laying the Foundation for Socialism*. London: Verso.

Pinker, Steven. 2018. *Enlightenment Now: The Case for Reason, Science, Humanism and Progress*. London: Penguin.

Pittelkow, Cameron, et al. 2014. 'Productivity Limits and Potentials of the Principles of Conservation Agriculture.' *Nature*. https://doi.org/10.1038/nature13809.

Ploeg, Jan Douwe van der. 2008. *The New Peasantries: Struggles for Autonomy and Sustainability in an Era of Empire and Globalization*. London: Earthscan.

———. 2013. *Peasants and the Art of Farming: A Chayanovian Manifesto*. Halifax: Fernwood.

Polimeni, John, et al. 2008. *The Jevons Paradox and the Myth of Resource Efficiency Improvements*. London: Routledge.

BIBLIOGRAPHY

Ponisio, Lauren, et al. 2014. 'Diversification Practices Reduce Organic to Conventional Yield Gap,' *Proceedings of the Royal Society B* 282:20141396.

Poore, J., and T. Nemecek. 2018. 'Reducing Food's Environmental Impacts Through Producers and Consumers,' *Science* 360(6392): 987–92.

Postel, Charles. 2007. *The Populist Vision*. Oxford: Oxford University Press.

Pournelle, Jennifer. 2019. 'Fields, Gardens and Staple States,' *Journal of Peasant Studies* 46(4): 878–84.

Powers, Richard. 2018. *The Overstory*. New York: Vintage.

Raban, Jonathan. 1986. *Coasting*. London: Picador.

Raskin, Ben, and Simone Osborn. 2019. *The Agroforestry Handbook*. Bristol: Soil Association.

Raworth, Kate. 2017. *Doughnut Economics: Seven Ways to Think Like a 21st-Century Economist*. London: Random House.

Rees, William, and Mathis Wackernagel. 1996. 'Urban Ecological Footprints: Why Cities Cannot Be Sustainable and Why They Are a Key to Sustainability.' *Environmental Impact Assessment Review* 16:223–48.

Ricardo, David. (1817) 2004. *The Principles of Political Economy and Taxation*. Mineola: Dover.

Rickson, R.J., et al. 2015. 'Input Constraints to Food Production: The Impact of Soil Degradation,' *Food Security* 7(2): 351–64.

Robbins, Peter. 2003. *Stolen Fruit: The Tropical Commodities Disaster*. London: Zed.

Rodney, Walter. (1972) 2018. *How Europe Underdeveloped Africa*. London: Verso.

Rosling, Hans. 2018. *Factfulness: Ten Reasons We're Wrong About the World – and Why Things Are Better Than You Think*. London: Sceptre.

Rosset, Peter, and Miguel Altieri. 2017. *Agroecology: Science and Politics*. Black Point: Fernwood.

Salaman, Redcliffe. (1949) 1985. *The History and Social Influence of the Potato*. Cambridge: Cambridge University Press.

Satterthwaite, David, et al. 2010. 'Urbanization and Its Implications for Food and Farming,' *Philosophical Transactions of the Royal Society B* 365:2809–20.

Sayer, Andrew. 2016. *Why We Can't Afford the Rich*. Bristol: Policy Press.

Schmidt, Christian, et al. 2017. 'Export of Plastic Debris by Rivers into the Sea,' *Environmental Science and Technology* 51(21): 12246–53.

Scoones, Ian. 1995. *Living with Uncertainty: New Directions in Pastoral Development in Africa*. London: Intermediate Technology Publications.

Scott, James. 1985. *Weapons of the Weak: Everyday Forms of Peasant Resistance*. New Haven: Yale University Press.

———. 2009. *The Art of Not Being Governed: An Anarchist History of Upland Southeast Asia*. New Haven: Yale University Press.

———. 2017. *Against the Grain: A Deep History of the Earliest States*. New Haven: Yale University Press.

Scruton, Roger. 2004. *News from Somewhere: On Settling*. London: Continuum.

Sen, Amartya. 1981. *Poverty and Famines: An Essay on Entitlement and Deprivation*. Oxford: Oxford University Press.

Shalizi, Cosma. 2011. 'Scaling and Hierarchy in Urban Economies,' *PNAS*. https://arxiv.org/abs/1102.4101.

Shepard, Mark. 2013. *Restoration Agriculture: Real-World Permaculture for Farmers*. Austin: Acres USA.

Shrubsole, Guy. 2019. *Who Owns England?* London: William Collins.

Slobodian, Quinn. 2018. *Globalists: The End of Empire and the Birth of Neoliberalism*. Cambridge, MA: Harvard University Press.

Smaje, Chris. 2015. 'The Strong Perennial Vision: A Critical Review,' *Agroecology and Sustainable Food Systems* 39(5): 471–99.

Smil, Vaclav. 2010. *Energy Myths and Realities: Bringing Science to the Energy Policy Debate*. Washington, DC: AEI Press.

———. 2017. *Energy and Civilization: A History*. Cambridge, MA: MIT Press.

———. 2019. *Growth: From Microorganisms to Megacities*. Cambridge, MA: MIT Press.

Smith, Adam. (1776) 1993. *Wealth of Nations*. Oxford: Oxford University Press.

Smith, Jo, et al. 2012. 'Reconciling Productivity with Protection of the Environment: Is Temperate Agroforestry the Answer?' *Renewable Agriculture and Food Systems* 28(1): 80–92.

Smith, Stephen. 2005. *Ending Global Poverty: A Guide to What Works*. Basingstoke: Palgrave Macmillan.

Soil Association. 2010. *A Rock and a Hard Place: Peak Phosphorus and the Threat to Our Food Security*. Bristol: Soil Association.

Solnit, Rebecca. 2010. *A Paradise Built in Hell: The Extraordinary Communities That Arise in Disaster*. London: Penguin.

Soper, Rachel. 2020. 'From Protecting Peasant Livelihoods to Essentializing Peasant Agriculture: Problematic Trends in Food Sovereignty Discourse,' *Journal of Peasant Studies* 47(2): 265–85.

Sowell, Thomas. 2006. *A Conflict of Visions: Ideological Origins of Political Struggles*. New York: Basic Books.

Srnicek, Nick, and Alex Williams. 2015. *Inventing the Future: Postcapitalism and a World Without Work*. London: Verso.

Stevenson, James, et al. 2013. 'Green Revolution Research Saved an Estimated 18 to 27 Million Hectares from Being Brought into Agricultural Production,' *PNAS* 110(21): 8363–8.

Stoll, Steven. 2017. *Ramp Hollow. The Ordeal of Appalachia*. New York: Hill and Wang.

Strange, Marty. 1984. 'The Economic Structure of a Sustainable Agriculture,' in *Meeting the Expectations of the Land*, edited by Wes Jackson et al. San Francisco: North Point, 115–25.

———. 1988. *Family Farming: A New Economic Vision*. Lincoln: University of Nebraska Press.

Streeck, Wolfgang. 2016. *How Will Capitalism End?* London: Verso.

Suwandi, Intan. 2019. *Value Chains: The New Economic Imperialism*. New York: Monthly Review Press.

Sverdrup, Harald, et al. 2012. 'The WORLD Model: Peak Metals, Minerals, Energy, Wealth, Food and Population.' https://lup.lub.lu.se/search/publication/4812977.

Tainter, Joseph. 1988. *The Collapse of Complex Societies*. Cambridge: Cambridge University Press.

Tawney, R.H. 1932. *Land and Labour in China*. London: George Allen & Unwin.

Therborn, Göran. 2017. *Cities of Power: The Urban, The National, The Popular, The Global*. London: Verso.

Thirsk, Joan. 1997. *Alternative Agriculture: A History*. Oxford: Oxford University Press.

Todaro, Michael, and Stephen Smith. 2015. *Economic Development*. Harlow: Pearson.

Tong, Dan, et al. 2019. 'Committed Emissions from Existing Energy Infrastructure Jeopardize 1.5°C Climate Target,' *Nature* 572: 373–77.

Trainer, Ted. 2019. 'Remaking Settlements for Sustainability: The Simpler Way,' *Journal of Political Ecology* 26(1): 202–23.

Tudge, Colin. 1998. *Neanderthals, Bandits and Farmers: How Agriculture Really Began*. New Haven: Yale University Press.

———. 2003. *So Shall We Reap*. London: Penguin.

Turner, Graham. 2008. 'A Comparison of *The Limits to Growth* with 30 Years of Reality.' *Global Environmental Change* 18:397–411.

UNDRR. 2019. *Global Assessment Report on Disaster Risk Reduction 2019*. Geneva: United Nations Office for Disaster Risk Reduction.

UNEP. 2014. *Decoupling 2: Technologies, Opportunities and Policy Options*. Paris: UNEP.

———. 2016. *Global Material Flows and Resource Productivity*. Paris: UNEP.

United Nations, Department of Economic and Social Affairs, Population Division. 2019. *World Population Prospects 2019: Highlights* (ST/ESA/SER.A/423).

UN Water. 2018. *The United Nations World Water Development Report 2018: Nature-Based Solutions for Water*. Paris: UNESCO.

Vandermeer, John. 2011. *The Ecology of Agroecosystems*. Sudbury: Jones and Bartlett.

Van Tassel, David, et al. 2010. 'Missing Domesticated Plant Forms: Can Artificial Selection Fll the Gap?' *Evolutionary Applications* 3:434–52.

van Vliet, Nathalie, et al. 2012. 'Trends, Drivers and Impacts of Changes in Swidden Cultivation in Tropical Forest-Agriculture Frontiers: A Global Assessment,' *Global Environmental Change* 22(2): 418–29.

Varvarousis, Angelos, and Giorgos Kallis. 2017. 'Commoning Against the Crisis,' in *Another Economy Is Possible*, edited by Manuel Castells et al. Cambridge: Polity, 128–59.

Vinten-Johansen, Peter, et al. 2003. *Cholera, Chloroform and the Science of Medicine: A Life of John Snow*. New York: Oxford University Press.

von Thünen, Johann. (1826) 1966. *von Thünen's Isolated State: An English Edition of Der Isolierte Staat*, edited by Peter Hall. Oxford: Pergamon.

Wainwright, Joel, and Geoff Mann. 2018. *Climate Leviathan: A Political Theory of Our Planetary Future*. London: Verso.

Wallace, Rob. 2016. *Big Farms Make Big Flu*. New York: Monthly Review Press.

Wallace, Rob, and Wallace, Rodrick. 2016. 'Ebola's Ecologies: Agro-economics and Epidemiology in West Africa,' *New Left Review* 102:43–55.

Wallerstein, Immanuel. 1974. *The Modern World-System*, 3 Vols. New York: Academic Press.

Warner, Anthony. 2018. *The Angry Chef: Bad Science and the Truth About Healthy Eating.* London: Oneworld.

WDI (World Development Indicators). n.d. https://databank.worldbank.org/reports.aspx?source=world-development-indicators.

Wesselbaum, Dennis, and Amelia Aburn. 2019. 'Gone with the Wind: International Migration,' *Global and Planetary Change* 178:96–109.

White, Lynn. 2018. *Rural Roots of Reform Before China's Conservative Change.* London: Routledge.

Wickham, Chris. 2005. *Framing the Early Middle Ages: Europe and the Mediterranean 400–800.* Oxford: Oxford University Press.

Wiebe, Keith, et al. 2015. 'Climate Change Impacts on Agriculture in 2050 Under a Range of Plausible Socioeconomic and Emissions Scenarios,' *Environmental Research Letters* 10:085010.

Wilson, Edward. 2001. *The Diversity of Life.* London: Penguin.

Wood, D., and Lenné, J. 2001. 'Nature's Fields: A Neglected Model for Increasing Food Production.' *Outlook on Agriculture* 30(3): 161–70.

Wood, Ellen Meiksins. 1988. *Peasant-Citizen and Slave: The Foundations of Athenian Democracy.* London: Verso.

Woolf, Steven, et al. 2018. 'Changes in Midlife Death Rates Across Racial and Ethnic Groups in the United States: Systematic Analysis of Vital Statistics,' *British Medical Journal* 362:k3096.

World Bank, FAO and IFAD. 2009. *Gender in Agriculture Sourcebook.* Washington, DC: The World Bank.

Worster, Donald. 1979. *Dust Bowl: The Southern Plains in the 1930s.* Oxford: Oxford University Press.

WWAP (World Water Assessment Programme). 2012. *The United Nations World Water Development Report 4: Managing Water Under Uncertainty and Risk.* Paris, UNESCO.

Zhan, Shaohua. 2020. 'The Land Question in 21st Century China,' *New Left Review* 122: 115–33.

Zhan, Shaohua, and Ben Scully. 2018. 'From South Africa to China: Land, Migrant Labor and the Semi-proletarian Thesis Revisited,' *Journal of Peasant Studies* 45(5–6): 1018–38.

Zibechi, Raúl. 2010. *Dispersing Power: Social Movements as Anti-State Forces.* Oakland: AK Press

Zuckerman, Larry. 1998. *The Potato.* London: Macmillan.

INDEX

ABOUT THE AUTHOR

CORDELIA ROWLATT

C hris Smaje has coworked a small farm in Somerset, southwest England, for the last 17 years. Previously, he was a university-based social scientist, working in the Department of Sociology at the University of Surrey and the Department of Anthropology at Goldsmiths College on aspects of social policy, social identities and the environment. Since switching focus to the practice and politics of agroecology, he's written for various publications, such as *The Land*, *Dark Mountain*, *Permaculture* magazine and Statistics Views, as well as academic journals such as *Agroecology* and *Sustainable Food Systems* and the *Journal of Consumer Culture*. Smaje writes the blog Small Farm Future, is a featured author at www.resilience.org and a current director of the Ecological Land Co-op.